MARK TWAIN

Pudd'nhead Wilson

&

Those Extraordinary Twins

WITH ESSAYS IN CRITICISM

Annotated with Critical Introduction

by

Yoo, Young-Jong

Shinasa

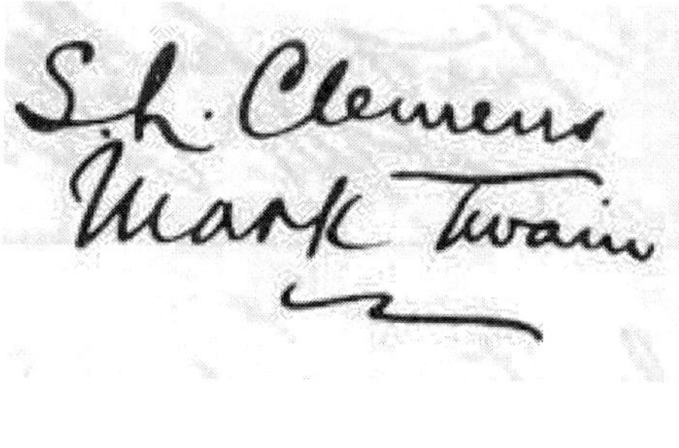
S. L. Clemens
Mark Twain

Contents

Critical Introduction

CRITICAL INTRODUCTION

I. Mark Twain (1835-1910) Introduction

Mark Twain의 본명은 Samuel Langhorne Clemens로 1835년 미국 남부와 북부의 경계선에 있던 Missouri주 Florida에서 태어났다. 그가 4살 때 그의 가족은 같은 주 Mississippi 강가에 있는 Hannibal이라는 작은 마을로 이주했다. 그는 여기서 소년시절을 보내며, 강을 오르내리는 증기선에 매료되었고 자신도 작은 뗏목을 타고 강 위를 돌아다녔다. 이때의 경험은 *The Adventures of Tom Sawyer*(1876)와 *Adventures of Huckleberry Finn*(1885)등 많은 작품들의 배경이 되었다. 그의 작품들에는 Mississippi강에 대한 애정이 강하게 드러나 있으며 Hannibal은 그가 만들어 낸 가상의 마을 St. Petersburg의 모델이 되었다.

1847년 아버지를 여읜 Twain은 학교를 그만 둔 후 인쇄 견습공이 되어 Missouri주 St. Louis부터 New York주에 이르기까지 다양한 곳을 돌아다녔다. 이때 그는 Thomas Jefferson Snodgrass라는 필명으로 해학적인 글들을 쓰기 시작했지만 성공을 거두지는 못했다. 남미로 가기위해 배를 타고 Mississippi강의 하류에 있는 New Orleans로 가던 그는 Horace Bixby라는 선장을 만나 그에게서 증기선을 조정하는 법을 배웠다. 1859년 그는 원래의 목적지인 남미로 내려가는 대신 Mississippi강을 항해하는 증기선의 선장이 되었다. 이때의 경험을 그는 *Life on the Mississippi*(1883)에 자세히 적어 놓았다.

1861년 남북전쟁이 발발하여 결국 Mississippi강의 증기선 운항이 중지되자 그는 남군의 민병대에 합류하였다가 일주일 만에

탈영해 형 Orion을 따라 서부로 떠난다. Nevada와 California주에서 금, 은광을 찾아 헤매며 서부 개척 시대의 다양한 경험을 한 그는 남서부 유머작가들로부터 영향을 받은 "The Celebrated Jumping Frog of Calavaras County"(1865)라는 단편을 발표하여 큰 인기를 얻는다. 그 후 그는 Union 신문사, Alta California 신문사의 특파원 자격을 얻어 유럽과 중동지역 등을 여행하고 유럽 문명을 풍자한 *Innocents Abroad*(1869)를 발표하여 전국적인 성공을 거둔다.

이렇듯 유명작가가 된 Twain은 1870년 결혼 하여 Connecticut주 Hartford에 정착한 후 이곳에서 20년 넘게 살며 그의 대표작들을 써냈다. 미국 서부 여행기인 *Roughing It* (1871), Charles Warner와 함께 공동으로 남북전쟁 후 재건시대의 사회상을 비판한 *The Gilded Age* (1873), *A True Story and Old Times on the Mississippi* (1874-75), *The Adventures of Tom Sawyer* (1876), *A Tramp Abroad* (1880), *The Prince and the Pauper* (1882), *Life on the Mississippi* (1883), *Adventures of Huckleberry Finn* (1884), *A Connecticut Yankee in King Arthur's Court* (1889) 등이 이 시기에 쓰여진 대표적인 작품들이다.

잇따른 문학적 성공에도 불구하고 그가 60살이 되고 또 *Pudd'nhead Wilson*이 출판된 1894년 그가 모든 재산을 쏟아 부었던 Paige Typesetter라는 식자기계와 Charles L. Webster & Co. 출판사가 실패함으로써 그는 결국 파산하게 된다. 부채를 갚기 위해 그는 세계강연여행을 시작하였고 그 일로 집을 떠나있던 중 그가 가장 사랑하던 딸인 Susy가 세상을 떠났다. 빚을 다 갚고 여행에서 돌아온 후 그는 전부터 건강에 문제가 있었던 그의 아내와 간질을 앓고 있었던 다른 딸 Jean의 죽음을 보아야 했다. 1898년 이후 연달아 비극적인 경험을 하게 된 그가 75살로 세상을 떠난 1910년까지 쓴 후기 작품들은 비극적인 세계관과 인류관을 보여주고 있다. 특히 그가 빚을 다 청산한 1898년 이후 쓰여진 단편 "The Man That

Corrupted Hadleyburg" (1900), 철학적 에세이 *What Is Man?* (1906), 소설 *The Mysterious Stranger* (1916년 유고집 간행) 등은 생전에 출판되지 않은 다른 미완성 작품들과 더불어 그의 비극적인 세계관을 대표한다.

Twain이 세상을 떠난지 이제 한 세기가 지났지만 미국문학에서 그처럼 중요한 위치를 차지하며 또한 전세계 독자들에게 친숙하게 알려진 작가는 드물 것이다. William Dean Howells가 그를 가리켜 "The Lincoln of American Literature"라고 부른 것에서, 그리고 Ernest Hemingway가 "모든 현대 미국 문학은 Huckleberry Finn이라는 이름의 Mark Twain이 쓴 한 권의 책에서 유래한다" 라고 말한 것에서 알 수 있듯이 Twain의 글은 미국적인 특성으로 가득 차 있다. 미국 남서부의 해학문학(Old Southwestern Humor) 전통과 지방색 문학(Regional Literature)의 전통을 이어받은 그는 구어체와 지역 방언의 사용 등을 통해 당대 미국인들의 경험과 미국의 풍경들을 다양하고 사실적이게 보여줌으로써 문체와 주제 모든 면에서 현대 미국 문학의 방향을 정립하는데 큰 역할을 했다. 그의 작품에 나타나는 미국사회내의 인종차별문제에 대한 비판과 미국사회에 대한 건강한 회의주의 역시 그를 대표적인 미국작가로 만드는데 손색이 없다. 그렇기 때문에 William L. Phelps는 "Mark Twain은 철두철미한 미국인이다. 만약 외국 사람이 미국정신의 실체를 알고 싶어 한다면 그의 작품을 읽게 하라. 그는 미국인들이 편애하는 Walt Whitman보다 몇 갑절 더 미국적인 작가이다"라고 주장하였다. 실제로 Sinclaire Lewis, Sherwood Anderson, Hemingway, William Faulkner, Jack Kerouac, J. D. Salinger, Saul Bellow, John Barth 등 현대 미국소설을 대표하는 작가들의 작품에서 그의 영향을 쉽게 찾아볼 수 있다.

II. *Pudd'nhead Wilson* Introduction

*Pudd'nhead Wilson*은 Twain의 작품 중에서 미국을 배경으로 하는 마지막 소설이다. 그가 소년시절을 보냈던 남북전쟁 전의 작은 마을 Hannibal에 배경을 두었다는 점에서 *The Adventures of Tom Sawyer*와 *Adventures of Huckleberry Finn*과 유사한 점이 있지만 *Puddn'head Wilson*은 이 두 소설보다 한층 더 어두운 분위기를 보여주고 있다. Twain이 일반적으로 유머작가라고 알려져 있기는 하지만 *Pudd'nhead Wilson*에서 그의 유머는 표면상에만 나타나 보이며 실제로는 비극적인 내용을 다루고 있다. 22장으로 나누어져 있는 이 소설은 남북전쟁이전 Missouri의 작은 마을인 Dawson's Landing에서의 23년간을 그리고 있으며 이 마을에서 일어난 일련의 사건들을 통해 미국 남부 작은 마을의 인종적 편견과 노예제도의 잔혹함, 혼혈의 문제, 타락한 남부의 귀족문화 등을 솔직하게 보여주고 있다.

1) Textual History

Twain이 "Those Extraordinary Twins"를 쓰기 시작한 것은 그가 57세인 1892년으로 그는 *A Connecticut Yankee in King Arthur's Court*를 쓴 이후 3년간 문학적 침체기를 겪고 있었다. 그 침체기는 여러 원인이 있었지만 가장 큰 원인은 경제적인 문제였다. 식자기계에 대한 투자 그리고 출판사업의 실패는 그를 경제적 파산상태로 몰아가고 있었다. 게다가 아내의 병 치료를 위한 휴양지로의 여행들로 인해 그는 글 쓸 시간을 찾기 힘들었다. 따라서 이 시기에 쓰여진 *The American Claimant*(1892), *Tom Sawyer Abroad*(1894), *Those Extraordinary Twins*는 문학적 성과라는 면에서 그가 쓴 다른 작품들에 많이 떨어진다고 평가 받고 있다.

*Pudd'nhead Wilson*을 쓰는 동안 Twain은 유럽에 살며 샴쌍둥이가 전시되고 있는 것을 보았다. 또한 1883년 *Life on the Mississippi*의 31장 "A Dying Man's Confession"을 쓸 때부터 지문이 사람을 식별할 수 있다는 사실에 관심을 가졌으며 1892년 London에서 출간된 Sir Francis Galton의 *Finger Prints*라는 책에서 지문감식에 대한 자세한 내용들을 읽었다. 그리고 노예제도와 혼혈문제는 그의 초기 작품부터 계속 관심을 기울여 오던 문제였다. 그는 미국남부의 잘못된 제도와 인간의 저속함 그리고 비열함이 이런 사회문제를 불러일으킨다고 생각했던 것이다.

Twain이 *Those Extraordinary Twins*의 서문 부분 "Author's Note to Those Extraordinary Twins"에서 밝히고 있듯이 *Pudd'nhead Wilson*의 원래 계획은 거의 모든 것에 반대이지만 "머리가 둘, 목이 둘, 네 팔과 한 몸, 그리고 한 쌍의 다리를 가진" 샴쌍둥이의 익살스러운 행동들에 대한 소극farce이었다. 하지만 David Wilson이 등장하면서 Tom Driscoll과 Roxana가 따라 나오게 되었고 결국 이야기는, Twain의 주장에 의하면, 자연스럽게 소극에서 비극으로 바뀌게 되었다. 소극에 살인사건이 어울리지 않고 또 한 작품 속에 두 이야기가 섞여 있다는 것을 깨닭고 Twain은 "한 이야기를 뿌리채 뽑아내고 다른 이야기만 남겨놓는 제왕절개수술"을 했다는 것이다. 즉, Twain은 샴쌍둥이에 관한 소극 부분을 잘라내고 나머지를 수정해 *Pudd'nhead Wilson*을 써낸 것이다. 이런 수정은 이야기에 근본적인 변화를 가져왔다. 분리된 샴쌍둥이의 비중이 줄어들고 Roxy, Tom, Wilson의 비중이 커진 것이다. 이런 집필과정으로 인해 *Pudd'nhead Wilson*의 곳곳에 샴쌍둥이 이야기의 흔적이 남아있게 되었고 그 때문에 일부 비평가들은 Twain을 부주의한 작가라는 비판하였다. 하지만 샴쌍둥이 이야기의 흔적들과 Those

Extraordinary Twins에 대한 지식은 *Pudd'nhead Wilson*의 복잡한 구조와 주제를 이해하는데 도움이 되기 때문에 Twain이 부주의하였다는 지적은 적당치 않다. Twain도 두 작품의 연관성을 주장하듯 1894년 11월 28일 미국에서 이 작품을 *The Tragedy of Pudd'nhead Wilson and The Comedy of Those Extraordinary Twins*라는 제목으로 처음 출간하였다.

2) Themes

*Pudd'nhead Wilson*이 처음 출판되었을 때 이 소설의 가장 큰 주제인 인종차별과 노예제도에 대한 비난이 주목받지 못하고 독자들에게 별로 인기를 끌지 못했다. 특히 *Those Extraordinary Twins* 원고를 수정함으로써 생긴 구조상의 오류는 이 작품을 많은 비평가와 독자들로부터 외면받게 만들었다. 하지만 20세기에 들어오면서 Twain의 후기 작품들에 대한 재평가가 시작되고 *Pudd'nhead Wilson*에 대한 관심도 커지게 되었다.

노예제도에 대한 Twain의 비판으로 인해 그의 작품들을 Harriet Beecher Stowe의 *Uncle Tom's Cabin*(1852) 같은 대표적 반노예제도 소설과 비교되기도 한다. 하지만 남북전쟁에 도화선이 된 Stowe의 소설과 달리 Twain의 반노예제도 소설들은 남북전쟁이 끝나 공식적으로 노예제도가 폐지된 지 20여년이 지나서야 출간되기 시작했다. 이미 없어진 노예제도를 반대하는 소설이라는 것이 비논리적으로 보이기는 하나 Twain의 소설은 사회적인 구속과 부당하고 억압받는 인간의 존엄성을 일깨우기 위한 은유로서뿐 만이 아니라 남북전쟁이후에도 엄연하게 존재하던 남부의 인종차별을 비판하고 있다.

*Pudd'nhead Wilson*도 남북전쟁이 끝난지 40년이 지나서야 출간되었다. 이것은 그때까지도 인종차별이 남부의 급박한 문제라는 것을 보여준다. 이 소설이 쓰여질 땐 미국이라는 국가에 남부를 다시 통합시키고 해방된 흑인들에게 설 곳을 만들어 주려는 남부재건 시도가 완전히 실패로 끝난 것이 명백해졌다. 흑백차별법(The Jim

Crow Laws)의 제정과 인종차별단체(Ku Klux Klan)의 등장은 남부 재건시대의 인종문제가 얼마나 복잡하게 얽혀버린 상태였는지를 상징적으로 보여주고 있다. 19세기 말 남부의 흑인들은 Roxy나 Tom/Chambers처럼 "down the river"로 팔려 가는 것을 두려워 할 필요는 없었지만 아직도 그들은 분명한 위협과 차별 속에서 살고 있었던 것이다. *Pudd'nhead Wilson*에 그려진 흑인들의 모습과 대화는 남부에서 차별을 받으며 살고 있는 흑인들의 비참한 모습을 보여주고 있는 것이다.

Twain은 이런 남부의 인종문제를 인간사이의 본질적 차이에 대한 문제 그리고 혼혈의 문제와 연결시킴으로써 더 복잡하게 만들어 버린다. 겉모습은 완벽한 백인이지만 몇 방울의 흑인 피가 섞여 있기 때문에 남부의 법과 관습에 따라 흑인으로 구분되는 인물들을 등장시킴으로써 Twain은 진정으로 흑인과 백인 사이의 차이점이 존재하는 것인가에 대한 의구심을 드러낸다. Tom/Chambers는 1/32의 흑인 피가 흐르기 때문에 완벽한 백인의 겉모습에 불구하고 노예가 된다. 하지만 흑인 선조에 대해 알려진 것이 없었다면 그는 이 소설에서처럼 백인으로 행세하며 살아갈 수 있었을 것이다. 이런 인종간 본질적 차이의 애매모호함은 Roxy가 자신의 "흑인"아기를 주인집 백인 아기와 바꿔치기 함으로써 더욱 강조된다. 아버지 Percy Driscoll 마저도 자신의 아이와 "흑인"아이를 구별하지 못할 정도로 인종간의 차이는 확실치 않은 것이다. 또한 이러한 바꿔치기는 현존하는 흑인과 백인의 차이가 본성nature 때문인지 아니면 양육nurture 때문인지에 대한 중대한 의문을 제기한다. 남부에서 흑인들은 본질적으로 백인들보다 열등하다고 여겨졌고 그렇기 때문에 백인들의 지배와 보호 필요성을 정당화 할 수 있었다. 하지만 Tom/Chamber의 비겁하고 사악함이 Roxy가 주장한 대로 "nigger in him" 때문에 생겨난 것인지 아니면 주인집 응석받이 아이로 키워졌기 때문인지 소설은 의문을 제기한다. Roxy는 Tom/Chambers에

섞인 한 방울이 흑인 피가 그를 그렇게 비겁하게 만들었다고 비난하지만 Twain은 그가 바뀌었을 때부터 시작된 양육방식에 잘못이 있다는 암시도 하고 있다. 이들 애매모호함은 남부의 법과 관습이 인위적인 것임을 지적한다.

Twain은 *Adventures of Huckleberry Finn*에서와 같이 이 소설에서도 남부의 낡은 인습과 도덕을 드러내 보인다. 특히 종교, 도덕, 법률, 문화라는 이름으로 사회에 편견과 그릇된 가치관을 퍼뜨리고 있는 남부사람들의 편협함을 비판하고 있다. Twain은 Wilson의 재치있는 농담을 알아듣지 못하고 20년이 넘게 그를 바보 취급한 남부 사람들을 풍자한다. 하지만 그들보다 더 심하게 그리고 심각하게 Twain이 비판하는 것은 남부의 가치를 지키고 있다고 생각하는 상류계층이다. Twain은 the First Families of Virginia로 대표되어지는 남부의 상류계층이 시대에 뒤쳐진 관례, 명예, 혈통을 강조하고 사회의 위계질서를 유지하려 함으로써 남부와 미국 전체를 타락시키고 생각한다. The First Families of Virginia로 인해 시작된 Roxy와 Tom/Chambers의 비극은 헛된 명예와 혈통에 대한 이들 가문의 집착이 Twain이 생각했던 미국 민주주의가 지향하는 이상인 자유와 평등 그리고 박애와 상반되는 것임을 보여주고 있다.

Pudd'nhead Wilson

Contents

There is no character, howsoever good and fine, but it can be destroyed by ridicule, howsoever poor and witless.[1] Observe the ass, for instance: his character is about perfect, he is the choicest spirit among all the humbler animals, yet see what ridicule has brought him to.[2] Instead of feeling complimented when we are called an ass, we are left in doubt.

\- Pudd'nhead Wilson's Calendar

1) howsoever: however의 옛말, "아무리 ~ 일지라도": 여기서 but은 부정문 뒤에서 필연적인 결과를 이끄는 역할을 한다.

2) ass: "당나귀"이지만 "바보", "고집쟁이"라는 비속어로 쓰이기도 한다.

A WHISPER TO THE READER

A person who is ignorant of legal matters is always liable to[3] make mistakes when he tries to photograph a court scene with his pen; and so I was not willing to let the law chapters in this book go to press without first subjecting them to rigid and exhausting revision and correction by a trained barrister if that is what they are called. These chapters are right, now, in every detail, for they were rewritten under the immediate eye[4] of William Hicks, who studied law part of a while[5] in southwest Missouri thirty-five years ago and then came over here to Florence for his health and is still helping for exercise and board in Macaroni Vermicelli's horse-feed shed, which is up the back alley as you turn around the corner out of the Piazza del Duomo just beyond the house where that stone that Dante used to sit on six hundred years ago is let into the wall when he let on to be watching them build Giotto's Campanile and yet always got tired looking as Beatrice passed along on her way to get a chunk of chestnut cake to defend herself with in case of a Ghibelline outbreak[6] before she got to school, at the same old stand where they sell the same old cake to this day and it is just as light and good as it was then, too, and this is not flattery, far from it. He was a little rusty[7] on his law, but he rubbed

---

1) liable to: ~하기가 쉽다
2) under the immediate eye: 직접적인 감독아래
3) part of a while: a while =잠시; part of a while =아주 잠시
4) Ghibelline outbreak: 황제당의 폭동, 중세 이탈리아에서 독일황제편을 들어 교황파에 반대했던 당
5) rusty: (쓰지않아) 서툴어진

up[8] for this book, and those two or three legal chapters are right and straight, now. He told me so himself.

Given under my hand this second day of January, 1893, at the Villa Viviani, village of Settignano, three miles back of Florence, on the hills the same certainly affording the most charming view to be found on this planet, and with it the most dreamlike and enchanting sunsets to be found in any planet or even in any solar system and given, too, in the swell room of the house, with the busts of Cerretani senators and other grandees of this line looking approvingly down upon me, as they used to look down upon Dante, and mutely asking me to adopt them into my family, which I do with pleasure, for my remotest ancestors are but spring chickens compared with these robed and stately antiques, and it will be a great and satisfying lift for me, that six hundred years will.

Mark Twain

6) rubbed up: 복습하다 = 다시 읽다

CHAPTER 1

Tell the truth or trump[1]—but get the trick.

- Pudd'nhead Wilson's Calendar

The scene of this chronicle is the town of Dawson's Landing, on the Missouri side of the Mississippi, half a day's journey, per steamboat, below St. Louis.

In 1830 it was a snug collection of modest one- and two-story frame dwellings, whose whitewashed exteriors were almost concealed from sight by climbing tangles of rose vines, honeysuckles, and morning-glories. Each of these pretty homes had a garden in front fenced with white palings and opulently stocked with hollyhocks, marigolds, touch-me-nots, prince's-feathers, and other old-fashioned flowers; while on the windowsills of the houses stood wooden boxes containing moss-rose plants and terra-cotta pots in which grew a breed of geranium whose spread of intensely red blossoms accented the prevailing pink tint of the rose-clad house-front like an explosion of flame. When there was room on the ledge outside of the pots and boxes for a cat, the cat was there—in sunny weather—stretched at full length, sleep and blissful, with her furry belly to the sun and a paw curved over her nose. Then that house was complete, and its contentment and peace were made manifest to the world by this symbol, whose testimony is infallible. A home without a cat—and a well-fed, well-petted, and properly revered cat—may be perfect home, perhaps, but how can it prove title?[2]

All along the streets, on both sides, at the outer edge of the brick sidewalks,

---

1) trump: 조작하다 (trump up)

2) title: the title of being a perfect home; how can it prove to the world that it is a perfect home의 의미

stood locust trees with trunks protected by wooden boxing, and these furnished shade for summer and a sweet fragrance in spring, when the clusters of buds came forth. The main street, one block back from the river, and running parallel with it, was the sole business street. It was six blocks long, and in each block two or three brick stores, three stories high, towered above interjected bunches of little frame shops. Swinging signs creaked in the wind, the street's whole length. The candy-striped pole, which indicates nobility proud and ancient along the palace-bordered canals of Venice, indicated merely the humble barbershop along the main street of Dawson's Landing. On a chief corner stood a lofty unpainted pole wreathed from top to bottom with tin pots and pans and cups, the chief tin-monger's noisy notice to the world (when the wind blew) that his shop was on hand for business at that corner.

The hamlet's front was washed by the clear waters of the great river; its body stretched itself rearward up a gentle incline; its most rearward border fringed itself out and scattered its houses about its base line of the hills; the hills rose high, enclosing the town in a half-moon curve, clothed with forests from foot to summit.

Steamboats passed up and down every hour or so. Those belonging to the little Cairo line and the little Memphis line[3] always stopped; the big Orleans liners stopped for hails only, or to land passengers or freight; and this was the case also with the great flotilla of "transients." These latter came out of a dozen rivers—the Illinois, the Missouri, the Upper Mississippi, the Ohio, the Monongahela, the Tennessee, the Red River, the White River, and so on; and were bound every whither and stocked with every imaginable comfort or necessity, which the Mississippi's communities could want, from the frosty Falls of St. Anthony down through nine climates to torrid New Orleans.

Dawson's Landing was a slave holding town, with a rich, slave-worked grain

---

3) the little Cairo line: Cairo는 오하이오강과 미시시피강이 합류하는 지점에 있는 남부 Illinois주의 마을. Illinois주는 Missouri주 옆에 붙어있으며 Missouri주와 반달리노예제도에 반대하였음. Memphis는 Atlanta주의 도시로 노예제도를 찬성하고 있었음. "line"은 steamboat의 노선

and pork country back of it. The town was sleepy and comfortable and contented. It was fifty years old, and was growing slowly—very slowly, in fact, but still it was growing.

The chief citizen was York Leicester Driscoll, about forty years old, judge of the county court. He was very proud of his old Virginian ancestry,[4)] and in his hospitalities and his rather formal and stately manners, he kept up its traditions. He was fine and just and generous. To be a gentleman—a gentleman without stain or blemish was his only religion, and to it he was always faithful. He was respected, esteemed, and beloved by all of the community. He was well off, and was gradually adding to his store.[5)] He and his wife were very nearly happy, but not quite, for they had no children. The longing for the treasure of a child had grown stronger and stronger as the years slipped away, but the blessing never came—and was never to come.

With this pair lived the judge's widowed sister, Mrs. Rachel Pratt, and she also was childless—childless, and sorrowful for that reason, and not to be comforted. The women were good and commonplace people, and did their duty, and had their reward in clear consciences and the community's approbation. They were Presbyterians, the judge was a freethinker.

Pembroke Howard, lawyer and bachelor, aged about forty, was another old Virginian grandee with proved descent from the First Families. He was a fine, brave, majestic creature, a gentleman according to the nicest requirements of the Virginia rule, a devoted Presbyterian, an authority on the "code," and a man always courteously ready to stand up before you in the field if any act or word of his had seemed doubtful or suspicious to you, and explain it with any weapon you might prefer from brad-awls to artillery. He was very popular with the people, and was the judge's dearest friend.

---

4) very proud of his old Virginian ancestry: 남부는 Virginia주로부터 정착되기 시작했고 Virginia주 출신의 조상을 가진 사람들은 자신들의 가문을 귀족처럼 생각하며 자랑스러워 하였다

5) He was well off, and was gradually adding to his store: well off=wealthy. 부유했으며 재산을 점점 늘리고 있었다

Then there was Colonel Cecil Burleigh Essex, another F.F.V.[6] of formidable caliber—however, with him we have no concern.

Percy Northumberland Driscoll, brother to the judge, and younger than he by five years, was a married man, and had had children around his hearthstone[7]; but they were attacked in detail by measles, croup, and scarlet fever, and this had given the doctor a chance with his effective antediluvian methods[8]; so the cradles were empty.[9] He was a prosperous man, with a good head for speculations[10], and his fortune was growing. On the first of February, 1830, two boy babes were born in his house: one to him, the other to one of his slave girls, Roxana by name. Roxana was twenty years old. She was up and around the same day, with her hands full, for she was tending both babes.

Mrs. Percy Driscoll died within the week. Roxy remained in charge of the children. She had her own way, for Mr. Driscoll soon absorbed himself in his speculations and left her to her own devices.[11]

In that same month of February, Dawson's Landing gained a new citizen. This was Mr. David Wilson, a young fellow of Scotch parentage. He had wandered to this remote region from his birthplace in the interior of the State of New York, to seek his fortune. He was twenty-five years old, college-bred, and had finished a post-college course in an Eastern law school a couple of years before.[12]

He was a homely, freckled, sandy-haired young fellow, with an intelligent blue eye that had frankness and comradeship in it and a covert twinkle of a pleasant sort. But for an unfortunate remark of his, he would no doubt have entered at once upon a successful career at Dawson's Landing. But he made his

---

6) F.F.V.: First Families of Virginia. 버지니아주에 첫 정착한 사람들을 조상으로 가진 가문

7) around his hearthstone: 그의 가정에

8) his effective antediluvian methods: 그의 효과적인 태고적 낡은 방식. "효과적"이라는 것은 반어적으로 쓰였으며 antediluvian은 "노아의 대홍수 이전의" 라는 뜻

9) so the cradles were empty: 요람이 비었다 (모두 죽었다)

10) a good head for speculations: 투기에 능한 머리를 가지고 있었다

11) She had her own way for Mr. Driscoll . . . left her to her own devices: have one's own way= 마음대로 하다; leave a person to his/her own devices =제멋대로 하게하다

12) college-bred: bred = breed의 과거형, 대학교육을 받은; a post-college course: 대학원 과정

fatal remark the first day he spent in the village, and it "gauged" him[13]. He had just made the acquaintance of a group of citizens when an invisible dog began to yelp and snarl and howl and make himself very comprehensively disagreeable, whereupon young Wilson said, much as[14] one who is thinking aloud—

"I wish I owned half of that dog."

"Why?" somebody asked.

"Because, I would kill my half."

The group searched his face with curiosity, with anxiety even, but found no light[15] there, no expression that they could read. They fell away from him as from something uncanny, and went into privacy to discuss him. One said—

"Pears[16] to be a fool."

"Pears?" said another. "Is, I reckon you better say."

"Said he wished he owned half of the dog, the idiot," said a third. "What did he reckon would become of the other half if he killed his half? Do you reckon he thought it would live?"

"Why, he must have thought it, unless he *is* the downrightest fool in the world; because if he hadn't thought that, he would have wanted to own the whole dog, knowing that if he killed his half and the other half died, he would be responsible for that half just the same as if he had killed that half instead of his own. Don't it look that way to you, gents?"

"Yes, it does. If he owned one half of the general dog, it would be so; if he owned one end of the dog and another person owned the other end, it would be so, just the same; particularly in the first case, because if you kill one half of a general dog, there ain't any man that can tell whose half it was, but if he owned one end of the dog, maybe he could kill his end of it and—"

"No, he couldn't, either; he couldn't and not be responsible if the other end

13) gauged: 평가하였다
14) much as: much like. – 처럼
15) found no light: 문제의 해명에 도움이 되는 것을 발견하지 못했다
16) 'pears to: appears to=~인 것 같다

died, which it would. In my opinion that man ain't in his righ mind."

"In my opinion he hain't got any mind."[17)]

No. 3 said.

"Well, he's a lummix, anyway."

"That's what he is" said No. 4, "he's a labrick—just a Simon-pure labrick,[18)] if ever there was one."

"Yes, sir, he's a dam fool,[19)] that's the way I put him up," said No. 5. "Anybody can think different that wants to, but those are my sentiments."

"I'm with you, gentlemen," said No. 6. "Perfect jackass—yes, and it ain't going too far to say he is a pudd'nhead.[20)] If he ain't a pudd'nhead, I ain't no judge, that's all."[21)]

Mr. Wilson stood elected. The incident was told all over the town, and gravely discussed by everybody. Within a week he had lost his first name; Pudd'nhead took its place. In time he came to be liked, and well liked too; but by that time the nickname had got well stuck on, and it stayed. That first day's verdict made him a fool, and he was not able to get it set aside, or even modified. The nickname soon ceased to carry any harsh or unfriendly feeling with it, but it held its place, and was to continue to hold its place for twenty long years.

---

17) he hain't *got* any mind: he ain't got any mind=he does not have any mind(지력). 그는 완전히 바보다.

18) a Simon-pure labrick: Simon-pure=real, gunuine 진짜, labrick=얼간이

19) dam fool: damn fool=바보 멍청이

20) pudd'nhead: puddinghead=얼간이, 바보

21) If he ain't a pudd'nhead, I ain't no judge: 만일 그가 바보가 아니라면 난 판단할 줄 조차 모르는 사람이다 (그가 바보임이 틀림없다)

CHAPTER 2

Adam was but human—this explains it all. He did not want the apple for the apple's sake, he only wanted it because it was forbidden. The mistake was in not forbidding the serpent; then he would have eaten the serpent.

- Pudd'nhead Wilson's Calendar

Pudd'nhead Wilson had a trifle of money when he arrived, and he bought a small house on the extreme western verge of the town. Between it and Judge Driscoll's house there was only a grassy yard, with a paling fence dividing the properties in the middle. He hired a small office down in the town and hung out a tin sign with these words on it:

DAVID WILSON
ATTORNEY AND COUNSELOR-AT-LAW
SURVEYING, CONVEYANCING, ETC.

But his deadly remark had ruined his chance—at least in the law. No clients came. He took down his sign, after a while, and put it up on his own house with the law features knocked out of it. It offered his services now in the humble capacities of land surveyor and expert accountant. Now and then he got a job of surveying to do, and now and then a merchant got him to straighten out his books.[1] With Scotch patience and pluck[2] he resolved to live down his reputation[3] and work

1) to straighten out his books: 장부를 정리하다
2) With Scotch patience and pluck: 스코틀랜드인의 인내심과 용기로

his way into the legal field yet. Poor fellow, he could foresee that it was going to take him such a weary long time to do it.

He had a rich abundance of idle time, but it never hung heavy on his hands,[4] for he interested himself in every new thing that was born into the universe of ideas, and studied it, and experimented upon it at his house. One of his pet fads was palmistry. To another one he gave no name, neither would he explain to anybody what its purpose was, but merely said it was an amusement. In fact, he had found that his fads added to his reputation as a pudd'nhead; therefore, he was growing chary of being too communicative about them. The fad without a name was one which dealt with people's finger-marks. He carried in his coat pocket a shallow box with grooves in it, and in the grooves strips of glass five inches long and three inches wide. Along the lower edge of each strip was pasted a slip of white paper. He asked people to pass their hands through their hair, (thus collecting upon them a thin coating of the natural oil,) and then make a thumb-mark on a glass strip, following it with the mark of the ball of each finger in succession. Under this row of faint grease- prints he would write a record on the strip of white paper—thus:

"JOHN SMITH, *right hand*"—

and add the day of the month and the year, then take Smith's left hand on another glass strip, and add name and date and the words "left hand." The strips were now returned to the grooved box, and took their place among what Wilson called his "records."

He often studied his records, examining and poring over[5] them with absorbing interest until far into the night; but what he found there—if he found anything—he revealed to no one. Sometimes he copied on

---

3) to live down his reputation: 바보라는 평판을 씻다
4) but it never hung heavy on his hands: 하지만 결코 따분하지는 않았다
5) poring over: pore over=열심히 읽다

paper the involved and delicate pattern left by the ball of the finger, and then vastly enlarged it with a pantograph so that he could examine its web of curving lines with ease and convenience.

One sweltering afternoon—it was the first day of July, 1830—he was at work over a set of tangled account books[6] in his workroom, which looked westward over a stretch of vacant lots, when a conversation outside disturbed him. It was carried on in yells, which showed that the people engaged in it were not close together:

"Say, Roxy, how does yo' baby come on?"[7] This from the distant voice. "Fustrate; How does you come on, Jasper?"[8] This yell was from close by.

"Oh, I's middlin'; hain't got noth'n to complain of, I's gwyne to come a-court'n you bime by, Roxy."[9]

"You is, you black mud-cat! Yah-yah-yah! I got somp'n better to do den 'sociat'n wid niggers as black as you is.[10] Is ole Miss Cooper's Nancy done give you de mitten?"[11] Roxy followed this sally with another discharge of carefree laughter.

"You's jealous, Roxy, dat's what's de matter wid you, you huzzy—yah-yah-yah! Dat's de time I got you!"[12]

---

6) a set of tangled account books: 뒤얽힌 (혼란스런, 엉망인) 회계장부 한 세트

7) how does yo' baby come on: How does your baby come on?=아이는 어때?

8) Fustrate: First-rate=일등급이야 (아주 좋아). Roxy와 Jasper는 흑인영어를 쓰며 사실주의 자인 마크 트웨인인 흑인영어를 그 발음과 비슷하게 적고 있다. 또한 흑인들의 비문법적인 영어도 그대로 사용한다.

9) I's middlin': I am middling=나는 보통이야; hain't got noth'n to complain of: ain't got nothing to complain of=don't have anything to complain of=불평할 게 없어; I's going to come a-court'n you bime by: I am going to come courting you by and by= 차차 네게 구애하러 갈 거야.

10) I got sump'n better to do den 'sociat'n wid niggers as black as you is: I got something better to do than associating with niggers=너처럼 검은 흑인과 사귀는 것보다 더 나은 일들이 있다.

11) give you the mitten: 널 퇴짜놓다

12) Dat's de time I got you!: That's the time I got you!=I got you this time의 의미. 네 말뜻을 알겠다 (Roxy가 질투하는 것이라고)

"Oh, yes, you got me, hain't you. 'Clah to goodness[13] if dat conceit o' yo'n strikes in, Jasper, it gwyne to kill you sho'. If you b'longed to me, I'd sell you down de river 'fo' you git too fur gone. Fust time I runs acrost yo' marster, I's gwyne to tell him so."[14]

This idle and aimless jabber went on and on, both parties enjoying the friendly duel and each well satisfied with his own share of the wit exchanged for wit they considered it.

Wilson stepped to the window to observe the combatants; he could not work while their chatter continued. Over in the vacant lots was Jasper, young, coal-black, and of magnificent build, sitting on a wheelbarrow in the pelting sun at work, supposably,[15] whereas he was in fact only preparing for it by taking an hour's rest before beginning. In front of Wilson's porch stood Roxy, with a local handmade baby-wagon, in which sat her two charges[16]—one at each end and facing each other. From Roxy's manner of speech, a stranger would have expected her to be black, but she was not. Only one-sixteenth of her was black, and that sixteenth did not show.[17] She was of majestic form and stature, her attitudes were imposing and statuesque, and her gestures and movements distinguished by a noble and stately grace. Her complexion was very fair, with the rosy glow of

---

13) 'Clah to goodness: 맙소사

14) if dat conceit o' yo'n strikes in . . it gwyne to kill you, sho': If that conceit of yours strikes in . . . it's going to kill you, sure=네 공상이 떠들기 시작한다면 널 죽이고 말거야, 정말로. I'd sell you down de river 'fo' you git too fur gone: I'd sell you down the river before you get too far gone=네가 많이 떠들기도 전에 널 강 아래 마을로 널 팔아 버렸을거야. Missouri주처럼 미시시피강 중류에 사는 노예들에게 "down the river"로 대변되는 the Deep South 주들에 팔리는 것은 지옥에 떨어지는 것 같이 공포스러운 일이었다. Missouri주 노예들은 대부분 집안일을 돌보았으나 the Deep South에 있는 노예들은 농장들에서 일했다. Fust time I runs acrost yo' master: First time I run across your master

15) supposably: supposedly

16) her two charges: 그녀가 돌보는 두 아이들

17) that sixteenth did not show: (Roxy는 1/16만 흑인피가 섞여있었고) 그 1/16은 보이지 않았다=흑인인 것처럼 보이지 않았다

vigorous health in her cheeks, her face was full of character and expression, her eyes were brown and liquid, and she had a heavy suit of fine soft hair which was also brown, but the fact was not apparent because her head was bound about with a checkered handkerchief and the hair was concealed under it. Her face was shapely, intelligent, and comely—even beautiful. She had an easy, independent carriage—when she was among her own caste—and a high and "sassy" way, withal; but of course she was meek and humble enough where white people were.

To all intents and purposes Roxy was as white as anybody, but the one-sixteenth of her which was black outvoted the other fifteen parts[18] and made her a negro. She was a slave, and salable as such. Her child was thirty-one parts white, and he, too, was a slave, and by a fiction of law and custom a negro. He had blue eyes and flaxen curls like his white comrade, but even the father of the white child was able to tell the children apart—little as he had commerce with them—by their clothes: for the white babe wore ruffled soft muslin and a coral necklace, while the other wore merely a coarse tow-linen shirt which barely reached to its knees, and no jewelry.

The white child's name was Thomas à Becket Driscoll, the other's name was Valet de Chambre[19]: no surname—slaves hadn't the privilege.[20] Roxana had heard that phrase somewhere, the fine sound of it had pleased her ear, and as she had supposed it was a name, she loaded it onto her darling. It soon got shortened to "Chambers," of course.

Wilson knew Roxy by sight, and when the duel of wit began to play

---

18) out-voted: 능가했다. 1/16의 흑인피가 나머지 15/16부분을 능가해서 그녀를 흑인으로 만들었다.

19) Valet de Chambre: 프랑스어로 "하인"이라는 뜻

20) slaves hadn't the privilege: 노예들은 그런 특권이 없었다. 아이들이 어렸을 때부터 노예로 팔렸기 때문에 또 많은 여자노예들이 백인 주인에게 겁탈을 당하고 아이를 낳았기 때문에 아이들에게 family name을 주지 못했다

out[21], he stepped outside to gather in a record or two. Jasper went to work energetically, at once—perceiving that his leisure was observed. Wilson inspected the children and asked—

"How old are they, Roxy?"

"Bofe de same age, sir—five months. Bawn de fust o' Febuary."[22]

"They're handsome little chaps. One's just as handsome as the other, too."

A delighted smile exposed the girl's white teeth, and she said:

"Bless yo' soul, Misto Wilson, it's pow'ful nice o' you to say dat, caze one of 'em ain't on'y a nigger.[23] Mighty prime little nigger, *I* allays says, but dat's caze it's mine, o' course."

"How do you tell them apart, Roxy, when they haven't any clothes on?"

Roxy laughed a laugh proportioned to her size, and said:

"Oh, *I* kin tell 'em 'part, Misto Wilson, but I bet Marse Percy couldn't, not to save his life."[24]

Wilson chatted along for a while, and presently got Roxy's fingerprints for his collection—right hand and left—on a couple of his glass strips; then labeled and dated them, and took the "records" of both children, and labeled and dated them also.

Two months later, on the third of September, he took this trio of finger-marks again. He liked to have a "series"—two or three "takings" at intervals during the period of childhood, these to be followed by others at intervals of several years. The next day—that is to say, on the

---

21) play out: 승부가 지어지다, 결말이 나다

22) Bofe de same age: Both the same age, Bawn de fust o' Febuary: Born the first of February

23) Misto Wilson: Mister Wilson, caze one of 'em ain't on'y a nigger: Because one of them isn't only a nigger

24) *I* kin tell 'em 'part: I can tell them apart, but I bet Marse Percy couldn't, not to save his life: Marse=Master 하지만 Percy주인님은 할 수 없을 겁니다, 주인님 생명을 걸고라도요 (=죽어도요)

fourth of September,—something occurred which profoundly impressed Roxana. Mr. Driscoll missed another small sum of money—which is a way of saying that this was not a new thing, but had happened before. In truth, it had happened three times before. Driscoll's patience was exhausted. He was a fairly humane man, toward slaves and other animals; he was an exceedingly humane man toward the erring of his own race.[25] Theft he could not abide, and plainly there was a thief in his house. Necessarily the thief must be one of his Negroes. Sharp measures must be taken. He called his servants before him. There were three of these, besides Roxy: a man, a woman, and a boy twelve years old. They were not related. Mr. Driscoll said:

"You have all been warned before. It has done no good. This time I will teach you a lesson. I will sell the thief. Which of you is the guilty one?"

25) toward the erring of his own race: 자신이 속한 인종 (=백인)의 실수에 대해서는

They all shuddered at the threat, for here they had a good home, and a new one was likely to be a change for the worse. The denial was general. None had stolen anything—not money, anyway—a little sugar, or cake, or honey, or something like that, that "Marse Percy wouldn't mind or miss," but not money—never a cent of money. They were eloquent in their protestations, but Mr. Driscoll was not moved by them. He answered each in turn with a stern "Name the thief!"

The truth was, all were guilty but Roxana; she suspected that the others were guilty, but she did not know them to be so. She was horrified to think how near she had come to being guilty herself; she had been saved in the nick of time by a revival in the colored Methodist church,[26)] a fortnight before, at which time and place she "got religion." The very next day after that gracious experience, while her change of style was fresh upon her and she was vain of her purified condition,[27)] her master left a couple of dollars unprotected on his desk, and she happened upon that temptation when she was polishing around with a dust-rag. She looked at the money a while with a steadily rising resentment, then she burst out with—

"Dad blame dat revival, I wisht it had a ben put off till tomorrow!"[28)]

Then she covered the tempter with a book, and another member of the kitchen cabinet got it. She made this sacrifice as a matter of religious etiquette; as a thing necessary just now, but by no means to be wrested into a precedent;[29)] no, a week or two would limber up[30)] her piety, then she would be rational again,

---

26) the colored Methodist church: 흑인 감리교회

27) while her change of style was fresh upon her and she was vain of her purified condition: 자신 삶의 방식의 변화가 아직 생생하고 그녀가 자신의 정화된 상태를 자랑스러워하고 있을 때

28) Dad blame dat revival: 젠장 그 부흥회 때문에 (Dad는 의미없음), I wisht it had a ben put off till tomorrow: I wished it had been put off till tomorrow=내일로 미뤄졌었으면, it=the revival

29) wrested into a precedent: 전례를 세우게 하다

30) limber up: 유연해지게 하다, 누그러지게 하다

and the next two dollars that got left out in the cold would find a comforter—and she could name the comforter.

Was she bad? Was she worse than the general run of her race?[31] No. They had an unfair show in the battle of life,[32] and they held it no sin to take military advantage of the enemy—in a small way; in a small way, but not in a large one. They would smouch provisions from the pantry whenever they got a chance; or a brass thimble, or a cake of wax, or an emery-bag, or a paper of needles, or a silver spoon, or a dollar bill, or small articles of clothing, or any other property of light value; and so far were they from considering such reprisals sinful, that they would go to church and shout and pray their loudest and sincerest with their plunder in their pockets. A farm smoke house had to be kept heavily padlocked, for even the colored deacon himself could not resist a ham when Providence showed him in a dream, or otherwise, where such a

thing hung lonesome, and longed for some one to love. But with a hundred hanging before him, the deacon would not take two—that is,

31) the general run of her race: 그녀가 속한 인종의 보통사람들
32) had an unfair show in the battle of life: 삶의 전쟁에서 불공평한 기회를 가졌다

on the same night. On frosty nights the humane Negro prowler would warm the end of the plank and put it up under the cold claws of chickens roosting in a tree; a drowsy hen would step on to the comfortable board, softly clucking her gratitude, and the prowler would dump her into his bag, and later into his stomach, perfectly sure that in taking this trifle from the man who daily robbed him of an inestimable treasure—his liberty—he was not committing any sin that God would remember against him in the Last Great Day.

"Name the thief!"

For the fourth time Mr. Driscoll had said it, and always in the same hard tone. And now he added these words of awful import:[33]

"I give you one minute"—He took out his watch—"if at the end of that time you have not confessed, I will not only sell all four of you, *but*—I will sell you DOWN THE RIVER!"

It was equivalent to condemning them to hell! No Missouri negro doubted this. Roxy reeled in her tracks, and the color vanished out of her face; the others dropped to their knees as if they had been shot; tears gushed from their eyes, their supplicating hands went up, and three answers came in the one instant:

"I done it!"

"I done it!"

"I done it!—have mercy, marster—Lord have mercy on us po' niggers!"[34)]

"Very good," said the master, putting up his watch, "I will sell you here, though you don't deserve it. You ought to be sold down the river."

The culprits flung themselves prone, in an ecstasy of gratitude, and kissed his feet, declaring that they would never forget his goodness and

33) these words of awful import: 무시무시한 뜻을 함축한 말들

never cease to pray for him as long as they lived. They were sincere, for like a god he had stretched forth his mighty hand and closed the gates of hell against them. He knew, himself, that he had done a noble and gracious thing, and he was privately well pleased with his magnanimity; and that night he set the incident down in his diary, so that his son might read it in after years, and be thereby moved to deeds of gentleness and humanity himself.

---

34) I done it!: I have done it=제가 했습니다, po' niggers: poor niggers

CHAPTER 3

Whoever has lived long enough to find out what life is, knows how deep a debt of gratitude we owe to Adam, the first great benefactor of our race. He brought death into the world.

- Pudd'nhead Wilson's Calendar

Percy Driscoll slept well the night he saved his house minions from going down the river, but no wink of sleep visited Roxy's eyes. A profound terror had taken possession of her. Her child could grow up and be sold down the river! The thought crazed her with horror. If she dozed, and lost herself for a moment, the next moment she was on her feet flying to her child's cradle to see if it was still there. Then she would gather it to her heart and pour out her love upon it in a frenzy of kisses, moaning, crying, and saying "Dey shant, oh, dey *shan't!*—yo' po' mammy will kill you fust!"[1)]

Once, when she was tucking it back in its cradle again, the other child nestled in its sleep and attracted her attention. She went and stood over it a long time, communing with herself:

"What has my po' baby done, dat he couldn't have yo' luck? He hain't done nuth'n.[2)] God was good to you; why warn't He good to him? Dey can't sell you down de river. I hates yo' pappy; he ain't got no heart[3)]—for niggers, he hain't,

---

1) Dey *shant:* They shan't=They shall not

2) He hani't done nuth'n: He ain't done nothing=He did not do anything 그는 아무 짓도 하지 않았다

3) yo' pappy: your papa; he ain't got no heart: he doesn't have heart 동정심이 없다. 흑인영어에서는 이중부정을 단순부정으로 많이 쓴다.

anyways. I hates him, en[4] I could kill him!" She paused awhile, thinking; then she burst into wild sobbings again, and turned away, saying, "Oh, I got to kill my chile, dey ain't no yuther way—killin' *him* wouldn't save de chile fum goin' down de river.[5] Oh, I got to do it, yo' po' mammy's got to kill you to save you, honey." she gathered her baby to her bosom now, and began to smother it with caresses—"Mammy's got to kill you—how *kin* I do it! But yo' mammy ain't gwyne to desert you, —no, no; *dah*,[6] don't cry—she gwyne *wid* you, she gwyne to kill herself, too.[7] Come along, honey, come along wid Mammy; we gwyne to jump in de river, den de troubles o' dis worl' is all over[8]—dey don't sell po' niggers down the river over *yonder*."[9]

She stared toward the door, crooning to the child and hushing it; midway she stopped, suddenly. She had caught sight of her new Sunday gown—a cheap curtain-calico thing, a conflagration of gaudy colors and fantastic figures. She surveyed it wistfully, longingly.

"Hain't ever wore it yet,"[10] she said, "en it's just lovely." Then she nodded her head in response to a pleasant idea, and added, "No, I ain't gwyne to be fished out[11], wid everybody lookin' at me, in dis mis'able ole linsey-woolsey."[12]

She put down the child and made the change. She looked in the glass and was astonished at her beauty. She resolved to make her

---

4) en: and

5) chile: child; dey ain't no yuther way: there is no other way; killin' him wouldn't save de chile fum goin' down de river: killing him (Master Percy) wouldn't save the child (her child) from going down the river

6) dah: there=자 (아기달랠 때 하는 말)

7) she gwyne wid you: she is going with you

8) den de troubles o' dis worl' is all over: then the troubles of this world is all over 그럼 이 세상에서의 고통은 다 끝난다

9) dey don't sell po' niggers down the river over *yonder*: 저 먼곳에서는 (heaven) 불쌍한 흑인들을 강 밑으로 팔지 않아

10) Hain't ever wore it yet: 아직 입어보지 않았다

11) fished out: (물에서) 낚여 올려지다, 꺼내지다.

12) in dis mis'able old linsey-woolsey: in this miserable linsey-woolsey (형편없는 린넨과 양모의 혼합 옷)

death-toilet[13] perfect. She handkerchief-turban and dressed her glossy wealth of hair "like white folks"; she added some odds and ends of rather lurid ribbon and a spray of atrocious artificial flowers; finally she threw over her shoulders a fluffy thing called a "cloud" in that day, which was of a blazing red complexion. Then she was ready for the tomb.

She gathered up her baby once more; but when her eye fell upon its miserably short little gray tow-linen shirt and noted the contrast between its pauper shabbiness and her own volcanic eruption of infernal splendors,[14] her mother-heart was touched, and she was ashamed.

"No, dolling[15] mammy ain't gwyne to treat you so. De angels isgwyne to 'mire you jist as much as dey does yo mammy.[16] Ain't gwyne to have 'em putt'n dey han's up 'fo' dey eyes en sayin' to David and Goliah en dem yuther prophets, Dat chile is dress' to indelicate fo' dis place. "[17]

13) death-toilet: 죽음을 위한 단장

14) her own volcanic irruption of infernal splendors: 그녀 자신의 새빨간 화려함의 화산같은 분출. 지옥의 붉은 불처럼 붉은 색조의 치장을 한 그녀의 화려함을 묘사

15) dolling: darling

16) to 'mire: to admire

17) Ain't gwyne to have 'em putt'n dey han's up 'fo' dey eyes en saying' to David en Goliah en dem yuther prophets: Does not going to have them put their hands up before their eyes and say to David and Goliah and the other prophets, Dat chile is dress' too indelicate fo' this place: That child is dressed too indelicate for this place, 그들(천사들)이 손으로 그들 눈을 가리고 다윗과 골리앗 그리고 다른 예언자들에게 "저 아이는 이 곳(천국)에 너무 어울리지 않는 옷을 입었다" 하고 말하게 하지 않을거야

By this time she had stripped off the shirt. Now she clothed the naked little creature in one of Thomas à Becket's snowy, long baby gowns, with its bright blue bows and dainty flummery of ruffles.

"Dah—now you's fixed."[18] She propped the child in a chair and stood off to inspect it. Straightway her eyes begun to widen with astonishment and admiration, and she clapped her hands and cried out, "Why, it do beat all!—I *never* knowed you was so lovely. Marse Tommy ain't a bit puttier[19]—not a single bit."

She stepped over and glanced at the other infant;' she flung a glance back at her own; then one more at the heir of the house. Now a strange light dawned in her eyes, and in a moment she was lost in thought. She seemed in a trance; when she came out of it, she muttered, "When I 'uz a-washin' 'em in de tub, yistiddy, he own pappy asked me which of 'em was his'n."[20]

She began to move around like one in a dream. She undressed Thomas à Becket, stripping him of everything, and put the tow-linen shirt on him. She put his coral necklace on her own child's neck. Then she placed the children side by side, and after earnest inspection she muttered—

"Now who would b'lieve clo'es could do de like o' dat?[21] Dog my cats[22] if it ain't all *I* kin do to tell t' other fum which, let alone his pappy."

She put her cub in Tommy's elegant cradle and said—

"You's young Marse *Tom* fum dis out, en I got to practice and git used to

---

18) Dah now you's fixed: There now you are fixed=자, 이제 다 준비되었다

19) puttier: prettier

20) When I 'uz a-washin' 'em in de tub, yistiddy, he own pappy asked me which of 'em was his'n: When I was washing them in the tub yesterday, his own papa asked me which of them was his

21) who would b'lieve clo'es could do de like o' dat?: who would believe clothes could do the like of that?=누가 옷이 이런 것을 할 수 있다고 믿을까?

22) Dog my cats: I'd be surprised의 의미

'memberin' to call you dat, honey[23], or I's gwyne to make a mistake some time en git us bofe into trouble. Dah—now you lay still en don't fret no mo', Marse Tom. oh, thank de good lord in heaven, you's saved, you's saved!—Dey ain't no man[24] kin ever sell mammy's po' little honey down de river now!"

She put the heir of the house in her own child's unpainted pine cradle, and said, contemplating its slumbering form uneasily—

"I's sorry for you, honey; I's sorry, God knows I is,—but what *kin* I do, what *could* I do? Yo' pappy would sell him to somebody, some time, en den he'd go down de river, sho', en I couldn't, couldn't, *couldn't* stan' it."[25]

She flung herself on her bed, and began to think and toss, toss and think. By and by she sat suddenly upright, for a comforting thought had flown through her worried mind—

"'Tain't no sin—*white* folks has done it! It ain't no sin, glory to goodness it ain't no sin! *Dey's* done it—yes, en dey was de biggest quality in de whole bilin', too—*kings*!"[26]

She began to muse; she was trying to gather out of her memory the dim particulars of some tale she had heard some time or other. At last she said—

"Now I's got it; now I 'member. It was dat ole nigger preacher dat tole it,[27] de time he come over here fum Illinois en preached in de nigger church. He said dey ain't nobody kin save his own self—can't do it by faith, can't do it by works, can't do it no way at all. Free grace is de *on'y*

---

23) You's: you are, fum this out: from this out 지금부터, git used to 'memberin': get used to remembering

24) dey ain't no man: there is no man=아무도, 누구도

25) *couldn't* stan' it: *couldn't* stand it=견딜수가 없다

26) en dey was de biggest quality in de whole bilin': and they were the biggest quality in the whole billing (bill, 목록)=그리고 그들은 모든 백인 중에서 가장 높은 지위의 사람들이었다

27) It was dat old nigger preacher dat tole it: It was that old nigger preacher that (=who) told it : 그 나이든 흑인 목사님이 그렇게 말했다.

way,[28] en dat don't come fum nobody but jis' de Lord;[29] en *He* kin give it to anybody He please, saint or sinner—*He* don't k'yer.[30] He do jis' as He's a mineter.[31] He s'lect out anybody dat suit Him, en put another one in his place, and make de fust one happy forever en leave t'other one to burn wid Satan. De preacher said it was jist like dey done in Englan' one time, long time ago. De queen she lef' her baby layin' aroun' one day, en went out callin'; an one 'o de niggers roun' 'bout de place dat was mos' white,[32] she come in en see de chile layin' aroun', en tuck en put her own chile's clo's on de queen's chile, en put de queen's chile's clo'es on her own chile, en den lef' her own chile layin' aroun', en tuck en toted de queen's chile home to de nigger quarter, en nobody ever foun' it out, en her chile was de king bimeby, en sole de queen's chile down de river one time when dey had to settle up de estate.[33] Dah, now—de preacher said it his own self, en it ain't no sin, caze white folks done it. *Dey* done it—yes, dey done it; en not on'y jis' common white folks nuther,[34] but de biggest quality dey is in de whole bilin'. Oh, I's so glad I 'member 'bout dat!"

She got light-hearted and happy, and went to the cradles, and spent what was left of the night "practicing." She would give her own child a light pat and say, humbly, "Lay still, Marse Tom," then give the real Tom a pat and say with severity, "Lay *still*, Chambers!—does you want me *to* take somep'n to you?"[35]

As she progressed with her practice, she was surprised to see how steadily and surely the awe which had kept her tongue reverent and

28) Free grace is de *on'y* way: Free grace is the only way=은총만이 유일한 방법이다. Calvinism의 교리

29) dat don't come fum nobody but jis' the Lord: that (=Free grace) doesn't come from nobody but just the Lord

30) *He* don't k'yer: He doesn't care

31) mineter: minister

32) mos': almost

33) bimeby: by and by=머지않아, settle up de estate: 재산을 정리하다

34) nuther: neither

35) Does you want me bring something *to* you?=무었을 가져다 주었으면 좋겠니? (뭐 원하는 것 있니?)

her manner humble toward her young master was transferring itself to her speech and manner toward the usurper, and how similarly handy she was becoming in transferring her motherly curtness of speech and peremptoriness of manner to the unlucky heir of the ancient house of Driscoll.

She took occasional rests from practicing, and absorbed herself in calculating her chances.

"Dey'll sell dese niggers today fo' stealin' de money, den dey'll buy some mo' dat don't know de chillen[36)]—so dat's all right. When I takes de chillen out to git de air, de minute I's roun' de corner I's gwyne to gaum dey mouths all roun' wid jam,[37)] den dey can't *nobody* notice dey's changed. Yes, I gwinter do dat till I's safe, if it's takes a year.

"Dey ain't but one man dat I's afeard of,[38)] en dat's dat Pudd'nhead Wilson. Dey calls him a pudd'nhead, en says he's a fool. My lan,[39)] dat man ain't no mo' fool den I is! He's de smartes' man in dis town, less'n[40)] it's Jedge Driscoll or maybe Pem. Howard. Blame dat man, he worries me wid dem ornery glasses o' his'n;[41)] *I* b'lieve he's a witch. But nemmine,[42)] I's gwyne to happen aroun' dah one o' dese days en let on dat I reckon he wants to print de chillen's fingers ag'in;[43)] en if *he* don't notice dey's changed, I bound dey ain't nobody gwyne to notice it, en den I's safe,

36) mo': more, chillen: children
37) to gaum dey mouths all roun' wid jam: to gum their mouths all around with jam=그 애들의 입주위를 온통 잼으로 발라놓다
38) I's afeard of: I am afraid of
39) My lan': my lord 같이 놀람 같은 것을 표현
40) less'n: less than
41) wid dem ornery glasses o' his'n: with those ornery glasses of his=그의 불길한 안경으로 나를 걱정시킨다
42) nemmine: nevermind
43) I's gwyne to happen aroun' dah one o' dese days en let on dat I reckon he wants to print de chillen's fingers ag'in: I am going to happen around there one of these days and let on (~인 체 하다) that I reckon he wants to print the children's fingers again=언제 그 사람 근처에 가서 그가 아이들의 지문을 또 채취하고 싶어할 것이라고 생각한 체 하겠다

sho'.[44] But I reckon I'll tote along a hoss-shoe[45] to keep off de witch-work."

The new negros gave Roxy no trouble, of course. The master gave her none, for one of his speculations was in jeopardy, and his mind was so occupied that he hardly saw the children when he looked at them, and all Roxy had to do was to get them both into a gale of laughter when he came about; then their faces were mainly cavities exposing gums, and he was gone again before the spasm passed and the little creatures resumed a human aspect.

Within a few days the fate of the speculation became so dubious that Mr. Percy went away with his brother, the judge, to see what could be done with it. It was a land speculation as usual, and it had gotten complicated with a lawsuit. The men were gone seven weeks. Before they got back, Roxy had paid her visit to Wilson, and was satisfied. Wilson took the fingerprints, labeled them with the names and with the date—October the first—put them carefully away, and continued his chat with Roxy, who seemed very anxious that he should admire the great advance in flesh and beauty which the babes had made since he took their fingerprints a month before. He complimented their improvement to her contentment; and as they were without any disguise of jam or other stain, she trembled all the while and was miserably frightened lest at any moment he—

But he didn't. He discovered nothing; and she went home jubilant, and dropped all concern about the matter permanently out of her mind

44) I bound: 맹세컨대, sho': sure

45) tote along a hoss-shoe: tote along a horse-shoe=편자를 가지고 가다 (Roxy는 다른 많은 흑인들처럼 horse-shoe가 악마를 쫓아낸다는 것 같은 미신을 믿음)

CHAPTER 4

Adam and Eve had many advantages, but the principal one was, that they escaped teething.

- Pudd'nhead Wilson's Calendar

There is this trouble about special providences—namely, there is so often a doubt as to which party was intended to be the beneficiary. In the case of the children, the bears, and the prophet, the bears got more real satisfaction out of the episode than the prophet did, because they got the children.

- Pudd'nhead Wilson's Calendar

This history must henceforth accommodate itself to the change which Roxana has consummated, and call the real heir "Chambers" and the usurping little slave, "Thomas à Becket"—shortening this latter name to "Tom," for daily use, as the people about him did.

"Tom" was a bad baby, from the very beginning of his usurpation. He would cry for nothing; he would burst into storms of devilish temper without notice, and let go scream after scream and squall after squall, then climax the thing with "holding his breath"—that frightful specialty of the teething nursling,[1] in the throes of which the creature exhausts its lungs, then is convulsed with noiseless squirmings and twistings and kickings in the effort to get its breath, while the lips turn blue and the mouth stands wide and rigid, offering for inspection one wee tooth set in the lower rim of a hoop of red gums; and when the

---

1) that frightful specialty of the teething nursling: 이나기 시작할 때쯤 된 젖먹이의 무시무시한 특기

appalling stillness has endured until one is sure the lost breath will never return, a nurse comes flying, and dashes water in the child's face, and—presto! the lungs fill, and instantly discharge a shriek, or a yell, or a howl which bursts the listening ear and surprises the owner of it into saying words which would not go well with a halo if he had one.[2] The baby Tom would claw anybody who came within reach of his nails, and pound anybody he could reach with his rattle. He would scream for water until he got it, and then throw cup and all on the floor and scream for more. He was indulged in all his caprices, howsoever troublesome and exasperating they might be; he was allowed to eat anything he wanted, particularly things that would give him the stomach-ache.

When he got to be old enough to begin to toddle about, and say broken words, and get an idea of what his hands were for, he was a more consummate pest[3] than ever. Roxy got no rest while he was awake. He would call for anything and everything he saw, simply saying, "Awnt it!" (want it), which was a command. When it was brought, he said in a frenzy, and motioning it away with his hands, "Don't awnt it! don't awnt it!" and the moment it was gone he set up frantic yells of "Awnt it! awnt it!" and Roxy had to give wings to her heels to get that thing back to him again before he could get time to carry out his intention of going into convulsions about it.

What he preferred above all other things was the tongs. This was because his "father" had forbidden him to have them lest he break windows and furniture with them. The moment Roxy's back was turned he would toddle to the presence of the tongs and say, "Like it!" and cock

---

2) a howl which bursts the listening ear: 듣고있는 귀를 파열시키는 고함; surprises the owner of it into saying words which would not go well with a halo if he had one: 만약 그(귀의) 주인에게 후광이 있다면(=성인같다면, 착하다면) 그것과 어울리지 않는 소리를 할만큼 놀라게 만들다

his eye to one side to see if Roxy was observing; then, "Awnt it!" and cock his eye again; then, "Hab it!" with another furtive glace; and finally, "Take it!"—and the prize was his. The next moment the heavy implement was raised aloft; the next, there was a crash and a squall, and the cat was off on three legs, to meet an engagement;[4] Roxy would arrive just as the lamp or a window went to irremediable smash.

Tom got all the petting, Chambers got none. Tom got all the delicacies, Chambers got mush and milk, and clabber without sugar. In consequence, Tom was a sickly child and Chambers wasn't. Tom was "fractious," as Roxy called it, and overbearing; Chambers was meek and docile.

With all her splendid common sense and practical everyday ability, Roxy was a doting fool of a mother. She was this toward her child—and she was also more than this: by the fiction created by herself, he was become her master; the necessity of recognizing this relation outwardly and of perfecting herself in the forms required to express the recognition, had moved her to such diligence and

---

3) consummate pest: 완전히 성가신 아이

4) the cat was off on three legs to meet an engagement: 고양이는 세 다리를 세우고 적과 싸우러 갔다 (물건 깨지는 소리에 놀라서, 급히 뛰쳐나갔다.)

faithfulness in practicing these forms that this exercise soon concreted itself into habit; it became automatic and unconscious; then a natural result followed: deceptions intended solely for others gradually grew practically into self-deceptions as well; the mock reverence became real reverence, the mock homage real homage; the little counterfeit rift of separation between imitation-slave and imitation-master widened and widened, and became an abyss, and a very real one—and on one side of it stood Roxy, the dupe of her own deceptions, and on the other stood her child, no longer a usurper to her, but her accepted and recognized master.

He was her darling, her master, and her deity all in one, and in her worship of him she forgot who she was and what he had been.

In babyhood Tom cuffed and banged and scratched Chambers unrebuked, and Chambers early learned that between meekly bearing it and resenting it the advantage all lay with the former policy. The few times that his persecutions had moved him beyond control and made him fight back had cost him very dear at headquarters; not at the hands of Roxy, for if she ever went beyond scolding him sharply for "forgett'n who his young marster was," she at least never extended her punishment beyond a box on the ear.[5] No, Percy Driscoll was the person. He told Chambers that under no provocation whatever was he privileged to lift his hand against his little master. Chambers overstepped the line three times, and got three such convincing canings from the man who was his father and didn't know it, that he took Tom's cruelties in all humility after that, and made no more experiments.

Outside of the house the two boys were together all through their boyhood. Chambers was strong beyond his years, and a good fighter;

---

5) box on the ear: 따귀

strong because he was coarsely fed and hard worked about the house, and a good fighter because Tom furnished him plenty of practice—on white boys whom he hated and was afraid of. Chambers was his constant bodyguard, to and from school; he was present on the playground at recess to protect his charge. He fought himself into such a formidable reputation, by and by, that Tom could have changed clothes with him, and "ridden in peace," like Sir Kay in Launcelot's armor.[6)]

He was good at games of skill, too. Tom staked him with marbles to play "keeps" with,[7)] and then took all the winnings away from him. In the winter season Chambers was on hand, in Tom's worn-out clothes, with "holy"[8)] red mittens, and "holy" shoes, and pants "holy" at the knees and seat, to drag a sled up the hill for Tom, warmly clad, to ride down on; but he never got a ride himself. He built snowmen and snow fortifications under Tom's directions. He was Tom's patient target when Tom wanted to do some snowballing, but the target couldn't fire back. Chambers carried Tom's skates to the river and strapped them on him, then trotted around after him on the ice, so as to be on hand when he wanted; but he wasn't ever asked to try the skates himself.

In summer the pet pastime of the boys of Dawson's Landing was to steal apples, peaches, and melons from the farmer's fruit wagons,—mainly on account of the risk they ran of getting their heads laid open with the butt of the farmer's whip. Tom was a distinguished adept at these thefts—by proxy. Chambers did his stealing, and got the peach stones, apple cores, and melon rhinds for his share.

---

6) "ridden in peace," like Sir Kay in Launcelot's armor: 랑슬롯의 갑옷을 입은 케이경처럼 평화롭게 여행할 수 있었다. (아더왕과 원탁의 기사이야기에 나오는 것으로 랑슬롯은 용맹스러운 기사였기 때문에 아무도 함부로 대하지 못했다. 케이경을 랑슬롯으로 알고 아무도 건드리지 않았다는 말)

7) play "keeps" with: 내기를 하다

8) "holy": holely(구멍뚫린)를 빗대어 쓴 말

Tom always made Chambers go in swimming with him, and stay by him as a protection. When Tom had had enough, he would slip out and tie knots in Chamber's shirt, dip the knots in the water and make them hard to undo, then dress himself and sit by and laugh while the naked shiverer tugged at the stubborn knots with his teeth.

Tom did his humble comrade these various ill turns partly out of native viciousness,[9)] and partly because he hated him for his superiorities of physique and pluck, and for his manifold cleverness. Tom couldn't dive, for it gave him splitting headaches. Chambers could dive without inconvenience, and was fond of doing it. He excited so much admiration, one day, among a crowd of white boys, by throwing back-somersaults from the stern of a canoe that it wearied Tom's spirit, and at last he shoved the canoe underneath Chambers while he was in the air—so he came down on his head in the canoe-bottom; and while he lay unconscious several of Tom's ancient adversaries saw that their long-desired opportunity was come, and they gave the false heir such a drubbing that with Chambers's best help he was hardly able to drag himself home afterward.

When the boys was fifteen and upwards, Tom was "showing off" in the river one day, when he was taken with a cramp, and shouted for help. It was a common trick with the boys—particularly if a stranger was present—to pretend a cramp and howl for help; then when the stranger came tearing hand-over-hand to the rescue,[10)] the howler would go on struggling and howling till he was close at hand, then replace the howl with a sarcastic smile and swim blandly away, while the town-boys assailed the dupe with a volley of jeers and laughter. Tom had never tried this joke as yet, but was supposed to be trying it now, so the boys held

---

9) native viciousness: 악한 본성. Twain은 여기에서 본성(nature)과 육성(nurture)의 차이점에 대해 지적하고 있다

10) tearing hand-over-hand to the rescue: 황급히 구하려 다가오면

warily back; but Chambers believed his master was in earnest; therefore, he swam out, and arrived in time, unfortunately, and saved his life.

This was the last feather.[11] Tom had managed to endure everything else, but to have to remain publicly and permanently under such an obligation as this to a nigger, and to this nigger of all niggers—this was too much. He heaped insults upon Chambers for "pretending" to think he was in earnest in calling for help, and said that anybody but a blockheaded nigger would have known he was funning and left him alone.

Tom's enemies were in strong force here, so they came out with their opinions quite freely. They laughed at him, and called him coward, liar, sneak, and other sorts of pet names, and told him they meant to call Chambers by a new name after this, and make it common in the town—"Tom Driscoll's Nigger-pappy"—to signify that he had had a second birth into this life, and that Chambers was the author of his new being.[12] Tom grew frantic under these taunts, and shouted—

"Knock their heads off, Chambers! Knock their heads off! What do you stand there with your hands in your pockets for?"

Chambers expostulated, and said,

"But, Marse Tom, dey's too many of 'em—dey's—"

"Do you hear me?"

"Please, Marse Tom, don't make me! Dey's so many of 'em dat—"

Tom sprang at him and drove his pocket knife into him two or three times before the boys could snatch him away and give the wounded lad a chance to escape. He was considerably hurt, but not seriously. If the blade had been a little longer, his career would have ended there.

Tom had long ago taught Roxy "her place." It had been many a day, now, since she had ventured a caress or a fondling epithet in his quarter.

---

11) This was the last feather: 이것은 최악의 (결정적인) 수치였다

12) Chambers was the author of his new being: Chambers가 Tom의 생명을 구했으니 그의 새로운 창조자(author)라는 의미

Such things, from a "nigger," were repulsive to him, and she had been warned to keep her distance and remember who she was. She saw her darling gradually cease from being her son, she saw that detail[13] perish utterly; all that was left was master—master, pure and simple, and it was not a gentle mastership, either. She saw herself sink from the sublime height of motherhood to the somber deeps of unmodified slavery.[14] The abyss of separation between her and her boy was complete. She was merely his chattel, now, his convenience, his dog, his cringing and helpless slave, the humble and unresisting victim of his capricious temper and vicious nature.

Sometimes she could not go to sleep, even when worn out with fatigue, because her rage boiled so high over the day's experiences with her boy. She would mumble and mutter to herself—

"He struck me, en I warn't no way to blame[15]—struck me in de face, right before folks. En he's al'ays callin' me nigger wench, en hussy, en all dem mean names, when I's doin' de very bes' I kin.[16] Oh, Lord, I done so much for him   I lif' him away up to whar he is[17]—en dis is what I git for it."[18]

Sometimes when some outrage of peculiar offensiveness stung her to the heart, she would plan schemes of vengeance and revel in the fancied spectacle of his exposure to the world[19] as an imposter and a slave; but in the midst of these joys fear would strike her: she had made him too strong;

---

13) that detail: being her son

14) sink from the sublime height of motherhood to the somber deeps of unmodified slavery: 숭고한 모성의 위치로부터 변하지 않은 노예 신분의 어두컴컴한 심연으로 추락

15) I warn't no way to blame: I wasn't no way to blame=나는 잘못이 전혀 없었다

16) en all dem mean names, when I's doin' de very bes' I kin: and all those mean names, when I am doing the very best I can=그리고 내가 최선을 다하고 있을 때도 그런 천한 욕을

17) I lif' him away up to whar he is: I lifted him away up to where he is=내가 그를 현재의 위치까지 올려놓았다

18) en dis is what I git for it: and this is what I get for it=그런데 이게 내가 받은 대접이다

19) the fancied spectacle of his exposure to the world: 그의 정체를 세상에 폭로하는 환상

she could prove nothing, and—heavens, she might get sold down the river for her pains! So her schemes always went for nothing,[20] and she laid them aside in impotent rage against the fates, and against herself for playing the fool on that fatal September day in not providing herself with a witness for use in the day when such a thing might be needed for the appeasing of her vengeance-hungry heart.

And yet the moment Tom happened to be good to her, and kind and this occurred every now and then—all her sore places were healed, and she was happy; happy and proud, for this was her son, her nigger son, lording it among the whites[21] and securely avenging their crimes against her race.

There were two grand funerals in Dawson's Landing that fall—the fall of 1845. One was that of Colonel Cecil Burleigh Essex, the other that of Percy Driscoll.

On his deathbed Driscoll set Roxy free and delivered his idolized ostensible son solemnly into the keeping of his brother, the Judge, and his wife. Those childless people were glad to get him. Childless people are not difficult to please.

Judge Driscoll had gone privately to his brother, a month before, and bought Chambers. He had heard that Tom had been trying to get his father to sell the boy down the river, and he wanted to prevent the scandal—for public sentiment did not approve of that way of treating family servants for light cause or for no cause.

Percy Driscoll had worn himself out in trying to save his great speculative landed estate, and had died without succeeding. He was hardly in his grave before the boom collapsed and left his hitherto envied young devil of an heir a pauper.[22] But that was nothing; his uncle told him he

---

20) went for nothing: 아무 소용도 없었다
21) lording it among the whites: 백인사이에서 큰소리치며
22) left his hitherto envied young devil of an heir a pauper: 지금까지 선망의 대상이었던 불

should be his heir and have all his fortune when he died; so Tom was comforted.

Roxy had no home now; so she resolved to go around and say good-bye to her friends and then clear out and see the world—that is to say, she would go chambermaiding on a steamboat, the darling ambition of her race and sex.

Her last call was on the black giant, Jasper. She found him chopping Pudd'nhead Wilson's winter provision of wood.

Wilson was chatting with him when Roxy arrived. He asked her how she could bear to go off chambermaiding and leave her boys; and chaffingly offered to copy off a series of their fingerprints, reaching up to their twelfth year, for her to remember them by; but she sobered in a moment, wondering if he suspected anything; then she said she believed she didn't want them. Wilson said to himself, "The drop of black blood in her is superstitious; she thinks there's some deviltry, some witch-business, about my glass mystery somewhere; she used to come here with an old horseshoe in her hand; it could have been an accident, but I doubt it."

쌍한 젊은 상속자를 거지로 만들었다

CHAPTER 5

Training is everything. The peach was once a bitter almond; cauliflower is nothing but cabbage with a college education.

- Pudd'nhead Wilson's Calendar

Remark of Dr. Baldwin's, concerning upstarts: We don't care to eat toadstools that think they are truffles.

- Pudd'nhead Wilson's Calendar

Mrs. York Driscoll enjoyed two years of bliss with that prize, Tom; bliss that was troubled a little at times, it is true, but bliss nevertheless; then she died, and her husband and his childless sister, Mrs. Pratt, continued this bliss-business at the old stand.[1] Tom was petted and indulged and spoiled to his entire content—or nearly that. This went on till he was nineteen, then he was sent to Yale. He went handsomely equipped with "conditions,"[2] but otherwise he was not an object of distinction there. He remained at Yale two years, and then threw up the struggle. He came home with his manners a good deal improved; he had lost his surliness and brusqueness, and was rather pleasantly soft and smooth, now; he was furtively, and sometimes openly, ironical of speech, and given to gently touching people on the raw,[3] but he did it with a good-natured semi-conscious air that carried it off safely and kept him from getting into trouble. He was as indolent as ever and showed no very

1) at the old stand: 예전 위치에서
2) conditions: (좋은) 조건들
3) touching people on the raw: 아픈데 (약점을) 건드리다

strenuous desire to hunt up an occupation. People argued from this that he preferred to be supported by his uncle until his uncle's shoes should become vacant.[4] He brought back one or two new habits with him, one of which he rather openly practiced—tippling—but concealed another, which was gambling. It would not do to gamble where his uncle could hear of it; he knew that quite well.

Tom's eastern polish was not popular among the young people. They could have endured it, perhaps, if Tom had stopped there; but he wore gloves, and that they couldn't stand, and wouldn't; so he was mainly without society. He brought home with him a suit of clothes of such exquisite style and cut and fashion—eastern fashion, city fashion—that it filled everybody with anguish and was regarded as a peculiarly wanton affront. He enjoyed the feeling which he was exciting, and paraded the town serene and happy all day; but the young fellows set a tailor to work that night, and when Tom started out on his parade next morning, he found the old deformed Negro bellringer straddling along in his wake[5] tricked out[6] in a flamboyant curtain-calico exaggeration of his finery, and imitating his fancy eastern graces as well as he could.

Tom surrendered, and after that clothed himself in the local fashion. But the dull country town was tiresome to him, since his acquaintanceship with livelier regions, and it grew daily more and more so. He began to make little trips to St. Louis for refreshment. There he found companionship to suit him, and pleasures to his taste, along with more freedom, in some particulars, than he could have at home. So, during the next two years, his

4) until his uncle's shoes should become vacant: 삼촌 재산이 다 사라질때까지
5) in his wake: 그의 바로 뒤에
6) tricked out: 잔뜩 꾸며서, 모양내서

visits to the city grew in frequency and his tarryings there grew steadily longer in duration.

He was getting into deep waters.[7] He was taking chances, privately, which might get him into trouble some day—in fact, did.

Judge Driscoll had retired from the Bench and from all business activities in 1850, and had now been comfortably idle three years. He was President of the Freethinkers' Society, and Pudd'nhead Wilson was the other member. The Society's weekly discussions were now the old lawyer's main interest in life. Pudd'nhead was still toiling in obscurity at the bottom of the ladder, under the blight of that unlucky remark which he had let fall twenty-three years before about the dog.

Judge Driscoll was his friend, and claimed that he had a mind above the average, but that was regarded as one of the judge's whims, and it failed to modify the public opinion. Or, rather, that was one of the reason why it failed, but there was another and better one. If the judge had stopped with bare assertion, it would have had a good deal of effect; but he made the mistake of trying to prove his position. For some years Wilson had been privately at work on a whimsical almanac, for his amusement—a calendar, with a little dab of ostensible philosophy, usually in ironical form, appended to each date; and the judge thought that these quips and fancies of Wilson's were neatly turned and cute;[8] so he carried a handful of them around one day, and read them to some of the chief citizens. But irony was not for those people; their mental vision was not focused for it. They read those playful trifles in the solidest earnest,[9] and decided without hesitancy that if there had ever been any doubt that Dave Wilson was a pudd'nhead which there hadn't this revelation removed that doubt for

7) He was getting into deep waters: 그는 수렁에 빠져들고 있었다

8) neatly turned and cute: 잘 표현되었고 재치있다

9) They read those playful trifles in the solidest earnest: 그들은 (Wilson의) 장난스러운 글들을 완전히 진지하게 읽었다.(irony를 전혀 이해하지 못하고 읽었다는 말)

good and all.[10] That is just the way, in this world; an enemy can partly ruin a man, but it takes a good-natured injudicious friend to complete the thing and make it perfect. After this the judge felt tenderer than ever toward Wilson, and surer than ever that his calendar had merit.

Judge Driscoll could be a freethinker and still hold his place in society because he was the person of most consequence in the community, and therefore could venture to go his own way and follow out his own notions. The other member of his pet organization was allowed the like liberty because he was a cipher in the estimation of the public, and nobody attached any importance to what he thought or did. He was liked, he was welcome enough all around, but he simply didn't count for anything.

The widow Cooper affectionately called "aunt Patsy" by everybody—lived in a snug and comely cottage with her daughter Rowena, who was nineteen, romantic, amiable, and very pretty, but otherwise of no consequence. Rowena had a couple of young brothers—also of no consequence.

The widow had a large spare room, which she let to a lodger, with board, when she could find one, but this room had been empty for a year now, to her sorrow. Her income was only sufficient for the family support, and she needed the lodging money for trifling luxuries. But now, at last, on a flaming June day, she found herself happy; her tedious wait was ended; her year-worn advertisement had been answered; and not by a village applicant, oh, no!—this letter was from away off yonder in the dim great world to the North: it was from St. Louis. She sat on her porch gazing out with unseeing eyes upon the shining reaches of the mighty Mississippi, her thoughts steeped in her good fortune. Indeed it was specially good fortune, for she was to have two lodgers instead of one.

She had read the letter to the family, and Rowena had danced away

---

10) for good and all: 영원히

to see to the cleaning and airing of the room by the slave woman, Nancy, and the boys had rushed abroad in the town to spread the great news, for it was matter of public interest, and the public would wonder and not be pleased if not informed. Presently Rowena returned, all aflush with joyous excitement, and begged for a re reading of the letter. It was framed thus:

> HONORED MADAM: My brother and I have seen your advertisement, by chance, and beg leave to take the room you offer.[11] We are twenty-four years of age and twins. We are Italians by birth, but have lived long in the various countries of Europe, and several years in the United States. Our names are Luigi and Angelo Capello. You desire but one guest; but, dear madam, if you will allow us to pay for two, we will not incommode you. We shall be down Thursday.

"Italians! How romantic! Just think, Ma—there's never been one in this town, and everybody will be dying to see them, and they're all *OURS*! Think of that!"

"Yes, I reckon they'll make a grand stir."

"Oh, indeed they will. The whole town will be on its head! Think—they've been in Europe and everywhere! There's never been a traveler in this town before, Ma, I shouldn't wonder if[12] they've seen kings!"

"Well, a body can't tell; but they'll make stir enough, without that."

"Yes, that's of course. Luigi—Angelo. They're lovely names; and so grand and foreign—not like Jones and Robinson and such. Thursday they are coming, and this is only Tuesday; it's a cruel long time to wait. Here comes Judge Driscoll in at the gate. He's heard about it. I'll go and open

---

11) beg leave to take the room you offer: 당신이 세놓는 방을 얻고 싶습니다
12) I shouldn't wonder if ~: ~했더라도 하나도 이상하지 않다

the door."

The judge was full of congratulations and curiosity. The letter was read and discussed. Soon Justice Robinson arrived with more congratulations, and there was a new reading and a new discussion. This was the beginning. Neighbor after neighbor, of both sexes, followed, and the procession drifted in and out all day and evening and all Wednesday and Thursday. The letter was read and re-read until it was nearly worn out; everybody admired its courtly and gracious tone, and smooth and practiced style, everybody was sympathetic and excited, and the Coopers were steeped in happiness all the while.

The boats were very uncertain, in low water,[13)] in those primitive times. This time the Thursday boat had not arrived at ten at night—so the people had waited at the landing all day for nothing; they were driven to their homes by a heavy storm without having had a view of the illustrious foreigners.

Eleven o'clock came; then twelve, and the Cooper house was the only one in the town that still had lights burning. The rain and thunder were booming yet, and the anxious family were still waiting, still hoping. At last there was a knock on the door, and the family jumped to open it. Two negro men entered, each carrying a trunk, and proceeded up stairs toward the guest room. Then entered the twins—the handsomest, the best dressed, the most distinguished-looking pair of young fellows the West had ever seen. One was a little fairer14) than the other, but otherwise they were exact duplicates.

---

13) in low water: 강물의 수위가 낮을 때
14) fairer: 피부색이 더 하얀

CHAPTER 6

Let us endeavor so to live that when we come to die even the undertaker will be sorry.

-Pudd'nhead Wilson's Calendar

Habit is habit, and not to be flung out of the window by any man, but coaxed downstairs a step at a time.

-Pudd'nhead Wilson's Calendar

At breakfast in the morning, the twins' charm of manner and easy and polished bearing made speedy conquest of the family's good graces. All constraint and formality quickly disappeared, and the friendliest feeling succeeded. Aunt Patsy called them by their Christian names[1)] almost from the beginning. She was full of the keenest curiosity about them, and showed it; they responded by talking about themselves, which pleased her greatly. It presently appeared that in their early youth they had known poverty and hardship. As the talk wandered along, the old lady watched for the right place to drop in a question or two concerning that matter, and when she found it, she said to the blonde twin, who was now doing the biographies in his turn while the brunette one rested—

"If it ain't asking what I ought not to ask, Mr. Angelo, how did you come to be so friendless and in such trouble when you were little? Do you mind telling? But don't, if you do."

"Oh, we don't mind it at all, madam; in our case it was merely misfortune, and nobody's fault. Our parents were well-to-do, there in

Italy, and we were their only child. We were of the old Florentine nobility"—Rowena's heart gave a great bound, her nostrils expanded, and a fine light played in her eyes—"and when the war broke out, my father was on the losing side and had to fly for his life. His estates were confiscated, his personal property seized, and there we were, in Germany, strangers, friendless, and in fact paupers. My brother and I were ten years old, and well educated for that age, very studious, very fond of our books, and well grounded in the German, French, Spanish, and English languages. Also, we were marvelous musical prodigies—if you will allow me to say it, it being only the truth.

"Our father survived his misfortunes only a month,[2] our mother soon followed him, and we were alone in the world. Our parents could have made themselves comfortable by exhibiting us as a show,[3] and they had many and large offers; but the thought revolted their pride, and they said they would starve and die first. But what they wouldn't consent to do, we had to do without the formality of consent. We were seized for the debts occasioned by their illness and their funerals, and placed among the attractions of a cheap museum in Berlin to earn the liquidation money. It took us two years to get out of that slavery. We traveled all about Germany, receiving no wages, and not even our keep. We had to exhibit for nothing, and beg our bread.

"Well, madam, the rest is not of much consequence. When we escaped from that slavery at twelve years of age, we were in some respects men. Experience had taught us some valuable things; among

---

1) their Christian names: 그들의 이름 (성이 아니라 이름을 부름으로 친근감 표시)

2) Our father survived his misfortunes only a month: 아버지는 그 재난들이 있은지 한달만에 돌아가셨다

3) by exhibiting us as a show: 우리를 구경거리로 전시해서 (Puddn'head Wilson의 시초가 된 Those Extraordinary Twins에서 이들은 샴 쌍둥이였다. Those Extraordinary Twins이 Pudd'nhead Wilson 이야기로 변경되면서 몇몇 곳에 첫 번째 이야기의 흔적이 남아있고 그래서 Mark Twain이 부주의했다고 비판하는 비평가들이 있다)

others, how to take care of ourselves, how to avoid and defeat sharks and sharpers,[4] and how to conduct our own business for our own profit and without other people's help. We traveled everywhere—years and years—picking up smatterings of strange tongues, familiarizing ourselves with strange sights and strange customs, accumulating an education of a wide and varied and curious sort. It was a pleasant life. We went to Venice—to London, Paris, Russia, India, China, Japan—"

At this point Nancy, the slave woman, thrust her head in at the door and exclaimed:

"Ole Missus, de house is plum jam full o' people, en dey's jes a-spilin' to see de gen'lemen!"[5] She indicated the twins with a nod of her head, and tucked it back out of sight again.

It was a proud occasion for the widow, and she promised herself high satisfaction in showing off her fine foreign birds before her neighbors and friends—simple folk who had hardly ever seen a foreigner of any kind, and never one of any distinction or style. Yet her feeling was moderate indeed when contrasted with Rowena's. Rowena was in the clouds, she walked on air; this was to be the greatest day, the most romantic episode in the colorless history of that dull country town, she was to be familiarly near the source of its glory and feel the full flood of it pour over her and about her; the other girls could only gaze and envy, not partake.

The widow was ready, Rowena was ready, so also were the foreigners.

The party moved along the hall, the twins in advance, and entered the open parlor door, whence issued a low hum of conversation. The

---

4) sharks and sharpers: 협잡꾼들과 사기꾼들

5) Ole Missus, de house is plum jam full o' people, en dey's jes' a-spilin' to see de gen'lemen: Old Misses, the house is plum jam full of people, and they are just spilling to see the gentlemen=마님, 집이 사람들로 가득 찼고 저 신사분들을 보려고 넘치고 있어요

twins took a position near the door, the widow stood at Luigi's side, Rowena stood beside Angelo, and the march-past and the introductions began. The widow was all smiles and contentment. She received the procession and passed it on to Rowena.

"Good mornin', Sister Cooper"—handshake.

"Good morning, Brother—Count Luigi Capello, Mr."—handshake, followed by a devouring stare and "I'm glad to see ye," on the part of, and a courteous inclination of the head and a pleasant "Most happy!" on the part of Count Luigi.

"Good mornin', Roweny"—handshake.

"Good morning, Mr. Higgins—present you to Count Angelo Capello." Handshake, admiring stare, "Glad to see ye"—courteous nod, smily "Most happy!" and Higgins passes on.

None of these visitors was at ease, but being honest people, they didn't pretend to be. None of them had ever seen a person bearing a title of nobility before, and none had been expecting to see one now, consequently the title came upon them as a kind of pile-driving surprise[6] and caught them unprepared. A few tried to rise to the emergency, and got out an awkward "My lord," or "Your lordship," or something of that sort, but the great majority were overwhelmed by the unaccustomed word and its dim and awful associations with gilded courts and stately ceremony and anointed kingship, so they only fumbled through the handshake and passed on, speechless. Now and then, as happens at all receptions everywhere, a more than ordinary friendly soul blocked the procession and kept it waiting while he inquired how the brothers liked the village, and how long they were going to stay, and if their family was well, and dragged in the weather, and hoped it would get cooler soon, and all that sort of thing, so as to

6) pile-driving surprise: 강렬한 놀라움

be able to say, when he got home, "I had quite a long talk with them;" but nobody did or said anything of a regrettable kind, and so the great affair went through to the end in a creditable and satisfactory fashion.

General conversation followed, and the twins drifted about from group to group, talking easily and fluently, and winning approval, compelling admiration, and achieving favor from all. The widow followed their conquering march with a proud eye, and every now and then Rowena said to herself with deep satisfaction, "And to think,[7] they are ours—all ours!"

There were no idle moments for mother or daughter. Eager inquiries concerning the twins were pouring into their enchanted ears all the time; each was the constant center of a group of breathless listeners; each recognized that she knew now for the first time the real meaning of that great word Glory, and perceived the stupendous value of it, and understand why men in all ages had been willing to throw away meaner happiness, treasure, life itself, to get a taste of its sublime and supreme joy. Napoleon and all his kind stood accounted for—and justified.

When Rowena had at last done all her duty by the people in the parlor, she went upstairs to satisfy the longings of an overflow meeting there, for the parlor was not big enough to hold all the comers. Again she was besieged by eager questioners, and again she swam in sunset seas of glory.[8] When the forenoon was nearly gone, she recognized with a pang that this most splendid episode of her life was almost over, that nothing could prolong it, that nothing quite its equal could ever fall to her fortune again. But never mind, it was sufficient unto itself, the grand occasion had moved on an ascending scale from the start, and was a noble and memorable success. If the twins could but do

7) And to think: 그리고 생각해보니 (to think of it)

some crowning act now to climax it, something unusual, something startling, something to concentrate upon themselves the company's loftiest admiration, something in the nature of an electric surprise—

Here a prodigious slam-banging broke out below, and everybody rushed down to see. It was the twins, knocking out a classic four-handed piece on the piano in great style. Rowena was satisfied; satisfied down to the bottom of her heart.

The young strangers were kept long at the piano. The villagers were astonished and enchanted with the magnificence of their performance, and could not bear to have them stop. All the music that they had ever heard before seemed spiritless prentice-work and barren of grace and charm when compared with these intoxicating floods of melodious sound. They realized that for once in their lives they were hearing masters.

8) sunset seas of glory: 영광의 황금빛 바다 (해가 질 때의 색깔)

CHAPTER 7

One of the most striking differences between a cat and a lie is that a cat has only nine lives.

- Pudd'nhead Wilson's Calendar

The company broke up reluctantly, and drifted toward their several homes, chatting with vivacity and all agreeing that it would be many a long day before Dawson's Landing would see the equal of this one again. The twins had accepted several invitations while the reception was in progress, and had also volunteered to play some duets at an amateur entertainment for the benefit of a local charity. Society was eager to receive them to its bosom. Judge Driscoll had the good fortune to secure them for an immediate drive,[1] and to be the first to display them in public. They entered his buggy with him and were paraded down the main street, everybody flocking to the windows and sidewalks to see.

The judge showed the strangers the new graveyard, and the jail, and where the richest man lived, and the Freemasons' hall, and the Methodist church, and the Presbyterian church, and where the Baptist church was going to be when they got some money to build it with, and showed them the town hall and the slaughterhouse, and got out the independent fire company in uniform and had them put out an imaginary fire; then he let them inspect the muskets of the militia company, and poured out an exhaustless stream of enthusiasm over all these splendors,

1) to secure them for an immediate drive: 즉석 드라이브를 위해 그들을 확보하다.

and seemed very well satisfied with the responses he got, for the twins admired his admiration, and paid him back the best they could, though they could have done better if some fifteen or sixteen hundred thousand previous experiences of this sort in various countries had not already rubbed off a considerable part of the novelty of it.

The judge laid himself hospitably out to make them have a good time, and if there was a defect anywhere, it was not his fault. He told them a good many humorous anecdotes, and always forgot the nub, but they were always able to furnish it, for these yarns were of a pretty early vintage, and they had had many a rejuvenating pull at them before. And he told them all about his several dignities, and how he had held this and that and the other place of honor or profit, and had once been to the legislature, and was now president of the Society of Freethinkers. He said the society had been in existence four years, and already had two members, and was firmly established. He would call for the brothers in the evening, if they would like to attend a meeting of it.

Accordingly he called for them, and on the way he told them all about Pudd'nhead Wilson, in order that they might get a favorable impression of him in advance and be prepared to like him. This scheme succeeded—the favorable impression was achieved. Later it was confirmed and solidified when Wilson proposed that out of courtesy to the strangers the usual topics be put aside and the hour be devoted to conversation upon ordinary subjects and the cultivation of friendly relations and good-fellowship,—a proposition which was put to vote and carried.

The hour passed quickly away in lively talk, and when it was ended, the lonesome and neglected Wilson was richer by two friends than he had been when it began. He invited the twins to look in at his lodgings presently, after disposing of an intervening engagement, and they accepted with pleasure.

Toward the middle of the evening, they found themselves on the road to his house. Pudd'nhead was at home waiting for them and putting in his time puzzling over a thing which had come under his notice that morning. The matter was this. He happened to be up very early—at dawn, in fact; and he crossed the hall, which divided his cottage through the center, and entered a room to get something there. The window of the room had no curtains, for that side of the house had long been unoccupied, and through this window he caught sight of something which surprised and interested him. It was a young woman—a young woman where properly no young woman belonged; for she was in Judge Driscoll's house, and in the bedroom over the judge's private study or sitting room. This was young Tom Driscoll's bedroom. He and the judge, the judge's widowed sister Mrs. Pratt, and three Negro servants were the only people who belonged in the house. Who, then, might this young lady be? The two houses were separated by an ordinary yard,[2)] with a low fence running back through its middle from the street in front to the lane in the rear. The distance was not great, and Wilson was able to see the girl very well, the window shades of the room she was in being up, and the window also. The girl had on a neat and trim summer dress, patterned in broad stripes of pink and white, and her bonnet was equipped with a pink veil. She was practicing steps, gaits and attitudes, apparently; she was doing the thing gracefully, and was very much absorbed in her work. Who could she be, and how came she to be in young Tom Driscoll's room?

Wilson had quickly chosen a position from which he could watch the girl without running much risk of being seen by her, and he

---

2) an ordinary yard: 평범한 정원

remained there hoping she would raise her veil and betray her face. But she disappointed him. After a matter of twenty minutes she disappeared, and although he stayed at his post half an hour longer, she came no more.

Toward noon he dropped in at the judge's and talked with Mrs. Pratt about the great event of the day, the levèe of the distinguished foreigners at Aunt Patsy Cooper's. He asked after her nephew Tom, and she said he was on his way home and that she was expecting him to arrive a little before night, and added that she and the judge were gratified to gather from his letters that he was conducting himself very nicely and creditably—at which Wilson winked to himself privately. Wilson did not ask if there was a newcomer in the house, but he asked questions that would have brought light-throwing answers as to that matter if Mrs. Pratt had had any light to throw;[3] so he went away satisfied that he knew of things that were going on in her house of which she herself was not aware.

He was now awaiting for the twins, and still puzzling over the problem of who that girl might be, and how she happened to be in that young fellow's room at daybreak in the morning.

---

3) he asked questions that would have brought light-throwing answers as to that matter if Mrs. Pratt had had any light to throw: Mrs. Pratt이 그 일에 대해 알고 있는 것이 있었다면 그것에 대한 분명한 답을 가져왔을 질문들을 했다.

CHAPTER 8

The holy passion of Friendship is of so sweet and steady and loyal and enduring a nature that it will last through a whole lifetime if not asked to lend money.

- Pudd'nhead Wilson's Calendar

Consider well the proportions of things. It is better to be a young June-bug than an old bird of paradise.

- Pudd'nhead Wilson's Calendar

It is necessary now to hunt up[1)] Roxy.

At the time she was set free and went away chambermaiding, she was thirty-five. She got a berth as second chambermaid on a Cincinnati boat in the New Orleans trade, the "Grand Mogul." A couple of trips made her wonted and easy-going at the work, and infatuated her with the stir and adventure and independence of steamboat life. Then she was promoted and become head chambermaid. She was a favorite with the officers, and exceedingly proud of their joking and friendly ways with her.

During eight years she served three parts of the year on that boat, and the winters on a Vicksburg packet. But now for two months, she had had rheumatism in her arms, and was obliged to let the washtub alone. So she resigned. But she was well fixed—rich, as she would have described it; for she had lived a steady life, and had banked four dollars every month in New Orleans as a provision for her old age. She said in the start that she

1) to hunt up: 찾아내다

had "put shoes on one bar'footed nigger to tromple on her with,"[2] and that one mistake like that was enough; she would be independent of the human race thenceforth forevermore if hard work and economy could accomplish it.

When the boat touched the levee at New Orleans she bade good-bye to her comrades on the Grand Mogul and moved her kit ashore.

But she was back in a hour. The bank had gone to smash and carried her four hundred dollars with it. She was a pauper and homeless. Also disabled bodily, at least for the present. The officers were full of sympathy for her in her trouble, and made up a little purse for her.[3] She resolved to go to her birthplace; she had friends there among the Negroes, and the unfortunate always help the unfortunate, she was well aware of that; those lowly comrades of her youth would not let her starve.

She took the little local packet at Cairo, and now she was on the home-stretch. Time had worn away her bitterness against her son, and she was able to think of him with serenity. She put the vile side of him out of her mind, and dwelt only on recollections of his occasional acts of kindness to her. She gilded and otherwise decorated these, and made them very pleasant to contemplate. She began to long to see him. She would go and fawn upon him slavelike—for this would have to be her attitude, of course

and maybe she would find that time had modified him, and that he would be glad to see his long-forgotten old nurse and treat her gently. That would be lovely; that would make her forget her woes and her poverty.

Her poverty! That thought inspired her to add another castle to her dream: Maybe he would help her; maybe he would give her a trifle now and then—maybe a dollar, once a month, say; any little thing

2) put shoes on one bar' footed nigger to trample on her with: put shoes on one barefooted nigger to trample on ther with=맨발의 흑인에게 그녀를 짓밟을 신을 신겼다.(사기당할 가능성에 대해 반어적으로 말한 것인데 그녀가 저축했던 흑인은행이 파산함으로써 결국 실제가 되었다.

like that would help, oh, ever so much.

By the time she reached Dawson's Landing, she was her old self again; her blues were gone, she was in high feather.[4] She would get along, surely; there were many kitchens where the servants would share their meals with her, and also steal sugar and apples and other dainties for her to carry home—or give her a chance to pilfer them herself, which would answer just as well. And there was the church. She was a more rabid and devoted Methodist than ever, and her piety was no sham, but was strong and sincere. Yes, with plenty of creature comforts and her old place in the amen corner in her possession again, she would be perfectly happy and at peace thenceforward to the end.

She went to Judge Driscoll's kitchen first of all. She was received there in great form and with vast enthusiasm. Her wonderful travels, and the strange countries she had seen, and the adventures she had had, made her a marvel and a heroine of romance. The Negroes hung enchanted upon a great story of her experiences, interrupting her all along with eager questions, with laughter, exclamations of delight, and expressions of applause; and she was obliged to confess to herself that if there was anything better in this world than steamboating, it was the glory to be got by telling about it. The audience loaded her stomach with their dinners, and then stole the pantry bare to load up her basket.

Tom was in St. Louis. The servants said he had spent the best part of his time there during the previous two years. Roxy came every day, and had many talks about the family and its affairs. Once she asked why Tom was away so much. The ostensible "Chambers" said:

"De fac' is, ole marster kin git along better when young marster's away den he kin when he's in de town;[5] yes, en he love him better, too; so he

---

3) made up a little purse for her: 돈을 약간 모아 주었다.

4) she was in high feather: 신바람이 낫다, 팔팔해졌다.

5) De fac' is, ole marster kin git along better when young marster's away den he kin when he's

gives him fifty dollahs a month—"

"No, is dat so? Chambers, you's a-jokin', ain't you?"

"Clah to goodness I ain't, Mammy; Marse Tom tole me so his own self. But nemmine, t'ain't enough."[6)]

"My lan', what de reason t'ain't enough?"

"Well, I's gwyne to tell you, if you gimme a chanst, Mammy.[7)] De reason it ain't enough is becase Marse Tom gambles."

Roxy threw up her hands in astonishment, and Chambers went on—

"Ole marster found it out, because he had to pay two hundred dollahs for Marse Tom's gamblin' debts, en dat's true, Mammy, jes' as dead certain as you's bawn."[8)]

"Two—hund'd dollahs! Why, what is you talkin' 'bout? Two—hund'd—dollahs. Sakes alive,[9)] it's mos' enough to buy a tol'able good secondhand nigger wid.[10)] En you ain't lyin', honey?—You wouldn't lie to yo' old Mammy?"

"It's Gawd's own truth, jes' as I tell you—two hundred dollahs—I wisht I may never stir outen my tracks if it ain't so.[11)] En, oh, my lan', ole Marse was jes' a-hoppin'![12)] He was b'ilin' mad,[13)] I tell you! He tuck'n dissenhurrit him."[14)]

---

in de town: the fact is, the old master (Judge Driscoll) can get along better when young master (Tom) is away than he can when he is in the town=사실 주인님께서는 젊은 주인님이 마을에 계실 때보다 다른 곳에 가 계실 때 더 사이가 좋으세요

6) nemmine, 'tain't enough: nevermind, it isn't enough=$50이 충분치 못하다

7) if you gimme a chanst, Mammy: if you give me a chance, mommy=엄마가 내게 기회를 주면

8) jes' as dead certain as you's bawn: just as dead certain as you were born=엄마가 태어난 것만큼 엄연한 사실이다

9) Sakes alive: 맙소사

10) it's mos' enough to buy a tol'able good secondhand nigger wid: it's almost enough to buy a tolerable good secondhand nigger with=그건 꽤 괜찮은 나이든 흑인 노예를 사기에도 충분한 돈이야

11) I wisht I may never stir outen my tracks if it ain't so: I wish I may never stir out of my tracks if it isn't so=만약 그게 사실이 아니라면 이 자리에서 다시는 움직이지 않도록 빌겠다 (거짓말이라면 이 자리에 쓰러져 죽겠다)

12) ole Marse was jes' a-hoppin': Old Master was just hopping=주인님은 격노했다

13) b'ilin' mad: boiling mad=화가 끓어오르듯 났다

14) He tuck'n dissenhurrit him: 그의 상속권을 박탈했다

He licked his chops with relish after that stately word. Roxy struggled with I a moment, then gave it up and said—

"Disen *whiched* him?"

"Dissenhurrit him."

"What's dat? What do you mean?"

"Means he busted de will."[15]

"Bus-ted de will! He wouldn't ever treat him so! Take it back, you mis'able imitation nigger dat I bore in sorrow en tribbilation."[16]

Roxy's pet castle an occasional dollar from Tom's pocket—was tumbling to ruin before her eyes. She could not abide such a disaster as that; she couldn't endure the thought of it. Her remark amused Chambers:

"Yah-yah-yah! Jes listen to dat! If I's imitation, what is you? Bofe of us is imitation *white*[17]—dat's what we is—en pow'ful good imitation, too—Yah-yah-yah!—We don't 'mount to noth'n as imitation *niggers*;[18] en as

---

15) Means he busted de will: It means he busted the will=그가 유언장을 찢었다는 뜻 이지요

16) tribbilation: tribulation=고난

17) Bofe of us is imitation *white*: Both of us is imitation white (1/16과 1/32의 피가 섞인 두 사람 모두 백인과 똑같이 생겼으므로)

18) We don't 'mount to noth'n as imitation niggers: We don't amount to anything as imitation

for—"

"Shet up yo' foolin', 'fo' I knock you side de head,[19] en tell me 'bout de will. Tell me t'ain't busted—do, honey, en I'll never forgit you."

"Well, *t'ain't*—'ca'se dey's a new one made,[20] en Marse Tom's all right ag'in. But what is you in sich a sweat 'bout it for,[21] Mammy? T'ain't none o' your business I don't reckon."

"T'ain't none o' my business? Whose business is it den, I'd like to know? Wuz I his mother tell[22] he was fifteen years old, or wusn't I?—you answer me dat. En you speck I could see him turned out po' and ornery on de worl' en never care noth'n' 'bout it? I reckon if you'd ever be'n a mother yo'self, Valet de Chambers, you wouldn't talk sich foolishness as dat."

"Well, den, ole Marse forgive him en fixed up de will ag'in[23]—do dat satisfy you?"

Yes, she was satisfied now, and quite happy and sentimental over it. She kept coming daily, and at last she was told that Tom had come home. She began to tremble with emotion, and straightway sent to beg him to let his "po' ole nigger Mammy have jes one sight of him en die for joy."

Tom was stretched at his lazy ease on a sofa when Chambers brought the petition. Time had not modified his ancient detestation of the humble drudge and protector of his boyhood; it was still bitter and uncompromising. He sat up and bent a severe gaze upon the face of the

---

niggers=우린 가짜 흑인으로는 아무 가치도 없어요 (Roxy가 그를 imitation nigger라고 부른 것에 대해 하얀 피부의 그들이 전혀 흑인같이 생기지 않았다고 대답)

19) Shet up yo' foolin', 'fo' I knock you side de head: Shut up your fooling, before I knock you side of the head=내가 네 머리통을 치기 전에 멍청이 같은 소리를 멈춰라

20) 'ca'se dey's a new one made: because there is a new one (=will) made

21) what is you in sich a sweat 'bout it for: why are you in such a sweat about it=왜 이 일을 그렇게 걱정하세요

22) Wuz I his mother tell: Was I his mother till

23) ole Marse forgive him en fixed up de will ag'in: old Master forgave him and fixed up the will again=주인님이 그를 용서하고 유언장을 다시 고쳤다

young fellow whose name he was unconsciously using and whose family rights he was enjoying. He maintained the gaze until the victim of it had become satisfactorily pallid with terror, then he said—

"What does the old rip want with me?"

The petition was meekly repeated.

"Who gave you permission to come and disturb me with the social attentions of niggers?"

Tom had risen. The other young man was trembling now, visibly. He saw what was coming, and bent his head sideways, and put up his left arm to shield it. Tom rained cuffs upon the head and its shield, saying no word: the victim received each blow with a beseeching, "Please, Marse Tom!—oh, please, Marse Tom!" Seven blows—then Tom said, "Face the door—march!" He followed behind with one, two, three solid kicks. The last one helped the pure-white slave over the door-sill, and he limped away mopping his eyes with his old, ragged sleeve. Tom shouted after him, "Send her in!"

Then he flung himself panting on the sofa again and rasped out the remark, "He arrived just at the right moment; I was full to the brim with bitter thinkings, and nobody to take it out of. How refreshing it was! I feel better."

Tom's mother entered now, closing the door behind her, and approached her son with all the wheedling and supplicating servilities that fear and interest can impart to the words and attitudes of the born slave. She stopped a yard from her boy and made two or three admiring exclamations over his manly stature and general handsomeness, and Tom put an arm under his head and hoisted a leg over the sofa back in order to look properly indifferent.

"My lan', how you is growed,[24] honey! 'Clah to goodness, I wouldn't

---

24) how you is growed: how you are grown=이렇게 많이 자라다니 (how much you have grown)

a-knowed you,[25] Marse Tom! 'Deed I wouldn't! Look at me good; does you 'member old Roxy? Does you know yo' old nigger mammy, honey? Well now, I kin lay down en die in peace, 'ca'se I's seed—"[26]

"Cut it short, damn it, cut it short! What is it you want?"

"You heah dat? Jes' the same old Marse Tom, al'ays so gay and funnin' wid de ole mammy. I'uz jes' as shore—"[27]

"Cut it short, I tell you, and get along! What do you want?"

This was a bitter disappointment. Roxy had for so many days nourished and fondled and petted her notion that Tom would be glad to see his old nurse, and would make her proud and happy to the marrow with a cordial word or two, that it took two rebuffs to convince her that he was not funning, and that her beautiful dream was a fond and foolish variety, a shabby and pitiful mistake. She was hurt to the heart, and so ashamed that for a moment she did not quite know what to do or how to act. Then her breast began to heave, the tears came, and in her forlornness she was moved to try that other dream of hers—an appeal to her boy's charity; and so, upon the impulse, and without reflection, she offered her supplication—

"Oh, Marse Tom, de po' ole mammy is in sich hard luck dese days;[28] en she's kinder crippled in de arms and can't work, en if you could gimme a dollah—on'y jes one little dol—"[29]

Tom was on his feet so suddenly that the supplicant was startled into a jump herself.

"A dollar!—give you a dollar! I've a notion to strangle you![30] Is *that*

---

25) I wouldn't a-knowed you: I wouldn't have known you=못알아 볼 뻔 했어요

26) Well now, I kin lay down en die in peace, 'ca'se I's seed: I can lie down and die in peace, because I have seen=이제 누워서 편히 죽을 수 있겠어요, 이제 (도련님을) 보았기 때문에

27) heah: hear, al'ays so gay and funnin' wid de ole mammy: always so gay and funny with the old mammy, I'uz jes as shore: I was just as sure

28) dese days: these days

29) gimme a dollah on'y jes one little dol : give me a dollar only just one little dol(lar)—

30) I've a notion to strangle you: 네 목을 조르고 싶은 기분이야

your errand here? Clear out! And be quick about it!"

Roxy backed slowly toward the door. When she was halfway she stopped, and said mournfully—

"Marse Tom, I nussed you when you was a little baby, en I raised you all by myself tell[31] you was 'most a young man; en now you is young en rich, en I is po' en gitt'n ole,[32] en I come heah b'leavin' dat you would he'p de ole mammy 'long down de little road dat's lef' twix her en de grave,[33] en—"

Tom relished this tune less than any that had preceded it,[34] for it began to wake up a sort of echo in his conscience; so he interrupted and said with decision, though without asperity, that he was not in a situation to help her, and wasn't going to do it.

"Ain't you ever gwyne to he'p me, Marse Tom?"[35]

"No! Now go away and don't bother me any more."

Roxy's head was down, in an attitude of humility. But now the fires of her old wrongs flamed up in her breast and began to burn fiercely. She raised her head slowly, till it was well up, and at the same time her great frame unconsciously assumed an erect and masterful attitude, with all the majesty and grace of her vanished youth in it. She raised her finger and punctuated with it.[36]

"You has said de word. You has had yo' chance, en you has trompled it under yo' foot. When you git another one, you'll git down on yo' knees en

---

31) tell: till

32) gitt'n ole: getting old

33) en I come heah b'leavin' dat you would he'p de ole mammy 'long down de little road dat's lef' twix her en de grave: and I came here believing that you would help the old mammy along down the little road that's left between her and the grave=그래서 나는 도련님께서 이 늙은 유모가 죽을때까지 얼마 남지 않은 길을 여행하는 동안 도와 주실거라고 믿으며 찾아왔지요

34) Tom relished this tune less than any that had preceded it: Tom은 이 소리를 먼저 들었던 다른 어떤 말들보다 더 듣기 싫어했다

35) Ain't you ever gwyne to he'p me, Marse Tom?: Aren't you ever going to help me, Master Tom?

36) punctuated with it: 그것에 힘을 주었다

beg for it!"

A cold chill went to Tom's heart, he didn't know why; for he did not reflect that such words, from such an incongruous source, and so solemnly delivered, could not easily fail of that effect. However, he did the natural thing: he replied with bluster and mockery.

"*You'll* give me a chance—*you*! Perhaps I'd better get down on my knees now! But in case I don't—just for argument's sake—what's going to happen, pray?"[37]

"Dis is what is gwyne to happen, I's gwyne as straight to yo' uncle as I kin walk, en tell him every las' thing[38] I knows 'bout you."

Tom's cheek blenched, and she saw it. Disturbing thoughts began to chase each other through his head. "How can she know? And yet she must have found out—she looks it.[39] I've had the will back only three months, and am already deep in debt again, and moving heaven and earth to save myself from exposure and destruction, with a reasonably fair show of getting the thing covered up if I'm let alone,[40] and now this fiend has gone and found me out somehow or other. I wonder how much she knows? Oh, oh, oh, it's enough to break a body's heart! But I've got to humor he—there's no other way."

Then he worked up a rather sickly sample of a gay laugh and a hollow chipperness of manner, and said—[41]

"Well, well, Roxy dear, old friends like you and me mustn't quarrel. Here's your dollar—now tell me what you know."

He held out the wildcat bill;[42] she stood as she was, and made no

---

37) pray?: please?=제발 (알려주겠소)?

38) every las' thing: 모든 것을 남김없이

39) she looks it: she looks like it=그렇게 보여

40) if I'm let alone: 방해만 안받으면

41) Then he worked up a rather sickly sample of a gay laugh and a hollow chipperness of manner, and said: 그리고 그는 좀 생기없는 웃음과 공허하게 활발한 태도를 애써 만들어내며 말했다

42) wildcat bill: 무허가(공인되지 않은) 지폐, 수상한 지폐

movement. It was her turn to scorn persuasive foolery now, and she did not waste it. She said, with a grim implacability in voice and manner which made Tom almost realize that even a former slave can remember for ten minutes insults and injuries returned for compliments and flatteries received, and can also enjoy taking revenge for them when the opportunity offers—

"What does I know? I'll tell you what I knows. I knows enough to bu'st dat will to flinders—[43]en more, mind you,[44] more!"

Tom was aghast.

"More?" he said, "What do you call more? Where's there any room for more?"

Roxy laughed a mocking laugh, and said scoffingly, with a toss of her head, and her hands on her hips—

"Yes!—oh, I reckon! '*Cose* you'd like to know—wid yo' po' little ole rag dollah.[45] What you reckon I's gwyne to tell *you* for—you ain't got no money.[46] I's gwyne to tell yo' uncle—en I'll do it dis minute, too—he'll gimme *five* dollahs for de news, en mighty glad,[47] too."

She swung herself around disdainfully, and started away. Tom was in a panic. He seized her skirts, and implored her to wait. She turned and said, loftily—

"Look-a-heah,[48] what 'uz it I tole you?"

"You—you—I don't remember anything. What was it you told me?"

"I tole you dat de next time I give you a chance you'd git down on yo' knees en beg for it."

---

43) to bu'st dat will to flinders: 유언장을 산산조각으로 찢어버리다
44) mind you: 잘 들어
45) wid yo' po' little ole rag dollah: with your poor little old rag dollar=너의 낡은 걸레같은 돈으로
46) What you reckon I's gwyne to tell you for?: What you reckon I am going to tell you for?=내가 왜 네게 알려줄꺼라고 생각하지?, you ain't got no money: 돈도 없는데
47) mighty glad: very glad
48) Look-a-heah: Look here=이것 봐

Tom was stupefied for a moment. He was panting with excitement. Then he said—

"Oh, Roxy, you wouldn't require your young master to do such a horrible thing. You can't mean it."

"I'll let you know mighty quick whether I means it or not! You call me names, en as good as spit on me when I comes here, po' en ornery en 'umble,[49] to praise you for bein' growed up so fine and handsome, en tell you how I used to nuss you[50] en tend you en watch you when you 'uz sick en hadn't no mother but me in de whole worl', en beg you to give de po' ole nigger a dollah for to git her som'n' to eat,[51] en you call me names[52]—*names*, dad blame you![53] Yassir, I gives you jes' one chance mo', and dat's *now*, en it las' on'y a half a second[54]—you hear?"

Tom slumped to his knees and began to beg, saying—

"You see I'm begging, and it's honest begging, too! Now tell me, Roxy, tell me."

The heir of two centuries of unatoned insult and outrage looked down on him[55] and seemed to drink in deep draughts of satisfaction.[56] Then she said—

"Fine nice young white gen'l'man kneelin' down to a nigger wench! I's wanted to see dat jes' once befo' I's called.[57] Now, Gabr'el, blow de hawn,

---

49) po' en ornery en 'umble: poor and ornery and humble=가난하고 비천하고 초라해져서

50) how I used to nuss you: how I used to nurse you=어떻게 너를 길렀으며

51) som'n' to eat: something to eat

52) call me names: 날 욕했다

53) dad blame you!: 천벌 받을 것!

54) it las' on'y a half a second: it lasts only half a second=이 기회(=무릎꿇고 빌을)는 1/2 초 동안만 계속될거다

55) The heir of two centuries of unatoned insult and outrage looked down on him: 2세기에 걸친 속죄받지 않은 모욕과 폭행의 상속자 (=2세기에 걸친 노예사를 말함)가 그를 내려다 보았다

56) seemed to drink in deep draughts of satisfaction: 만족을 가슴 가득히 들여 마시는 것 같았다

57) I's wanted to see dat jes' once befo' I's called: I wanted to see that just once before I am called=내가 신으로부터 불리어지기 전에 (=죽기전에) 그걸 (=백인이 흑인에게 무릎꿇

I's ready . . .[58] Git up!"

Tom did it. He said, humbly—

"Now, Roxy, don't punish me any more. I deserved what I've got, but be good and let me off with that. Don't go to uncle. Tell me—I'll give you the five dollars."

"Yes, I bet you will; en you won't stop dah, nuther.[59] But I ain't gwyne to tell you heah—"

"Good gracious, no!"

"Is you 'feared o' de ha'nted house?"[60]

"N-no."

"Well, den, you come to de ha'nted house 'bout ten or 'leven tonight,[61] en climb up de ladder, 'ca'se de sta'rsteps is broke down,[62] en you'll find me. I's a-roostin' in de ha'nted house 'ca'se I can't 'ford to roos' nowher's else."[63] She started toward the door, but stopped and said, "Gimme de dollah bill!" He gave it to her. She examined it and said, "H'm—like enough de bank's bu'sted."[64] She started again, but halted again. "Has you got any whisky?"

"Yes, a little."

"Fetch it!"

He ran to his room overhead and brought down a bottle which was two-thirds full. She tilted it up and took a drink. Her eyes sparkled

---

는 것) 꼭 한번 보고 싶었다

58) Now, Gabr'el, blow de hawn, I's ready: Now, Gabriel, blow the horn, I am ready. Gabriel 천사님 이제 나팔을 불어주소서, 저는 준비되었습니다. (Gabriel 천사s는 심판의 나팔을 분다고 함)

59) en you won't stop dah, nuther: and you won't stop there, neither=그리고 거기서 그치지 않을 것이다

60) Is you 'feared o' de ha'nted house?: Are you afraid of the haunted house?

61) 'bout ten or 'leven tonight: about ten or eleven tonight

62) 'ca'se de sta'rsteps is broke down: because the stairs are broken down

63) I's a-roostin' in de ha'nted house 'ca'se I can't 'ford to roos' nowher's else: I am roosting in the haunted house because I can afford to roost anymore else=다른 머물 곳이 없어 그 유령의 집에 머물고 있다

64) like enough de bank's bu'sted: 아마 은행이 망한 것 같군

with satisfaction, and she tucked the bottle under her shawl, saying—

"It's prime. I'll take it along."

Tom humbly held the door for her, and she marched out as grim and erect as a grenadier.[65)]

---

65) she marched out as grim and erect as a grenadier: 그녀는 근위병처럼 단호하고 꼿꼿이 걸어 나갔다

CHAPTER 9

Why is it that we rejoice at birth and grieve at a funeral? It is because we are not the person involved.

- Pudd'nhead Wilson's Calendar

It is easy to find fault, if one has that disposition. There was once a man who, not being able to find any other fault with his coal, complained that there were too many prehistoric toads in it.

- Pudd'nhead Wilson's Calendar

Tom flung himself on the sofa, and put his throbbing head in his hands, and rested his elbows on his knees. He rocked himself back and forth and moaned.

"I've knelt to a nigger wench!" he muttered. "I thought I had struck the deepest depths of degradation before, but oh, dear, it was nothing to this. . . . Well, there is one consolation, such as it is[1)]—I've struck bottom this time; there's nothing lower."

But that was a hasty conclusion.

At ten that night he climbed the ladder in *the* haunted house, pale, weak, and wretched. Roxy was standing in the door of one of the rooms, waiting, for she had heard him.

This was a two-story log house which had acquired the reputation a few years ago of being haunted, and that was the end of its usefulness. Nobody would live in it afterward, or go near it by night, and most

1) such as it is: 변변치는 못하지만

people even gave it a wide berth[2] in the daytime. As it had no competition, it was called the haunted house. It was getting crazy and ruinous, now, from long neglect. It stood three hundred yards beyond Pudd'nhead Wilson's house, with nothing between but vacancy. It was the last house in the town at that end.

Tom followed Roxy into the room. She had a pile of clean straw in the corner for a bed, some cheap but well-kept clothing was hanging on the wall, there was a tin lantern freckling the floor with little spots of light, and there were various soap and candle boxes scattered about, which served for chairs. The two sat down. Roxy said—

"Now den, I'll tell you straight off, en I'll begin to k'leck[3] de money later on; I ain't in no hurry. What does you reckon I's gwyne to tell you?"

"Well, you—you—oh, Roxy, don't make it too hard for me! Come right out and tell me you've found out somehow what a shape I'm in on account of dissipation and foolishness."

"Disposition en foolishness! *No* sir, dat ain't it. Dat jist ain't nothin' at all, 'longside o' what I knows."[4]

Tom stared at her, and said—

"Why—Roxy, what do you mean?"

She rose, and gloomed above him like a Fate.[5]

"I means dis en it's de Lord's truth. You ain't no more kin to ole Marse Driscoll den I is![6]—*dat's* what I means!" and her eyes flamed with triumph.

"What?"

---

2) gave it a wide berth: 피했다

3) k'leck: collect

4) Dat jist ain't nothin' at all, 'longside o' what I knows: That just isn't anything at all, alongside of what I know=내가 알고 있는 것에 비하면 그건 아무 것도 아니다

5) gloomed above him like a Fate: 운명의 여신처럼 그에게 어두운 표정을 지었다

6) You ain't no more kin to ole Marse Driscoll den I is: You are no more kin to old Master Driscoll than I am=너는 Driscoll 주인님에게 나보다 조금도 더 친척이 아니다 (그가

"Yassir, en dat ain't all! You's a *nigger*!—*bawn* a nigger and a *slave*![7]—en you's a nigger en a slave dis minute;8) en if I opens my mouf ole Marse Driscoll'll sell you down de river befo' you is two days older den what you is now!"[9]

"It's a thundering lie, you miserable old blatherskite!"[10]

"It ain't no lie, nuther. It's jes' de truth, en nothin' but de truth, so he'p me.[11] Yassir—you's my *son*—"

"You devil!—"

—"en dat po' boy dat you's be'n a-kickin' en a-cuffin' today is Percy Driscoll's son en yo' *marster*—"[12]

"You beast!"

—"En *his* name is Tom Driscoll, en *yo* name's Valet de Chambers, en you ain't got no fambly name, beca'se niggers don't *have* 'em!"

Tom sprang up and seized a billet of wood and raised it, but his mother only laughed at him, and said—

"Set down, you pup![13] Does you think you kin skyer me?[14] It ain't in you, nor de likes of you.[15] I reckon you'd shoot me in de back, maybe, if

---

Driscoll의 친척이 아니다는 말)

7) bawn a nigger and a slave!: 흑인 그리고 노예로 태어났다

8) en you's a nigger en a slave dis minute: and you are a nigger and a slave this minute=너는 지금도 흑인이고 노예다

9) if I opens my mouf ole Marse Driscoll'll sell you down de river befo' you is two days older den what you is now!: if I open my mouth, old Master Driscoll will sell you down the river before you are two days older than what you are now!=만약 내가 입을 열면 Driscoll 주인님이 이틀이 지나기도 전에 널 강 밑마을로 팔아버릴 것이다

10) blatherskite: 허풍쟁이

11) It's just de truth, en nothin' but de truth, so he'p me: It's the truth, and nothing but the truth, so help me (God): 법정에서 진실만을 이야기하겠다고 증인 선서할 때 쓰는 말

12) En dat po' boy dat you's be'n a-kickin' en a-cuffin' today is Percy Driscoll's son en yo' marster: And that poor boy that you've been kicking and cuffing today is Percy Driscoll's son and your master 그리고 네가 오늘 발로 차고 손으로 친 그 불쌍한 아이가 Percy Driscoll의 아들이고 네 주인이다

13) Set down: Sit down

14) kin skyer: can scare

15) It ain't in you, nor de likes of you: 나를 나무토막으로 칠 용기는 너나 너와 비슷한 이들에겐 없다

you got a chance, for dat's jist yo' style—*I* knows you, thoo en thoo[16]—but I don't mind gitt'n killed, beca'se all dis is down in writin' and it's in safe hands, too, en de man dat's got it knows whah to look for de right man when I gits killed.[17] Oh, bless yo' soul, if you puts yo' mother up for as big a fool as *you* is, you's pow'ful mistaken,[18] I kin tell you! Now den, you set still en behave yo'self; en don't you git up ag'in till I tell you!"

Tom fretted and chafed awhile in a whirlwind of disorganizing sensations and emotions, and finally said with something like settled conviction—[19]

"The whole thing is moonshine—[20] now, then, go ahead and do your worst; I'm done with you."

Roxy made no answer. She took the lantern and started toward the door. Tom was in a cold panic in a moment.

"Come back, come back!" he wailed. "I didn't mean it, Roxy; I take it all back, and I'll never say it again! Please come back, Roxy!"

The woman stood a moment, then she said gravely—

"Dah's one thing you's got to stop, Valet de Chambers. You can't call me *Roxy*, same as if you was my equal. Chillen don't speak to dey mammies[22] like dat. You'll call me Ma or mammy, dat's what you'll call me—leastways when dey ain't nobody aroun'.[23] *Say* it!"

It cost Tom a struggle, but he got it out.

"Dat's all right. Don't you ever forgit it ag'in, if you knows what's good for you. Now den, you had said you wouldn't ever call it lies en

16) thoo en thoo: through and through=완벽히
17) whah to look for de right man when I gits killed: where to look for the right man when I get killed
18) you's pow'ful mistaken: You are powerful(ly) mistaken=크게 잘못 생각한 거야.
19) with something like settled conviction: 약간 확신을 갖고
20) moonshine: nonsense=헛소리
21) dey mammies: their mothers
22) leastways when dey ain't nobody aroun': leastwise when there isn't nobody around=적어도

moonshine ag'in. I'll tell you dis, for a warnin': if you ever does say it ag'in, it's de *las'* time[24] you'll ever say it to me; I'll tramp as straight to de judge as I kin walk, en tell him who you is, en *prove* it. Does you b'lieve me when I says dat?"

"Oh," groaned Tom, "I more than believe it; I *know* it."

Roxy knew her conquest was complete. She could have proven nothing to anybody, and her threat of writings was a lie; but she knew the person she was dealing with, and had made both statements without any doubt as to the effect they would produce.

She went and sat down on her candle-box, and the pride and pomp of her victorious attitude made it a throne. She said—

"Now den, Chambers, we's gwyne to talk business, en dey ain't gwyne to be no mo' foolishness.[25] In de fust place, you gits fifty dollahs a month; you's gwyne to han' over half of it to yo' ma. Plank it out!"[26]

But Tom had only six dollars in the world. He gave her that, and promised to start fair on next month's pension.

"Chambers, how much is you in debt?"

Tom shuddered, and said—

"Nearly three hundred dollars."

"How is you gwyne to pay it?"

Tom groaned out—

"Oh, I don't know; don't ask me such awful questions."

But she stuck to her point until she wearied a confession out of him:[27] he had been prowling about in disguise, stealing small valuables from

---

근처에 아무도 없을 땐

23) de *las'* time: the last time

24) we's gwyne to talk business, en dey ain't gwyne to be no mo' foolishness: We are going to talk business, and there isn't going to be any more foolishness=이제 진지하게 이야기 하겠다, 그리고 더 이상 어리석은 짓은 말아

25) Plank it out!: 당장 내놔!

26) But she stuck to her point until she wearied a confession out of him: 그녀는 그가 고백할 때까지 집요하게 물었다

private houses; in fact, had made a good deal of a raid on his fellow villagers a fortnight before, when he was supposed to be in St. Louis; but he doubted if he had sent away enough stuff to realize the required amount, and was afraid to make a further venture in the present excited state of the town. His mother approved of his conduct, and offered to help, but this frightened him. He tremblingly ventured to say that if she would retire from the town he should feel better and safer, and could hold his head higher[28)]—and was going on to make an argument, but she interrupted and surprised him pleasantly by saying she was ready; it didn't make any difference to her where she stayed, so that she got her share of the pension regularly. She said she would not go far, and would call at the haunted house once a month for her money. Then she said—

"I don't hate you so much now, but I've hated you a many a year—and anybody would. Didn't I change you off, en give you a good fambly en a good name, en made you a white gen'l'man en rich, wid store clothes on[29)]—en what did I git for it? You despised me all de time, en was al'ays sayin' mean hard things to me befo' folks, en wouldn't ever let me forgit I's a nigger—en—en—"

She fell to sobbing, and broke down. Tom said—

"But you know I didn't know you were my mother; and besides—"

"Well, nemmine 'bout dat,[30)] now; let it go. I's gwyne to forgit it." Then she added fiercely, "En don't ever make me remember it ag'in, or you'll be sorry, *I* tell you."

When they were parting, Tom said, in the most persuasive way he could command—

"Ma, would you mind telling me who was my father?"

---

27) could hold his head higher: 머리를 높이 들고 다닐 수 있다, 떳떳하게 다닐 수 있다

28) wid store clothes on: 파는 옷을 입은 (여기서는 집에서 만든 것이 아니라 파는 고급 옷을 뜻함)

29) nemmine 'bout dat: nevermind about that=그것에 대해 신경쓰지 말아라

He had supposed he was asking an embarrassing question. He was mistaken. Roxy drew herself up[31] with a proud toss of her head, and said:

"Does I mine tellin' you? No, dat I don't! You ain't got no 'casion to be shame' o' yo' father,[32] *I* kin tell you. He wuz de highest quality in dis whole town ole Virginny stock.[33] Fust famblies, he wuz. Jes as good stock as de Driscolls en de Howards, de bes' day dey ever seed."[34] She put on a little prouder air, if possible, and added impressively: "Does you 'member Cunnel Cecil Burleigh Essex,[35] dat died de same year yo' young Marse Tom Driscoll's pappy died, en all de Masons en Odd Fellers en Churches turned out en give him de bigges' funeral dis town ever seed? Dat's de man."

Under the inspiration of her soaring complacency the departed graces of her earlier days returned to her, and her bearing took to itself a dignity and state that might have passed for queenly if her surroundings had been a little more in keeping with it.

"Dey ain't another nigger in dis town dat's as highbawn as you is.[36] Now den, go 'long! En jes' you hold yo' head up as high as you want to you has de right, en dat I kin swah."[37]

---

30) Roxy drew herself up: Roxy는 꼿꼿이 섰다

31) You ain't got no 'casion to be shame' o' yo' father: You haven't got any occasion to be ashamed of your father=네 아버지에 대해 창피하게 생각할 일은 전혀 없다

32) He wuz de highest quality in dis whole town ole Virginny stock: He was the highest quality in this whole town old Virginia stock=그는 이 마을 전체에서 가장 훌륭한 신분을 가지신 분이셨다 옛 버지니아 혈통의.

33) de bes' day dey ever seed: the best day they ever saw=가장 훌륭한

34) Does you 'member Cunnel Cecil Burleigh Essex: Do you remember Colonel Cecil Burleigh Essex=Cecil Breleigh Essex 대령님을 기억하니

35) Dey ain't another nigger in dis town dat's as highbawn as you is: There isn't another nigger in this town that's as highborn as you are=이 마을에 너처럼 명문태생의 흑인은 없다

36) dat I kin swah: that I can swear=그건 내가 맹세할 수 있다

CHAPTER 10

All say, "How hard it is that we have to die"— a strange complaint to come from the mouths of people who have had to live.

- Pudd'nhead Wilson's Calendar

When angry, count four; when very angry, swear.

- Pudd'nhead Wilson's Calendar

Every now and then, after Tom went to bed, he had sudden wakings out of his sleep, and his first thought was, "Oh, joy, it was all a dream!" Then he laid himself heavily down again, with a groan and the muttered words, "A nigger!—I am a nigger!—Oh, I wish I was dead!"

He woke at dawn with one more repetition of this horror, and then he resolved to meddle no more with that treacherous sleep. He began to think. Sufficiently bitter thinkings they were. They wandered along something after this fashion:

"Why were niggers *and* whites made? What crime did the uncreated first nigger commit that the curse of birth was decreed for him? And why is this awful difference made between white and black? . . . How hard the nigger's fate seems, this morning!—yet until last night such a thought never entered my head."

He sighed and groaned an hour or more away. Then "Chambers" came humbly in to say that breakfast was nearly ready. "Tom" blushed scarlet to see this aristocratic white youth cringe to him, a nigger, and call him "Young Marster." He said, roughly—

"Get out of my sight!" and when the youth was gone, he muttered, "He has done me no harm, poor wretch, but he is an eyesore to me now, for he is Driscoll, the young gentleman, and I am a—oh, I wish I was dead!"

A gigantic iruption, like that of Krakatoa a few years ago, with the accompanying earthquakes, tidal waves, and clouds of volcanic dust, changes the face of the surrounding landscape beyond recognition, bringing down the high lands, elevating the low, making fair lakes where deserts had been, and deserts where green prairies had smiled before. The tremendous catastrophe which had befallen Tom had changed his moral landscape in much the same way. Some of his low places he found lifted to ideals, some of his ideas had sunk to the valleys, and lay there with the sackcloth and ashes of pumice stone and sulphur on their ruined heads.

For days he wandered in lonely places, thinking, thinking, thinking—trying to get his bearings.[1] It was new work. If he met a friend, he found that the habit of a lifetime had in some mysterious way vanished—his arm hung limp, instead of involuntarily extending the hand for a shake. It was the "nigger" in him asserting its humility, and he blushed and was abashed. And the "nigger" in him was surprised when the white friend put out his hand for a shake with him. He found the "nigger" in him involuntarily giving the road, on the sidewalk, to a white rowdy and loafer. When Rowena, the dearest thing his heart knew, the idol of his secret worship, invited him in, the "nigger" in him made an embarrassed excuse and was afraid to enter and sit with the dread white folks on equal terms.[2] The "nigger" in him went shrinking and skulking here and there and yonder, and fancying it saw suspicion and maybe detection in all faces, tones, and

---

1) trying to get his bearings: 그의 환경에 익숙해지려고 노력하며
2) on equal terms: 대등하게, 동등하게

gestures. So strange and uncharacteristic was Tom's conduct that people noticed it, and turned to look after him when he passed on; and when he glanced back as he could not help doing, in spite of his best resistance—and caught that puzzled expression in a person's face, it gave him a sick feeling, and he took himself out of view as quickly as he could. He presently came to have a hunted sense and a hunted look, and then he fled away to the hilltops and the solitudes. He said to himself that the curse of Ham[3] was upon him.

He dreaded his meals; the "nigger" in him was ashamed to sit at the white folks' table, and feared discovery all the time; and once when Judge Driscoll said, "What's the matter with you? You look as meek as a nigger," he felt as secret murderers are said to feel when the accuser says, "Thou art the man!" Tom said he was not well, and left the table.

His ostensible "aunt's" solicitudes and endearments were become a terror to him, and he avoided them.

And all the time, hatred of his ostensible "uncle" was steadily growing in his heart; for he said to himself, "He is white; and I am his chattel, his property, his goods, and he can sell me, just as he could his dog."

For as much as a week after this, Tom imagined that his character had undergone a pretty radical change. But that was because he did not know himself.

In several ways his opinions were totally changed, and would never go back to what they were before, but the main structure of his character was not changed, and could not be changed.[4] One or two very important features of it were altered, and in time effects would result

---

3) the curse of Ham: 성경의 창세기에 나오는 노아의 둘째아들로 노아의 저주를 받고 흑인종의 시초가 되었다는 주장이 있다

4) but the main structure of his character was not changed, and could not be changed: 하지만 그의 성격의 중심 구성(=본성)은 바뀌지 않았고 바뀔수도 없었다

from this, if opportunity offered—effects of a quite serious nature, too. Under the influence of a great mental and moral upheaval, his character and his habits had taken on the appearance of complete change, but after a while with the subsidence of the storm, both began to settle toward their former places. He dropped gradually back into his old frivolous and easygoing ways and conditions of feeling and manner of speech, and no familiar of his could have detected anything in him that differentiated him from the weak and careless Tom of other days.

The theft-raid which he had made upon the village turned out better than he had ventured to hope. It produced the sum necessary to pay his gaming debts, and saved him from exposure to his uncle and another smashing of the will.

He and his mother learned to like each other fairly well. She couldn't love him, as yet, because there "warn't nothing to him,"[5] as she expressed it, but her nature needed something or somebody to rule over, and he was better than nothing. Her strong character and aggressive and commanding ways compelled Tom's admiration in spite of the fact that he got more illustrations of them than he needed for his comfort.[6] However, as a rule her conversation was made up of racy tattle[7] about the privacies of the chief families of the town (for she went harvesting among their kitchens every time she came to the village), and Tom enjoyed this. It was just in his line.[8] She always collected her half of his pension punctually, and he was always at the haunted house to have a chat with her on these occasions. Every

---

5) there "warn't nothing to him,": there wasn't nothing to him=그에겐 아무것도 없었다 (그는 가치없는 존재였다.)

6) he got more illustrations of them than he needed for his comfort: 그의 안락함을 위해 필요한 것 보다 더 많은 강한 성격과 공격적이고 명령적인 것들의 실례를 보았다(Roxydml 강한 성격과 공격적이고 명력적인 것들이 그를 편치 않게 하였다)

7) racy tattle: 선정적인 수다

8) It was just in his line: 이게 그의 성격에 딱 맞는 일이었다.

now and then, she paid him a visit there on between-days also.

Occasionally he would run up to St. Louis for a few weeks, and at last temptation caught him again. He won a lot of money, but lost it, and with it a deal more besides, which he promised to raise as soon as possible.

For this purpose he projected a new raid on his town. He never meddled with any other town, for he was afraid to venture into houses whose ins and outs he did not know, and the habits of whose households he was not acquainted with. He arrived at the haunted house in disguise on the Wednesday before the advent of the twins—after writing his aunt Pratt that he would not arrive until two days later—and laying in hiding there with his mother until toward daylight Friday morning, when he went to his uncle's house and entered by the back way with his own key, and slipped up to his room where he could have the use of the mirror and toilet articles.[9] He had a suit of girl's clothes with him in a bundle as a disguise for his raid, and was wearing a suit of his mother's clothing, with black gloves and veil. By dawn he was tricked out for his raid,[10] but he caught a glimpse of Pudd'nhead Wilson through the window over the way, and knew that Pudd'nhead had caught a glimpse of him. So he entertained Wilson with some airs and graces and

9) toilet articles: 화장품
10) By dawn he was tricked out for his raid: 동틀 녘까지 그는 도둑질을 할 변장을 마쳤다

attitudes for a while, then stepped out of sight and resumed the other disguise, and by and by went down and out the back way and started downtown to reconnoitre the scene of his intended labors.

But he was ill at ease. He had changed back to Roxy's dress, with the stoop of age added to the disguise, so that Wilson would not bother himself about a humble old women leaving a neighbor's house by the back way in the early morning, in case he was still spying. But supposing Wilson had seen him leave, and had thought it suspicious, and had also followed him? The thought made Tom cold. He gave up the raid for the day, and hurried back to the haunted house by the obscurest route he knew. His mother was gone; but she came back, by and by, with the news of the grand reception at Patsy Cooper's, and soon persuaded him that the opportunity was like a special Providence, it was so inviting and perfect. So he went raiding, after all, and made a nice success of it while everybody was gone to Patsy Cooper's. Success gave him nerve and even actual intrepidity; insomuch, indeed, that after he had conveyed his harvest to his mother in a back alley, he went to the reception himself, and added several of the valuables of that house to his takings.

After this long digression we have now arrived once more at the point where Pudd'nhead Wilson, while waiting for the arrival of the twins on that same Friday evening, sat puzzling over the strange apparition of that morning—a girl in young Tom Driscoll's bedroom; fretting, and guessing, and puzzling over it, and wondering who the shameless creature might be.

CHAPTER 11

There are three infallible ways of pleasing an author and the three form a rising scale of compliment: 1,to tell him you have read one of his books; 2,to tell him you have read all of his books; 3; to ask him to let you read the manuscript of his forthcoming book. No. 1 admits you to his respect; No. 2 admits you to his admiration; No. 3 carries you clear into his heart.

- Pudd'nhead Wilson's Calendar

As to the Adjective: when in doubt, strike it out.[1]

- Pudd'nhead Wilson's Calendar

The twins arrived presently, and talk began. It flowed along chattily and sociably, and under its influence the new friendship gathered ease and strength. Wilson got out his Calendar, by request, and read a passage or two from it, which the twins praised quite cordially. This pleased the author so much that he complied gladly when they asked him to lend them a batch of the work to read at home. In the course of their wide travels, they had found out that there are three sure ways of pleasing an author; they were now working the best of the three.

There was an interruption now. Young Driscoll appeared, and joined the party. He pretended to be seeing the distinguished strangers for the first time when they rose to shake hands; but this was only a blind,[2] as he had already had a glimpse of them, at the reception, while robbing the house. The twins made mental note

---

1) strike it out: 지워버려라

that he was smooth-faced and rather handsome, and smooth and undulatory in his movements—graceful, in fact. Angelo thought he had a good eye; Luigi thought there was something veiled and sly about it. Angelo thought he had a pleasant free-and-easy way of talking; Luigi thought it was more so than was agreeable. Angelo thought he was a sufficiently nice young man; Luigi reserved his decision. Tom's first contribution to the conversation was a question which he had put to Wilson a hundred times before. It was always cheerily and good-natured put, and always inflicted a little pang, for it touched a secret sore; but this time the pang was sharp, since strangers were present:

"Well, how does the law come on? Had a case yet?"

Wilson bit his lip, but answered, "No—not yet," with as much indifference as he could assume. Judge Driscoll had generously left the law feature out of Wilson's biography which he had furnished to the twins. Young Tom laughed pleasantly, and said—

"Wilson's a lawyer, gentlemen, but he doesn't practice now."

The sarcasm bit, but Wilson kept himself under control, and said without passion:

"I don't practice, it is true. It is true that I have never had a case, and have had to earn a poor living for twenty years as an expert accountant in a town where I can't get a hold of a set of books to untangle as often as I should like.[3] But it is also true that I did fit myself well for the practice of the law. By the time I was your age, Tom, I had chosen a profession, and was soon competent to enter upon it." Tom winced. "I never got a chance to try my hand at it, and I may never get a chance;

---

2) a blind: 눈속임

3) where I can't get a hold of a set of books to untangle as often as I should like: 내가 원하는 만큼 정리할 장부조차도 찾아낼 수 없는 마을에서

and yet if I ever do get it, I shall be found ready, for I have kept up my law-studies all these years."

"That's it; that's good grit! I like to see it. I've a notion to throw all my business your way.[4] My business and your law practice ought to make a pretty gay team, Dave," and the young fellow laughed again.

"If you will throw—" Wilson had thought of the girl in Tom's bedroom, and was going to say, "If you will throw the surreptitious and disreputable part of your business my way, it may amount to something,"[5] but thought better of it and said, "However, this matter doesn't fit well in a general conversation."

"All right, we'll change the subject; I guess you were about to give me another dig,[6] anyway, so I'm willing to change. How's the Awful Mystery flourishing these days?

Wilson's got a scheme for driving plain window glass panes out of the market by decorating it with greasy finger-marks, and getting rich by selling it at famine prices to the crowned heads over in Europe to outfit their palaces with. Fetch it out,[7] Dave."

Wilson brought three of his glass strips, and said:

"I get the subject to pass the fingers of his right through his hair, so as to get a little coating of the natural oil on them, and then press the balls of them on the glass. A fine an delicate print of the lines in the skin results, and is permanent, if it doesn't come in contact with something able to rub it off. You begin, Tom."

"Why, I think you took my finger-marks once or twice before."

"Yes, but you were a little boy the last time, only about twelve years old."

---

4) I've a notion to throw all my business your way: 내 사업들을 다 당신한테 맡길 생각이 있다
5) it may amount to something: 대단하게 될 것이다
6) dig: 비꼬기
7) Fetch it out: 가져와라

"That's so. Of course, I've changed entirely since then, and variety is what the crowned heads want, I guess."

He passed his fingers through his crop of short hair, and pressed them one at a time on the glass. Angelo made a print of his fingers on another glass, and Luigi followed with a third. Wilson marked the glasses with names and dates, and put them away. Tom gave one of his little laughs, and said—

"I thought I wouldn't say anything, but if variety is what you are after, you have wasted a piece of glass. The hand print of one twin is the same as the hand print of the fellow twin."

"Well, it's done now, and I like to have them both, anyway," said Wilson, returned to his place.

"But look here, Dave," said Tom, "you used to tell people's fortunes, too, when you took their finger-marks. Dave's just an all-round genius a genius of the first water,[8] gentlemen a great scientist running to seed here in this village, a prophet with the kind of honor that prophets generally get at home—for here they don't give shucks for his scientifics, and they call his skull a notion factory[9]—hey, Dave, ain't it so? But never mind, he'll make his mark someday—finger mark, you know, he-he! But really, you want to let him take a shy at your palms once;[10] it's worth twice the price of admission or your money's returned at the door. Why, he'll read your wrinkles as easy as a book, and not only tell you fifty or sixty things that's going to happen to you, but fifty or sixty thousand that ain't. Come, Dave, show the gentlemen what an

---

8) a genius of the first water: 일류 (최우수) 천재
9) they call his skull a notion factory: 그들은 그의 머리를 허황된 생각 제작소라고 부른다
10) let him take a shy at your palms once: 그에게 당신들의 손바닥을 보여줘 봐라

inspired jack-at-all-science[11] we've got in this town and don't know it."

Wilson winced under this nagging and not very courteous chaff, and the twins suffered with him and for him. They rightly judged, now, that the best way was to relieve him would be to take the thing in earnest and treat it with respect, ignoring Tom's rather overdone raillery; so Luigi said:

"We have seen something of palmistry in our wanderings, and know very well what astonishing things it can do. If it isn't a science, and one of the greatest of them too, I don't know what its other name ought to be. In the Orient—"

Tom looked surprised and incredulous. He said—

"That jugglery a science? But really, you ain't serious, are you?"

"Yes, entirely so. Four years ago we had our hands read out to us as if our plans had been covered with print."

"Well, do you mean to say there was actually anything in it?" asked Tom, his incredulity beginning to weaken a little.

"There was this much in it," said Angelo: "what was told us of our characters was minutely exact—we could not have bettered it ourselves.[12] Next, two or three memorable things that had happened to us were laid bare[13]—things which no one present but ourselves could have known about."

"Why, it's rank sorcery!"[14] exclaimed Tom, who was now becoming very much interested. "And how did they make out with what was going to happen to you in the future?"

"On the whole, quite fairly," said Luigi. "Two or three of the most

---

11) jack-at-all-science: 만물박사 과학자
12) we could have not have bettered it ourselves: 우리 자신도 더 잘 할 수 없었을 것이다
13) laid bare: 드러났다
14) it's rank sorcery!: 마법 같다!

striking things foretold have happened since; much the most striking one of all happened within that same year. Some of the minor prophesies have come true; some of the minor and some of the major ones have not been fulfilled yet, and of course may never be—still, I should be more surprised if they failed to arrive than if they didn't."[15)]

Tom was entirely sobered, and profoundly impressed. He said, apologetically—

"Dave, I wasn't meaning to belittle that science; I was only chaffing—chattering, I reckon I better say. I wish you would look at their palms. Come, won't you?"

"Why certainly, if you want me to; but you know I've had no chance to become an expert, and don't claim to be one. When a past event is somewhat prominently recorded in the palm, I can generally detect that, but minor ones often escape me—not always, of course, but often but I haven't much confidence in myself when it comes to reading the future. I am talking as if palmistry was a daily study with me, but that is not so. I haven't examined half a dozen hands in the last half a dozen years; you see, the people got to joking about it, and I stopped to let the talk die down.[16)] I'll tell you what we'll do, Count Luigi: I'll make a try at your past, and if I have any success there—no, on the whole, I'll let the future alone; that's really the affair of an expert."

He took Luigi's hand. Tom said—

"Wait don't look yet, Dave! Count Luigi, here's paper and pencil. Set down that thing that you said was the most striking one that was foretold to you and happened less than a year afterward, and give it to me so I can see if Dave finds it in your hand."

---

15) I should be more surprised if they failed to arrive than if they didn't: 그 예견들이 이루어지지 않는다면 더 놀랄 것이다
16) die down: 차차 사라져 버리다

Luigi wrote a line privately, and folded up the piece of paper, and handed it to Tom, saying—

"I'll tell you when to look at it, if he finds it."

Wilson began to study Luigi's palm, tracing life lines, heart lines, head lines, and so on, and noting carefully their relations with the cobweb of finer and more delicate marks and lines that enmeshed them on all sides; he felt of the fleshy cushion at the base of the thumb and noted its shape; he felt of the fleshy side of the hand between the wrist and the base of the little finger and noted its shape also; he painstakingly examined the fingers, observing their form, proportions, and natural manner of disposing themselves when in repose. All this process was watched by the three spectators with absorbing interest, their heads bent together over Luigi's palm, and nobody disturbing the stillness with a word. Wilson now entered upon a close survey of the palm again, and his revelations began.[17)]

He mapped out Luigi's character and disposition, his tastes, aversions, proclivities, ambitions, and eccentricities in a way which sometimes made Luigi wince and the others laugh, but both twins declared that the chart was artistically drawn and was correct.

Next, Wilson took up Luigi' history. He proceeded cautiously and with hesitation now, moving his finger slowly along the great lines of the palm, and now and then halting it at a "star" or some such landmark, and examining that neighborhood minutely. He proclaimed one or two past events, Luigi confirmed his correctness, and the search went on. Presently Wilson glanced up suddenly with a surprised expression.

"Here is a record of an incident which you would perhaps not wish me to—"

"Bring it out," said Luigi, good-naturedly. "I promise you it shan't

---

17) his revelations began: 그가 발견한 것들을 말하기 시작했다

embarrass me."

But Wilson still hesitated, and did not seem quite to know what to do. Then he said—

"I think it is too delicate a matter to—to—. I believe I would rather write it or whisper it to you, and let you decide for yourself whether you want it talked out or not."

"That will answer," said Luigi. "Write it."

Wilson wrote something on a slip of paper and handed it to Luigi, who read it to himself and said to Tom—

"Unfold your slip and read it, Mr. Driscoll."

Tom said:

"It was prophesied that I would kill a man. It came true before the year was out." Tom added, "Great Scott!"[18]

Luigi handed Wilson's paper to Tom, and said:

"Now read this one." Tom read:

"You have killed someone—but whether man, woman, or child, I don not make out." "Caesar's ghost!"[19] commented Tom, with astonishment. "It beats anything that was ever heard of! Why, a man's own hand is his deadliest enemy![20] Just think of that—a man's own hand keeps a record of the deepest and fatalest secrets of his life, and is treacherously ready to expose himself to any black-magic stranger that comes along. But what do you let a person look at your hand for, with that awful thing printed in it?"

"Oh," said Luigi, reposefully, "I don't mind it. I killed the man for good reasons, and I don't regret it."

"What were the reasons?"

---

18) Great Scott: 이런!, 맙소사! 같이 놀람을 나타내는 표현

19) Caesar's ghost!: Great Scott과 같이 놀람을 나타내는 표현

20) a man's own hand is his deadliest enemy: (비밀을 남에게 숨김없이 드러내기 때문에) 자신의 손이 자신의 가장 무서운 적이다

"Well, he needed killing."

"I'll tell you why he did it, since he won't say himself," said Angelo, warmly. "He did it to save my life, that's what he did it for. So it was a noble act, and not a thing to be hid in the dark."

"So it was, so it was," said Wilson. "To do such a thing to save a brother's life is a great and fine action."

"Now come," said Luigi, "it is very pleasant to hear you say these things, but for unselfishness, or heroism, or magnanimity, the circumstances won't stand scrutiny. You overlook one detail; suppose I hadn't saved Angelo's life, what would have become of mine? If I had let the man kill him, wouldn't he have killed me, too?[21] I saved my own life, you see."

"Yes, that is your way of talking," said Angelo, "but I know you—I don't believe you thought of yourself at all. I keep that weapon yet that Luigi killed the man with, and I'll show it to you some time. That incident makes it interesting, and it had a history before it came into Luigi's hands which adds to its interest. It was given to Luigi by a great Indian prince, the Gaikowar of Baroda, and it had been in his family two or three centuries. It killed a good many disagreeable people who troubled the hearthstone at one time or another. It isn't much to look at, except it isn't shaped like other knives, or dirks, or whatever it may be called—here, I'll draw it for you." He took a sheet of paper and made a rapid sketch. "There it is—a broad and murderous blade, with edges like a razor for sharpness. The devices engraved on it are the ciphers or names of its long line of possessors—I had Luigi's name added in Roman letters myself with our coat of arms, as you see. You notice what a curious

21) suppose I hadn't saved Angelo's life, what would have become of mine? If I had let the man kill him, wouldn't he have killed me, too? 만약 내가 Angelodml 생명을 구하지 않았다면 내 생명은 어떻게 되었을 것인가? 만약 그가 Angelo를 살해하게 놔두었다면, 나 역시

handle the thing has. It is solid ivory, polished like a mirror, and is four or five inches long—round, and as thick as a large man's wrist, with the end squared off flat, for your thumb to rest on; for you grasp it, with your thumb resting on the blunt end—so—and lift it aloft and strike downwards. The Gaikowar showed us how thc thing was done when he gave it to Luigi, and before that night was ended, Luigi had used the knife, and the Gaikowar was a man short by reason of it.[22) The sheath is magnificently ornamented with gems of great value. You will find a sheath more worth looking at than the knife itself, of course."

Tom said to himself:

"It's lucky I came here. I would have sold that knife for a song; I supposed the jewels were glass."

"But go on; don't stop," said Wilson. "Our curiosity is up now, to hear about the homicide. Tell us about that."

"Well, briefly, the knife was to blame for that, all around. A native servant slipped into our room in the palace in the night, to kill us and steal the knife on account of the fortune encrusted on its sheath, without a doubt. Luigi had it under his pillow; we were in bed together. There was a dim night-light burning. I was asleep, but Luigi was awake, and he thought he detected a vague form nearing the bed. He slipped the knife out of the sheath and was ready and unembarrassed by hampering bedclothes, for the weather was hot and we hadn't any. Suddenly that native rose at the bedside, and bent over me with his right hand lifted and a dirk in it aimed at my throat; but Luigi grabbed his wrist, pulled him downward, and drove his own knife into the man's neck. That is the whole story."

살해당하지 않았겠는가? 이 둘이 첫 원고에서 샴쌍둥이였다는 것을 알려주는 문장

22) the Gaikowar was a man short by reason of it: 그것 때문에 Gaikowar 집안에는 한 사람이 적어졌다

Wilson and Tom drew deep breaths, and after some general chat about the tragedy, Pudd'nhead said, taking Tom's hand—

"Now, Tom, I've never had a look at your palms, as it happens; perhaps you've got some little questionable privacies that need—hel-lo!"

Tom had snatched away his hand, and was looking a good deal confused.

"Why, he's blushing!" said Luigi.

Tom darted an ugly look at him, and said sharply:

"Well, if I am, it ain't because I'm a murderer!" Luigi's dark face flushed, but before he could speak or move, Tom added with anxious haste: "Oh, I beg a thousand pardons. I didn't mean that; it was out before I thought, and I'm very, very sorry—you must forgive me!"

Wilson came to the rescue, and smoothed things down as well as he could; and in fact was entirely successful as far as the twins were concerned, for they felt sorrier for the affront put upon him by his guest's outburst of ill manners than for the insult offered to Luigi. But the success was not so pronounced with the offender.[23)] Tom tried to seem at his ease, and he went through the motions fairly well, but at bottom he felt resentful toward all the three witnesses of his exhibition; in fact, he felt so annoyed at them for having witnessed it and noticed it that he almost forgot to feel annoyed at himself for placing it before them. However, something presently happened which made him almost comfortable, and brought him nearly back to a state of charity and friendliness. This was a little spat between the twins; not much of a spat, but still a spat; and before they got far with it, they were in a decided condition of irritation with each other. Tom was charmed; so pleased, in deed, that he cautiously did what he could to increase the

---

23) But the success was not so pronounced with the offender: 하지만 무례를 행한 사람(Tom)

irritation while pretending to be actuated by more respectable motives. By his help the fire got warmed up to the blazing point, and he might have had the happiness of seeing the flames show up in another moment, but for the interruption of a knock on the door—an interruption which fretted him as much as it gratified Wilson. Wilson opened the door.

The visitor was a good-natured, ignorant, energetic middle-aged Irishman named John Buckstone, who was a great politician in a small way, and always took a large share in public matters of every sort. One of the town's chief excitements, just now, was over the matter of rum. There was a strong rum party and a strong anti-rum party. Buckstone was training with the rum party, and he had been sent to hunt up the twins and invite them to attend a mass meeting of that faction. He delivered his errand, and said the clans were already gathering in the big hall over the market house. Luigi accepted the invitation cordially. Angelo less cordially, since he disliked crowds, and did not drink the powerful intoxicants of America. In fact, he was even a teetotaler sometimes when it was judicious to be one.

The twins left with Buckstone, and Tom Driscoll joined the company with them uninvited.

In the distance, one could see a long wavering line of torches drifting down the main street, and could hear the throbbing of the bass drum, the clash of cymbals, the squeaking of a fife or two, and the faint roar of remote hurrahs. The tail end of this procession was climbing the market house stairs when the twins arrived in its neighborhood; when they reached the hall, it was full of people, torches, smoke, noise, and enthusiasm. They were conducted to the platform by Buckstone—Tom Driscoll still following—and were delivered to the

---

에 대한 (Wilson의 화해시도) 성공은 그리 확실하지 않았다

chairman in the midst of a prodigious explosion of welcome. When the noise had moderated a little, the chair proposed that "our illustrious guests be at once elected, by complimentary acclamation, to membership in our ever-glorious organization, the paradise of the free and the perdition of the slave."

This eloquent discharge opened the floodgates of enthusiasm again, and the election was carried with thundering unanimity. Then arose a storm of cries:

"Wet them down![24] Wet them down! Give them a drink!"

Glasses of whisky were handed to the twins. Luigi waves his aloft, then brought it to his lips; but Angelo set his down. There was another storm of cries—

"What's the matter with the other one?" "What is the blonde one going back on us for?"[25] "Explain! Explain!"

The chairman inquired, and then reported—

"We have made an unfortunate mistake, gentlemen. I find that the Count Angelo Capello is opposed to our creed—is a teetotaler, in fact,

---

24) Wet them down!: 취하게 만들라

25) What is the blond one going back on us for?: 왜 저 금발은 우리를 배신하는가? What for=왜, go back on=배신하다, 저버리다

and was not intending to apply for membership with us. He desires that we reconsider the vote by which he was elected. What is the pleasure of the house?"[26]

There was a general burst of laughter, plentifully accented with whistlings and cat calls, but the energetic use of the gavel presently restored something like order. Then a man spoke from the crowd and said that while he was very sorry that the mistake had been made, it would not be possible to rectify it at the present meeting. According to the bylaws, it must go over to the next regular meeting for action. He would not offer a motion, as none was required. He desired to apologize to the gentlemen in the name of the house, and begged to assure him that as far as it might lie in the power of the Sons of Liberty, his temporary membership in the order would be made pleasant to him.

This speech was received with great applause, mixed with cries of—

"That's the talk!" "He's a good fellow, anyway, if he is a teetotaler!" "Drink his health!" "Give him a rouser, and no heeltaps!"[27]

Glasses were handed around, and everybody on the platform drank Angelo's health, while the house bellowed forth in song:

"For he's a jolly good fel-low,
For he's a jolly good fel-low,
For he's a jolly good fe-el-low,
Which nobody can deny."

Tom Driscoll drank. It was his second glass, for he had drunk Angelo's the moment that Angelo had set it down. The two drinks made him very merry—almost idiotically so—and he began to take a most lively and prominent part in the proceedings, particularly in the

26) What is the pleasure of the house?: 회원들은 어떻게 하였으면 좋겠는가?
27) Give him a rouser, and no heeltaps!: 그에게 깨우침을 주자, 한 방울도 남기지 않고 마셔라!

music and cat calls and side-remarks.

The chairman was still standing at the front, the twins at his side. The extraordinarily close resemblance of the brothers to each other suggested a witticism to Tom Driscoll, and just as the chairman began a speech he skipped forward and said, with an air of tipsy confidence, to the audience—

"Boys, I move that he keeps still and lets this human philopena snip you out a speech."[28)]

The descriptive aptness of the phrase caught the house,[29)] and a mighty burst of laughter followed.

Luigi's southern blood[30)] leaped to the boiling point in a moment under the sharp humiliation of this insult delivered in the presence of four hundred strangers. It was not in the young man's nature to let the matter pass, or to delay the squaring of the account.[31)] He took a couple of strides and halted behind the unsuspecting joker. Then he drew back and delivered a kick of such titanic vigor that it lifted Tom clear over the footlights and landed him on the heads of the front row of the Sons of Liberty.

Even a sober person does not like to have a human being emptied on[32)] him when he is not doing any harm; a person who is not sober cannot endure such an attention at all. The nest of Sons of Liberty that Driscoll landed in had not a sober bird in it; in fact there was probably not an entirely sober one in the auditorium. Driscoll was promptly and indignantly flung on the heads of Sons in the next row, and these Sons

---

28) this human philopena snip you out a speech: 이 열매 반쪽 같은 인간들이 한마디 하게 하자. philopena=아몬드처럼 핵이 둘 있는 열매로 Angelo와 Luigi가 샴쌍둥이었던 첫 원고의 흔적이 보임

29) The descriptive aptness of the phrase caught the house: 묘사의 적절함이 청중을 사로잡았다

30) Luigi's southern blood: Luigi의 남부기질 (라틴계의 남부 유럽 사람들은 게르만계의 북부 유럽 사람들 보다 열정적이라고 여겨졌다

31) the squaring of the account: 대차를 청산하다, 앙갚음하다

32) emptied on ~: ~위로 쏟아지다

passed him on toward the rear, and then immediately began to pummel the front row Sons who had passed him to them. This course was strictly followed by bench after bench as Driscoll traveled in his tumultuous and airy flight toward the door; so he left behind him an ever-lengthening wake of raging and plunging and fighting and swearing humanity. Down went group after group of torches, and presently, above the deafening clatter of the gavel, roar of angry voices, and crash of succumbing benches, rose the paralyzing cry of

"FIRE!"

The fighting ceased instantly; the cursing ceased; for one distinctly defined moment, there was a dead hush, a motionless calm, where the tempest had been; then with one impulse the multitude awoke to life and energy again, and went surging and struggling and swaying, this way and that, its outer edges melting away through windows and doors and gradually lessening the pressure and relieving the mass.

The fire-boys were never on hand so suddenly before; for there was no distance to go this time, their quarters being in the rear end of the market house, There was an engine company and a hook-and-ladder company. Half of each was composed of rummies and the other half of anti-rummies, after the moral and political share-and-share-alike fashion of the frontier town of the period. Enough anti-rummies were loafing in quarters to man the engine and the ladders. In two minutes they had their red shirts and helmets on—they never stirred officially in unofficial costume—and as the mass meeting overhead smashed through the long row of windows and poured out upon the roof of the arcade, the deliverers were ready for them with a powerful stream of water, which washed some of them off the roof and nearly drowned the rest. But water was preferable to fire, and still the stampede from the windows continued, and still the pitiless drenching assailed it until the building was empty; then the fire-boys mounted to the hall and flooded it with water enough to annihilate forty times as much fire as there was there: for a village fire company does not often get a chance to show off, and so when it does get a chance, it makes the most of it.33) Such citizens of that village as were of a thoughtful and judicious temperament did not insure against fire; they insured against the fire company.

33) when it does get a chance, it makes the most of it: 기회가 생겼을 때 최대한 활용했다

CHAPTER 12

Courage is resistance to fear, mastery of fear—not absence of fear. Except a creature be part coward, it is not a compliment to say it is brave, it is merely a loose misapplication of the word. Consider the flea!—incomparably the bravest of all the creatures of God, if ignorance of fear were courage. Whether you are asleep or awake he will attack you, caring nothing for the fact that in bulk and strength you are to him as are the massed armies of the earth to a sucking child; he lives both day and night and all days and nights in the very lap of peril and the immediate presence of death, and yet is no more afraid than is the man who walks the streets of a city that was threatened by an earthquake ten centuries before. When we speak of Clive, Nelson, and Putnam as men who "didn't know what fear was," we ought always to add the flea—and put him at the head of the procession.[1]

-Pudd'nhead Wilson's Calendar

Judge Driscoll was in bed and asleep by ten o'clock on Friday night, and he was up and gone a-fishing before daylight in the morning with his friend Pembroke Howard. These two had been boys together in Virginia when that state still ranked as the chief and most imposing member of the Union,[2] and they still coupled the proud and affectionate adjective "old" with her name when they spoke of her. In Missouri a recognized superiority attached to any person who hailed from Old Virginia; and this superiority was exalted to supremacy when a person of such nativity could also

1) put him at the head of the procession: 행렬의 맨 앞에 놓아야 한다

2) when that state still ranked as the chief and most imposing member of the Union: Virginia주가 아직 남부연합의 수장이자 가장 두드러진 일원이었을 때

prove descent from the First Families of that great commonwealth. The Howards and Driscolls were of this aristocracy. In their eyes, it was a nobility. It had its unwritten laws, and they were as clearly defined and as strict as any that could be found among the printed statues of the land. The F.F.V. was born a gentleman; his highest duty in life was to watch over that great inheritance and keep it unsmirched. He must keep his honor spotless. Those laws were his chart; his course was marked out on it; if he swerved from it by so much as half a point of the compass, it meant shipwreck to his honor; that is to say, degradation from his rank as a gentleman. These laws required certain things of him which his religion might forbid: then his religion must yield—the laws could not be relaxed to accommodate religions or anything else. Honor stood first; and the laws defined what it was and wherein it differed in certain details from honor as defined by church creeds and by the social laws and customs of some of the minor divisions of the globe that had got crowded out when the sacred boundaries of Virginia were staked out.

If Judge Driscoll was the recognized first citizen of Dawson's Landing, Pembroke Howard was easily its recognized second citizen. He was called "the great lawyer"—an earned title.[3)] He and Driscoll were of the same age—a year or two past sixty.

Although Driscoll was a freethinker and Howard a strong and determined Presbyterian, their warm intimacy suffered no impairment in consequence. They were men whose opinions were their own property and not subject to revision and amendment, suggestion or criticism, by anybody, even their friends.

---

3) an earned title: (Virginia 혈통이라는 것과 다르게) 획득한 칭호

The day's fishing finished, they came floating downstream in their skiff, talking national politics and other high matters, and presently met a skiff coming up from town, with a man in it who said:

"I reckon you know one of the new twins gave your nephew a kicking last night, Judge?"

"Did *what*?"

"Gave him a kicking."

The old judge's lips paled, and his eyes began to flame. He choked with anger for a moment, then he got out what he was trying to say

"Well—well—go on! Give me the details!"

The man did it. At the finish the judge was silent a minute, turning over in his mind the shameful picture of Tom's flight over the footlights; then he said, as if musing aloud—

"Hm—I don't understand it. I was asleep at home. He didn't wake me. Thought he was competent to manage his affair without my help, I reckon." His face lit up with pride and pleasure at that thought, and he said with a cheery complacency, "I like that—it's the true old blood[4)] —hey, Pembroke?"

Howard smiled an iron smile and nodded his head approvingly. Then the news-bringer spoke again—

"But Tom beat the twin on the trial."

The judge looked at the man wonderingly, and said

"The trial? What trial?"

"Why, Tom had him up before Judge Robinson for assault and battery."

The old man shrank suddenly together like one who has received a death-stroke. Howard sprang for him as he sank forward in a swoon, and took him in his arms, and bedded him on his back in the boat. He

---

4) it's the true old blood: 이게 진정한 남부신사야

sprinkled water in his face, and said to the startled visitor—

"Go, now—don't let him come to and find you here. You see what an effect your heedless speech has had; you ought to have been more considerate than to blurt out such a cruel piece of slander as that."

"I'm right down sorry I did it, now, Mr. Howard, and I wouldn't have done it if I had thought; but it ain't a slander; it's perfectly true, just as I told him."

He rowed away. Presently the old judge came out of his faint and looked up piteously into the sympathetic face that was bent over him.

"Say it ain't true, Pembroke; tell me it ain't true!" he said, in a weak voice.

There was nothing weak in the deep organ-tones that responded—

"You know it's a lie as well as I do, old friend. He is of the best blood of the Old Dominion."[5)]

"God bless you for saying it!" said the old gentleman fervently. "Ah, Pembroke, it was such a blow!"

Howard stayed by his friend, and saw him home, and entered the house with him. It was dark, and past supper-time, but the judge was not thinking of supper; he was eager to hear the slander refuted from headquarters, and as eager to have Howard hear it, too. Tom was sent for, and he came immediately. He was bruised and lame, and was not a happy-looking object. His uncle made him sit down, and said—

"We have been hearing about your adventure, Tom, with a handsome lie added to it for embellishment. Now pulverize that lie to dust! What measures have you taken? How does the thing stand?"

Tom answered guilelessly: "It don't stand at all; it's all over. I had him up in court and beat him. Pudd'nhead Wilson defended him—first case he ever had, and lost it. The judge fined the miserable hound five

---

5) He is of the best blood of the Old Dominion: 그는 Virginia주에서 최고의 가문출신이다.

dollars for the assault."

Howard and the judge sprang to their feet with the opening sentence—why, neither knew; then they stood gazing vacantly at each other. Howard stood a moment, then sat mournfully down without saying anything. The judge's wrath began to kindle, and he burst out—

"You cur! You scum! You vermin! Do you mean to tell me that blood of my race has suffered a blow and crawled to a court of law about it? Answer me!"

Tom's head drooped, and he answered with an eloquent silence. His uncle stared at him with a mixed expression of amazement and shame and incredulity that was sorrowful to see. At last he said—

"Which of the twins was it?"

"Count Luigi."

"You have challenged him?"

"N—no," hesitated Tom, turning pale.

"You will challenge him tonight. Howard will carry it."[6]

Tom began to turn sick, and to show it. He turned his hat round and round in his hand, his uncle glowering blacker and blacker upon him as the heavy seconds drifted by; then at last he began to stammer, and said piteously—

"Oh, please, don't ask me to do it, uncle! He is a murderous devil. I—I'm afraid of him!"

Old Driscoll's mouth opened and closed three times before he could get it to perform its office;[7] then he stormed out:

"A coward in my family! A Driscoll a coward! Oh, what have I done to deserve this infamy!" He tottered to his secretary in the corner,[8]

---

the Old Dominion은 Virginia주를 부르는 말

6) Howard will carry it: Howard가 결투신청을 전달해 줄 것이다

7) before he could get it to perform its office: 그가 말을 할 수 있기까지

8) He tottered to his secretary in the corner: 그는 구석에 있는 책상까지 비틀거리며 걸어갔다

repeating that lament again and again in heartbreaking tones, and got out of a drawer a paper, which he slowly tore to bits, scattering the bits absently in his track as he walked up and down the room, still grieving and lamenting. At last he said:

"There it is, shreds and fragments once more—my will. Once more you have forced me to disinherit you, you base son of a most noble father! Leave my sight! Go—before I spit on you!"

The young man did not tarry. Then the judge turned to Howard:

"You will be my second, old friend?"[9)]

"Of course."

"There is pen and paper. Draft the cartel, and lose no time."

"The Count shall have it in his hands in fifteen minutes," said Howard.

Tom was very heavy-hearted. His appetite was gone with his property and his self-respect. He went out the back way and wandered down the obscure lane, grieving, and wondering if any course of future conduct, however discreet and carefully perfected and watched over, could win back his uncle's favor and persuade him to reconstruct once more that generous will which had just gone to ruin before his eyes. He finally concluded that it could. He said to himself that he had accomplished this sort of triumph once already, and that what had been done once could be done again. He would set about it. He would bend every energy to the task, and he would score that triumph once more, cost what it might to his convenience, limit as it might his frivolous and liberty-loving life.

"To begin," he says to himself, "I'll square up with the proceeds of my raid, and then gambling has got to be stopped—and stopped short

---

9) You will be my second, old friend?: (결투에서) 내 보조인이 되어주겠나, 친구?

off.[10] It's the worst vice I've got—from my standpoint, anyway, because it's the one he can most easily find out, through the impatience of my creditors. He thought it expensive to have to pay two hundred dollars to them for me once. Expensive—that! Why, it cost me the whole of his fortune—but, of course, he never thought of that; some people can't think of any but their own side of a case. If he had known how deep I am in now, the will would have gone to pot without waiting for a duel to help. Three hundred dollars! It's a pile! But he'll never hear of it, I'm thankful to say. The minute I've cleared it off, I'm safe; and I'll never touch a card again. Anyway, I won't while he lives, I make oath to that. I'm entering on my last reform—I know it yes, and I'll win; but after that, if I ever slip again I'm gone."

10) stopped short off: 뚝 끊다

CHAPTER 13

When I reflect upon the number of disagreeable people who I know have gone to a better world, I am moved to lead a different life.

- Pudd'nhead Wilson's Calendar

OCTOBER. This is one of the peculiarly dangerous months to speculate in stocks in. The others are July, January, September, April, November, May, March, June, December, August, and February.

- Pudd'nhead Wilson's Calendar

Thus mournfully communing with himself, Tom moped along the lane past Pudd'nhead Wilson's house, and still on and on between fences enclosing vacant country on each hand till he neared the haunted house, then he came moping back again, with many sighs and heavy with trouble. He sorely wanted cheerful company. Rowena! His heart gave a bound at the thought, but the next thought quieted it—the detested twins would be there.

He was on the inhabited side of Wilson's house, and now as he approached it, he noticed that the sitting room was lighted. This would do; others made him feel unwelcome sometimes, but Wilson never failed in courtesy toward him, and a kindly courtesy does at least save one's feelings, even if it is not professing to stand for a welcome.[1] Wilson heard footsteps at his threshold, then the clearing of a throat.

"It's that fickle-tempered, dissipated young goose—poor devil, he

---

1) even if it is not professing to stand for a welcome: 만일 그 예절바름이 환영의 의미를 보여주는 것은 아닐지라도

find friends pretty scarce today, likely, after the disgrace of carrying a personal assault case into a law-court."

A dejected knock. "Come in!"

Tom entered, and dropped into a chair, without saying anything. Wilson said kindly—

"Why, my boy, you look desolate. Don't take it so hard. Try and forget you have been kicked."

"Oh, dear," said Tom, wretchedly, "it's not that, Pudd'nhead—it's not that. It's a thousand times worse than that—oh, yes, a million times worse."

"Why, Tom, what do you mean? Has Rowena—"

"Flung me? No, but the old man has."

Wilson said to himself, "Aha!" and thought of the mysterious girl in the bedroom. "The Driscolls have been making discoveries!" Then he said aloud, gravely:

"Tom, there are some kinds of dissipation which—"

"Oh, shucks, this hasn't got anything to do with dissipation. He wanted me to challenge that derned Italian savage, and I wouldn't do it."

"Yes, of course he would do that," said Wilson in a meditative matter-of-course way, "but the thing that puzzled me was, why he didn't look to that last night,[2] for one thing, and why he let you carry such a matter into a court of law at all, either before the duel or after it. It's no place for it. It was not like him. I couldn't understand it. How did it happen?"

"It happened because he didn't know anything about it. He was asleep when I got home last night."

"And you didn't wake him? Tom, is that possible?"

---

2) why he didn't look to that last night: 왜 어제 밤 그 일에 관심를 안 기울였는지

Tom was not getting much comfort here. He fidgeted a moment, then said:

"I didn't choose to tell him—that's all. He was going a-fishing before dawn, with Pembroke Howard, and if I got the twins into the common calaboose—and I thought sure I could—I never dreamed of their slipping out on a paltry fine for such an outrageous offense—well, once in the calaboose they would be disgraced, and uncle wouldn't want any duels with that sort of characters, and wouldn't allow any. "

"Tom, I am ashamed of you! I don't see how you could treat your good old uncle so. I am a better friend of his than you are; for if I had known the circumstances I would have kept that case out of court until I got word to him and let him have the gentleman's chance."

"You would?" exclaimed Tom, with lively surprise. "And it your first case! And you know perfectly well there never would have been any case if he had got that chance, don't you? And you'd have finished your days a pauper nobody,[3)] instead of being an actually launched and recognized lawyer today. And you would really have done that, would you?"

"Certainly."

Tom looked at him a moment or two, then shook his head sorrowfully and said

"I believe you upon my word I do. I don't know why I do, but I do. Pudd'nhead Wilson, I think you're the biggest fool I ever saw."

"Thank you."

"Don't mention it."

"Well, he has been requiring you to fight the Italian, and you have refused. You degenerate remnant of an honorable line! I'm thoroughly ashamed of you, Tom!"

---

3) And you'd have finished your days a pauper nobody: 그래서 당신 삶을 별볼일없는 가난뱅이로 끝냈을 것이라고

"Oh, that's nothing! I don't care for anything, now that the will's torn up again."

"Tom, tell me squarely—didn't he find any fault with you for anything but those two things—carrying the case into court and refusing to fight?"

He watched the young fellow's face narrowly, but it was entirely reposeful, and so also was the voice that answered:

"No, he didn't find any other fault with me. If he had had any to find, he would have begun yesterday, for he was just in the humor for it.[4] He drove that jack-pair[5] around town and showed them the sights, and when he came home he couldn't find his father's old silver watch that don't keep time and he thinks so much of, and couldn't remember what he did with it three or four days ago when he saw it last, and when I suggested that it probably wasn't lost but stolen, it put him in a regular passion, and he said I was a fool which convinced me, without any trouble, that that was just what he was afraid had happened, himself, but did not want to believe it, because lost things stand a better chance of being found again than stolen ones."

"Whe-ew!" whistled Wilson. "Score another one the list."[6]

"Another what?"

"Another theft!"

"Theft?"

"Yes, theft. That watch isn't lost, it's stolen. There's been another raid on the town and just the same old mysterious sort of thing that has happened once before, as you remember."

"You don't mean it!"

---

4) for he was just in the humor for it: 그(Judge Driscoll)가 (Tom에게 못마땅한) 그런 기분에 있었으므로

5) that jack-pair: playing cards의 Jack에 있는 한 쌍의 그림 같은 Angelo와 Luigi

6) Score another one the list: (도둑맞은 집) 목록에 하나가 더 늘었다

"It's as sure as you are born! Have you missed anything yourself?"

"No. That is, I did miss a silver pencil case that Aunt Mary Pratt gave me last birthday—"

"You'll find it stolen—that's what you'll find."

"No, I shan't; for when I suggested theft about the watch and got such a rap, I went and examined my room, and the pencil case was missing, but it was only mislaid, and I found it again."

"You are sure you missed nothing else?"

"Well, nothing of consequence. I missed a small plain gold ring worth two or three dollars, but that will turn up. I'll look again."

"In my opinion you'll not find it. There's been a raid, I tell you. Come in! "

Mr. Justice Robinson entered, followed by Buckstone and the town constable, Jim Blake. They sat down, and after some wandering and aimless weather-conversation Wilson said—

"By the way, we've just added another to the list of thefts, maybe two. Judge Driscoll's old silver watch is gone, and Tom here has missed a gold ring."

"Well, it is a bad business," said the justice, "and gets worse the further it goes. The Hankses, the Dobsons, the Pilligrews, the Ortons, the Grangers, the Hales, the Fullers, the Holcombs, in fact everybody that lives around about Patsy Cooper's had been robbed of little things like trinkets and teaspoons and such like small valuables that are easily carried off. It's perfectly plain that the thief took advantage of the reception at Patsy Cooper's when all the neighbors were in her house and all their niggers hanging around her fence for a look at the show, to raid the vacant houses undisturbed. Patsy is miserable about it; miserable on account of the neighbors, and particularly miserable on account of her foreigners, of course; so miserable on their account that she hasn't any room to worry about her own little losses."

"It's the same old raider," said Wilson. "I suppose there isn't any doubt about that."

"Constable Blake doesn't think so."

"No, you're wrong there," said Blake. "The other times it was a man; there was plenty of signs of that, as we know, in the profession, thought we never got hands on him; but this time it's a woman."

Wilson thought of the mysterious girl straight off. She was always in his mind now. But she failed him again.[7] Blake continued:

"She's a stoop-shouldered old woman with a covered basket on her arm, in a black veil, dressed in mourning. I saw her going aboard the ferryboat yesterday. Lives in Illinois, I reckon; but I don't care where she lives, I'm going to get her—she can make herself sure of that."

"What makes you think she's the thief?"

"Well, there ain't any other, for one thing; and for another, some of the nigger draymen that happened to be driving along saw her coming out of or going into houses, and told me so—and it just happens that they was *robbed*, every time."

It was granted that this was plenty good enough circumstantial evidence. A pensive silence followed, which lasted some moments, then Wilson said:

"There's one good thing, anyway. She can't either pawn or sell Count Luigi's costly Indian dagger."

"My!" said Tom. "Is that gone?"

"Yes."

"Well, that was a haul![8] But why can't she pawn it or sell it?"

"Because when the twins went home from the Sons of Liberty

---

7) But she failed him again: 그러나 그녀는 또 그를 실망시켰다. 처음에는 그녀의 정체에 대해 생각했으나 알아내지 못했고 이번에는 그녀가 범인일 것이라고 생각했으나 틀려서

8) that was a haul!: 굉장한 건데!

meeting last night, news of the raid was sifting in from everywhere, and Aunt Patsy was in distress to know if they had lost anything. They found that the dagger was gone, and they notified the police and pawnbrokers everywhere. It was a great haul, yes, but the old woman won't get anything out of it, because she'll get caught."

"Did they offer a reward?" asked Buckstone.

"Yes, five hundred dollars for the knife, and five hundred more for thief."

"What a leather-headed idea!"[9] exclaimed the constable. "The thief dasn't go near them, nor send anybody. Whoever goes is going to get himself nabbed, for there ain't any pawnbroker that's going to lose the chance to—"

If anybody had noticed Tom's face at that time, the gray-green color of it might have provoked curiosity; but nobody did. He said to himself: "I'm gone! I never can square up;[10] the rest of the plunder won't pawn or sell for half of the bill. Oh, I know it—I'm gone, I'm gone and this time it's for good. Oh, this is awful—I don't know what to do, nor which way to turn!"

"Softly, softly," said Wilson to Blake. "I planned their scheme for them at midnight last night, and it was all finished up ship shape by two this morning. They'll get their dagger back, and then I'll explain to you how the thing was done."

There were strong signs of a general curiosity, and Buckstone said

"Well, you have whetted us up pretty sharp, Wilson, and I'm free to say that if you don't mind telling us in confidence—"

"Oh, I'd as soon tell as not,[11] Buckstone, but as long as the twins and I agreed to say nothing about it, we must let it stand so. But you can

---

9) What a leather-headed idea!: 참 멍청한 생각이군!

10) I never can square up: 난 결코 (빚을 다 갚고) 바로 설 수 없을 것이다

11) I'd as soon tel as no: 기꺼이 말해주고 싶다.

take my word for it, you won't be kept waiting three days. Somebody will apply for that reward pretty promptly, and I'll show you the thief and the dagger both very soon afterward."

The constable was disappointed, and also perplexed. He said

"It may all be—yes, and I hope it will, but I'm blamed if I can see my way through it. It's too many for yours truly[12)]."

The subject seemed about talked out. Nobody seemed to have anything further to offer. After a silence the justice of the peace[13)] informed Wilson that he and Buckstone and the constable had come as a committee, on the part of the Democratic party, to ask him to run for mayor for the little town was about to become a city and the first charter election was approaching. It was the first attention which Wilson had ever received at the hands of any party; it was a sufficiently humble one, but it was a recognition of his début into the town's life and activities at last; it was a step upward, and he was deeply gratified. He accepted, and the committee departed, followed by young Tom.

---

12) yours truly: me
13) the justice of the peace: 치안판사

CHAPTER 14

The true Southern watermelon is a boon apart, and not to be mentioned with commoner things. It is chief of this world's luxuries, king by the grace of God over all the fruits of the earth. When one has tasted it, he knows what the angels eat. It was not a Southern watermelon that Eve took: we know it because she repented.

- Pudd'nhead Wilson's Calendar

About the time that Wilson was bowing the committee out, Pembroke Howard was entering the next house to report. He found the old judge sitting grim and straight in his chair, waiting.

"Well, Howard—the news?"

"The best in the world."

"Accepts, does he?" and the light of battle gleamed joyously in the Judge's eye.

"Accepts? Why, he jumped at it."[1]

"Did, did he? Now that's fine that's very fine. I like that. When is it to be?"

"Now! Straight off! Tonight! An admirable fellow—admirable!"

"Admirable? He's a darling! Why, it's an honor as well as a pleasure to stand up before such a man. Come—off with you! Go and arrange everything and give him my heartiest compliments. A rare fellow, indeed; an admirable fellow, as you have said!"

Howard hurried away, saying—

"I'll have him in the vacant stretch between Wilson's and the

---

1) he jumped at it: 쾌히 응했다

haunted house within the hour, and I'll bring my own pistols."

Judge Driscoll began to walk the floor in a state of pleased excitement; but presently he stopped, and began to think—began to think of Tom. Twice he moved toward the secretary, and twice he turned away again; but finally he said—

"This may be my last night in the world—I must not take the chance. He is worthless and unworthy, but it is largely my fault. He was entrusted to me by my brother on his dying bed, and I have indulged him to his hurt,[2] instead of training him up severely and making a man of him, I have violated my trust, and I must not add the sin of desertion to that. I have forgiven him once already, and would subject him to a long and hard trial before forgiving him again, if I could live; but I must not run that risk. No, I must restore the will. But if I survive the duel, I will hide it away, and he will not know, and I will not tell him until he reforms, and I see that[3] his reformation is going to be permanent."

He re-drew the will, and his ostensible nephew was heir to a fortune again. As he was finishing his task, Tom, wearied with another brooding tramp, entered the house and went tip-toeing past the sitting-room door. He glanced in, and hurried on, for the sight of his uncle was nothing but terrors for him tonight. But his uncle was writing! That was unusual at this late hour. What could he be writing? A chill anxiety settled down upon Tom's heart. Did that writing concern him? He was afraid so. He reflected that when ill luck begins, it does not come in sprinkles, but in showers. He said he would get a glimpse of that document or know the reason why. He heard someone coming, and stepped out of sight and hearing. It was Pembroke

2) I have indulged him to his hurt: 그에게 해가되게 버릇없이 길렀다
3) I see that ~: I see (to it) that=꼭 ~ 시키다

Howard. What could be hatching?[4)]

Howard said, with great satisfaction—

"Everything's right and ready. He's gone to the battle ground with his second and the surgeon—also with his brother. I've arranged it all with Wilson—Wilson's his second. We are to have three shots apiece."

"Good! How is the moon?"

"Bright as day, nearly. Perfect for the distance—fifteen yards. No wind—not a breath; hot and still."

"All good; all first-rate. Here, Pembroke, read this, and witness it."

Pembroke read and witnessed the will, then gave the old man's hand a hearty shake and said—

"Now that's right, York—but I knew you would do it. You couldn't leave that poor chap to fight along without means or profession, with certain defeat before him, and I knew you wouldn't, for his father's sake if not for his own."

"For his dead father's sake, I couldn't, I know; for poor Percy—but you know what Percy was to me. But mind—Tom is not to know of this unless I fall tonight."

"I understand. I'll keep the secret."

---

4) What could be hatching?: 무슨 일이 꾸며지고 있는 것일까?

The judge put the will away, and the two started for the battleground. In another minute the will was in Tom's hands. His misery vanished, his feelings underwent a tremendous revulsion. He put the will carefully back in its place and spread his mouth and swung his hat once, twice, three times around his head, in imitation of three rousing huzzahs, no sound issuing from his lips. He fell to communing with himself excitedly and joyously, but every now and then he let off another volley of dumb hurrahs.

He said to himself: "I've got the fortune again, but I'll not let on that I know about it.[5] And this time I'm gong to hang on to it. I take no more risks. I'll gamble no more, I'll drink no more, because—well, because I'll not go where there is any of that sort of thing going on, again. It's the sure way, and the only sure way; I might have thought of that sooner—well, yes, if I had wanted to. But now—dear me, I've had a bad scare this time, and I'll take no more chances. Not a single chance more. Land! I persuaded myself this evening that I could fetch him around without any great amount of effort, but I've been getting more and more heavy-hearted and doubtful straight along, ever since. If he tells me about this thing, all right; but if he doesn't, I shan't let on. I—well, I'd like to tell Pudd'nhead Wilson, but—no, I'll think about that; perhaps I won't." He whirled off another dead huzzah, and said, "I'm reformed, and this time I'll stay so, sure!"

He was about to close with a final grand silent demonstration, when he suddenly recollected that Wilson had put it out of his power to pawn or sell the Indian knife, and that he was once more in awful peril of exposure by his creditors for that reason. His joy collapsed utterly, and he turned away and moped toward the door moaning and lamenting over the bitterness of his luck. He dragged himself upstairs,

5) I'll not let on that I know about it: 그 유언장에 대해 알고 있는 것을 누설하지 않을 것

and brooded in his room a long time, disconsolate and forlorn, with Luigi's Indian knife for a text.[6] At last he sighed and said:

"When I supposed these stones were glass and this ivory bone, the thing hadn't any interest for me because it hadn't any value, and couldn't help me out of my trouble. But now—why, now it is full of interest; yes, and of a sort to break a body's heart. It's a bag of gold that has turned to dirt and ashes in my hands. It could save me, and save me so easily, and yet I've got to go to ruin. It's like drowning with a life preserver in my reach. All the hard luck comes to me, and all the good luck goes to other people—Pudd'nhead Wilson, for instance; even his career has got a sort of a little start at last, and what has he done to deserve it, I should like to know? Yes, he has opened his own road, but he isn't content with that, but must block mine. It's a sordid, selfish world, and I wish I was out of it." He allowed the light of the candle to play upon the jewels of the sheath, but the flashings and sparklings had no charm for his eye; they were only just so many pangs to his heart. "I must not say anything to Roxy about this thing," he said. "She is too daring. She would be for digging these stones out and selling them, and then—why, she would be arrested and the stones traced, and then—" The thought made him quake, and he hid the knife away, trembling all over and glancing furtively about, like a criminal who fancies that the accuser is already at hand.

Should he try to sleep? Oh, no, sleep was not for him; his trouble was too haunting, too afflicting for that. He must have somebody to mourn with. He would carry his despair to Roxy.

He had heard several distant gunshots, but that sort of thing was not uncommon, and they had made no impression upon him. He went out at the back door, and turned westward. He passed Wilson's house and

---

이다. let on=누설하다

proceeded along the lane, and presently saw several figures approaching Wilson's place through the vacant lots. These were the duelists returning from the fight; he thought he recognized them, but as he had no desire for white people's company, he stooped down behind the fence until they were out of his way.

Roxy was feeling fine. She said:

"Whah was you, child? Warn't you in it?"[7]

"In what?"

"In de duel."

"Duel? Has there been a duel?"

"Co'se dey has.[8] De ole Jedge has be'n havin' a duel wid one o' dem twins."[9]

"Great Scott!" Then he added to himself: "That's what made him remake the will; he thought he might get killed, and it softened him toward me. And that's what he and Howard were so busy about. . . . Oh dear, if the twin had only killed him, I should be out of my—"

"What is you mumblin' 'bout, Chambers? Whah was you? Didn't you know dey was gwyne to be a duel?"

"No, I didn't. The old man tried to get me to fight one with Count Luigi, but he didn't succeed, so I reckon he concluded to patch up the family honor himself."

He laughed at the idea, and went rambling on with a detailed account of his talk with the judge, and how shocked and ashamed the judge was to find that he had a coward in his family. He glanced up at last, and got a shock himself. Roxana's bosom was heaving with suppressed passion, and she was glowering down upon him with measureless

---

6) with Luigi's Indian knife for a text: Luigi의 Indian knife를 주제로
7) Warn't you in it?: Weren't you in it?=결투에 참여하지 않았니?
8) Co'se dey has: Of course, there has=물론 있었지
9) wid one o' dem twins: one of them (=those) twins

contempt written in her face.

"En you refuse' to fight a man dat kicked you, 'stid o' jumpin' at de chance![10] En you ain't got no mo' feelin' den to come en tell me, dat fetched sich a po' lowdown ornery rabbit into de worl'![11] Pah! it make me sick! It's de nigger in you, dat's what it is. Thirty-one parts o' you is white, en on'y one part nigger, en dat po' little one part is yo' soul.[12] 'Tain't wuth savin'; 'tain't wuth totin' out on a shovel en throwin' en de gutter.[13] You has disgraced yo' birth. What would yo' pa think o' you? It's enough to make him turn in his grave."

The last three sentences stung Tom into a fury, and he said to himself that if his father were only alive and in reach of assassination his mother would soon find that he had a very clear notion of the size of his indebtedness to that man, and was willing to pay it up in full, and would do it too, even at risk of his life; but he kept this thought to himself; that was safest in his mother's present state.

"What ever has come o' yo' Essex blood?[14] Dat's what I can't understan'. En it ain't on'y jist Essex blood dat's in you, not by a long sight—'deed it ain't! My great-great-great-gran'father en yo' great-great-great-great-gran'father was Ole Cap'n John Smith, de highest blood dat Ole Virginny ever turned out,[15] en his great-great-gran'mother, or somers along back dah, was

---

10) 'stid o' jumpin' at de chance!: Instead of jumping at the chance!=기회에 덥썩 뛰어드는 대신!

11) En you ain't got no mo' feelin' den to come en tell me, dat fetched sich a po' lowdown ornery rabbit into de worl'!: And you got no more feeling than to come and tell me, that fetched such a poor low down ornery rabbit into the world!

12) en dat po' little one part is yo' soul: and that poor little one part is your soul. Tom에게는 1/32 만 흑인 피가 섞여있는데 그것이 그의 영혼을 다 차지하고 있다는 말

13) 'Tain't wuth savin'; 'tain't wuth totin' out on a shovel en throwin' en de gutter: It isn't worth saving; it isn't worth toting out on a shovel and throwing in the gutter=이건 구원할 가치조차 없다; 이건 삽으로 떠서 시궁창에 던져버릴 가치조차 없다

14) What ever has 'come o' yo' Essex blood?: What ever has become of your Essex blood?=너의 Essex 혈통은 도대체 어떻게 된 거냐?

15) Ole Cap'n John Smith, de highest blood dat Ole Virginny ever turned out: Old Captain John Smith, the highest blood that Old Virginia ever turned out=Virginia 주가 여태껏 만들어 낸 최고의 혈통, Old Captain John Smith

Pocahontas de Injun queen, en her husbun' was a nigger king outen[16)] Africa—en yit here you is, a slinkin' outen a duel en disgracin' our whole line[17)] like a ornery lowdown hound! Yes, it's de nigger in you!"

She sat down on her candle-box and fell into a reverie. Tom did not disturb her; he sometimes lacked prudence, but it was not in circumstances of this kind, Roxana's storm went gradually down, but it died hard, and even when it seemed to be quite gone, it would now and then break out in a distant rumble, so to speak, in the form of muttered ejaculations. One of these was, "Ain't nigger enough in him to show in his fingernails, en dat takes mighty little—yit dey's enough to paint his soul."

Presently she muttered. "Yassir, enough to paint a whole thimbleful of 'em." At last her ramblings ceased altogether, and her countenance began to clear—a welcome sign to Tom, who had learned her moods and knew she was on the threshold of good humor now. He noticed that from time to time she unconsciously carried her finger to the end of her nose. He looked closer and said—

"Why, Mammy, the end of your nose is skinned. How did that come?"[18)]

She sent out the sort of whole hearted peal of laughter which God had vouchsafed in its perfection to none but the happy angels in heaven and the bruised and broken black slave on the earth, and said:

"Dad fetch dat duel, I be'n in it myself."[19)]

"Gracious! did a bullet to that?"

"Yassir, you bet it did!"

---

16) outen: out of

17) en yit here you is, a slinkin' outen a duel en disgracin' our whole line: and yet here you are, slinking out of a duel and disgracing our whole line=그런데 네가 여기 있다, 결투에서 살금살금 도망치며 우리 온 가문을 불명예스럽게 만드는

18) How did that come?: 왜 그렇게 되었어요?

19) Dad fetch dat duel, I be'n in it myself: 신이여 그 결투를 불러내보라, 내가 거기 있었다

"Well, I declare! Why, how did that happen?"

"Happened dis-away.[20] I 'uz a-sett'n' here kinder dozin' in de dark, en che-bang! goes a gun, right out dah I skips along out towards t'other end o' de house to see what's gwyne on, en stops by de ole winder[21] on de side towards Pudd'nhead Wilson's house dat ain't got no sash in it—but dey ain't none of 'em got any sashes, for as dat's concerned[22]—en I stood dah in de dark en look out, en dah in the moonlight, right down under me 'uz one o' de twins a-cussin'[23]—not much, but jist a-cussin' soft—it 'uz de brown one dat 'uz cussin,' 'ca'se he 'uz hit in de shoulder. En Doctor Claypool he 'uz a-workin' at him, en Pudd'nhead Wilson he 'uz a-he'pin', en ole Jedge Driscoll en Pem Howard 'uz a-standin' out yonder a little piece[24] waitin' for 'em to git ready agin. En treckly dey squared off en give de word,[25] en *bang-bang* went de pistols, en de twin he say, 'Ouch!'—hit him on de han' dis time—en I hear dat same bullet go '*spat*!' ag'in de logs under de winder; en de nex' time dey shoot, de twin say, 'Ouch!' ag'in, en I done it too, 'ca'se de bullet glance' on his cheekbone en skip up here en glance' on de side o' de winder en whiz right acrost my face en tuck de hide off'n my nose[26]—why, if I'd a' be'n jist a inch or a inch en a half furder, 't would a tuck de whole nose en disfiggered me.[27] Here's de bullet; I hunted her up."

---

20) dis-away: this way

21) winder: window

22) dey ain't none of 'em got any sashes, for as dat's concerned: there ain't none of them got any sashes, for as that's concerned=none of them got any sashes, if that's concerned

23) uz one o' de twins a-cussin: was one of the twins cursing

24) yonder a little piece: 좀 떨어져

25) En treckly dey squared off en give de word: 곧 싸울 자세를 취하고 (준비되었다고) 말했다

26) 'ca'se de bullet glance' on his cheekbone en skip up here en glance' on de side o' de winder en whiz right acrost my face en tuck de hide off'n my nose: because the bullet glanced on his cheekbone and skip up here and glanced on the side of the window and whiz right across my face and took the hide off my nose=왜냐하면 그 총알이 그의 광대뼈를 스치고 날아올라 창문 옆을 스친 후 내 얼굴 앞을 쌩하고 가로지르며 코끝을 벗겼다

27) if I'd a be'n jist a inch or a inch en a half furder, 't would a tuck de wholenose en disfiggered me: If I had been just an inch or an inch and a half further, it would have taken the whole

"Did you stand there all the time?"

"Dat's a question to ask, ain't it! What else would I do? Does I git a chance to see a duel every day?"

"Why, you were right in range! Weren't you afraid?"

The woman gave a sniff of scorn.

" 'Fraid! De Smith-Pocahontases ain't 'fraid o' nothin', let alone bullets."[28]

"They've got pluck enough, I suppose; what they lack is judgment. I wouldn't have stood there."

"Nobody's accusin' you!"

"Did anybody else get hurt?"

"Yes, we all got hit 'cep' de blon' twin en de doctor en de seconds.[29] De Jedge didn't git hurt, but I hear Pudd'nhead say de bullet snip some o' his ha'r[30] off."

"'George!"[31] said Tom to himself, "to come so near being out of my

---

nose and disfigured me=만약 내가 1인치나 1인치 반 정도 더 다가가 있었다면, 그 총알이 내 코를 완전히 날려 보내서 내 얼굴을 꼴사납게 만들었을 것이다

28) 'Fraid! De Smith-Pocahontases ain't 'fraid o' nothin', let alone bullets: Afraid! The Smith-Pocahontases isn't afraid of nothing, let alone bullets=두렵다고! Smith-Pocahontas 가문은 아무것도 두려워하지 않는다, 총알은 물론이고

29) we all got hit 'cep' de blon' twin en de doctor en de seconds: we all got hit except the blonde twin and the doctor and the seconds=금발의 쌍둥이와 의사와 보조인들 외에 우리 모두 다쳤다

30) ha'r: hair

31) George!: 이런!

trouble, and miss it by an inch. Oh dear, dear, he will live to find me out and sell me to some nigger trader yet—yes, and he would do it in a minute." Then he said aloud, in a grave tone:

"Mother, we are in an awful fix."

Roxana caught her breath with a spasm, and said

"Chile! What you hit a body so sudden for, like dat?[32] What's ben en gone en happen'?"

"Well, there's one thing I didn't tell you. When I wouldn't fight, he tore up the will again, and—"

Roxana's face turned a dead white, and she said:

"Now you's *done*!—done forever![33] Dat's de end. Bofe un us[34] is gwyne to starve to—"

"Wait and hear me through, can't you! I reckon that when he resolved to fight, himself, he thought he might get killed and not have a chance to forgive me any more in this life, so he made the will again, and I've seen it, and it's all right. But—"

"Oh, thank goodness, den we's safe ag'in! —safe! en so what did you want to come here en talk sich dreadful—"[35]

"Hold on, I tell you, and let me finish. The swag I gathered won't half square me up, and the first thing we know my creditors well, you know what'll happen."

Roxana dropped her chin and told her son to leave her alone she must think this matter out. Presently she said impressively:

"You got to go mighty keerful now, I tell you! En here's what you got to do. He didn't git killed, en if you gives him de least reason, he'll

32) What you hit a body so sudden for, like dat?: Why do you hit a body so sudden, like that?=왜 갑자기 그렇게 사람을 놀라게 하니?

33) you's done!: you are done!=넌 망했다!

34) Bofe un us: both of us

35) what did you want to come here en talk sich dreadful : why did you want to come here and talk such dreadful

bust de will ag'in, en dat's de *las'* time, now you hear me! So—you's got to show him what you kin do in de nex' few days. You got to be pison good,[36] en let him see it; you got to do everything dat'll make him b'lieve in you, en you got to sweeten aroun' ole Aunt Pratt, too—vshe's pow'ful strong with de Jedge, en de bes' frien' you got.[37] Nex', you'll go 'long away to Sent Louis,[38] en dat'll *keep* him in yo' favor. Den you go en make a bargain wid dem people. You tell 'em he ain't gwyne to live long—en dat's de fac', too—en tell 'em you'll pay 'em intrust,[39] en big intrust, too—ten per—what you call it?"

"Ten percent a month?"

"Dat's it. Den you take and sell yo' truck aroun', a little at a time, en pay de intrust. How long will it las'?"

"I think there's enough to pay the interest five or six months."

"Den you's all right. If he don't die in six months, dat don't make no diff'rence—Providence'll provide. You's gwyne to be safe—if you behaves." She bent an austere eye on him and added, "En you is gwyne to behave does you know dat?"

He laughed and said he was going to try, anyway. She did not unbend. She said gravely—

"Tryin' ain't de thing.[40] You's gwyne to do it. You ain't gwyne to steal a pin—'ca'se it ain't safe no mo'; en you ain't gwyne into no bad comp'ny—not even once, you understand; en you ain't gwyne to drink a drop—nary a single drop; en you ain't gwyne to gamble one single gamble—not one! Dis ain't what you's gwyne to *try* to do, it's what

36) pison good: very good

37) she's pow'ful strong with de Jedge, en de bes' frien' you got: she is powerful strong with the Judge, and the best friend you got=Aunt Pratt은 판사님에게 큰 영향을 끼치고, 너에겐 가장 훌륭한 한편이다

38) Sent Louis: Saint Louis

39) pay 'em intrust: pay them interest=이자를 치르다

40) Tryin' ain't de thing: Trying isn't the thing=노력하는 것만으로는 부족하다

you's gwyne to do. En I'll tell you how I knows it. Dis is how. I's gwyne to foller along to Sent Louis my own self;[41)]en you's gwyne to come to me every day o' your life, en I'll look you over; en if you fails in one single one o' dem things—jist *once*—I take my oath I'll come straight down to dis town en tell de Jedge you's a nigger en a slave—en prove it!" She paused, to let her words sink home.[42)] Then she added, "Chambers, does you b'lieve me when I says dat?"

Tom was sober enough now. There was no levity in his voice when he answered:

"Yes, Mother, I know, now, that I am reformed—and permanently. Permanently—and beyond the reach of any human temptation."

"Den g'long home en begin!"[43)]

---

41) I's gwyne to foller along to Sent Louis my own self: I am going to follow along to Saint Louis myself=내가 Saint Louis로 따라갈 것이다

42) She paused, to let her words sink home: 그녀의 말이 가슴을 찌르게 잠시 멈추었다

43) Den g'long home en begin!: Then go along home and begin!

CHAPTER 15

Nothing so needs reforming as other people's habits.

- Pudd'nhead Wilson's Calendar

Behold, the fool saith, "Put not all thine eggs in the one basket" — which is but a manner of saying, "Scatter your money and your attention"; but the wise man saith, "Put all your eggs in the one basket and—WATCH THAT BASKET!"

- Pudd'nhead Wilson's Calendar

What a time of it Dawson's Landing was having! All its life it had been asleep, but now it hardly got a chance for a nod, so swiftly did big events and crashing surprises come along in one another's wake: Friday morning, first glimpse of Real Nobility, also grand reception at Aunt Patsy Cooper's, also great robber-raid; Friday evening, dramatic kicking of the heir of the chief citizen in presence of four hundred people; Saturday morning, emergence as practicing lawyer of the long-submerged Pudd'nhead Wilson; Saturday night, duel between chief citizen and titled stranger.

The people took more pride in the duel than in all the other events put together, perhaps. It was a glory to their town to have such a thing happen there. In their eyes the principals had reached the summit of human honor. Everybody paid homage to their names; their praises were in all mouths. Even the duelists' subordinates came in for a handsome share of the public approbation: wherefore Pudd'nhead

Wilson was suddenly become a man of consequence.[1] When asked to run for the mayoralty Saturday night, he was risking defeat, but Sunday morning found him a made man[2] and his success assured.

The twins were prodigiously great now; the town took them to its bosom with enthusiasm. Day after day, and night after night, they went dining and visiting from house to house, making friends, enlarging and solidifying their popularity, and charming and surprising all with their musical prodigies, and now and then heightening the effects with samples of what they could do in other directions, out of their stock of rare and curious accomplishments. They were so pleased that they gave the regulation thirty days' notice, the required preparation for citizenship, and resolved to finish their days in this pleasant place. That was the climax. The delighted community rose as one man and applauded; and when the twins were asked to stand for seats in the forthcoming aldermanic board, and consented, the public contentment was rounded and complete.

Tom Driscoll was not happy over these things; they sunk deep, and hurt all the way down. He hated the one twin for kicking him, and the other one for being the kicker's brother.

Now and then the people wondered why nothing was heard of the raider, or of the stolen knife or the other plunder, but nobody was able to throw any light on that matter. Nearly a week had drifted by, and still the thing remained a vexed mystery.

On Saturday, Constable Blake and Pudd'nhead Wilson met on the street, and Tom Driscoll joined them in time to open their conversation for them. He said to Blake—

"You are not looking well, Blake; you seem to be annoyed about something. Has anything gone wrong in the detective business? I

---

1) a man of consequence: 중요한 사람

believe you fairly and justifiably claim to have a pretty good reputation in that line, isn't it so?"—which made Blake feel good, and look it; but Tom added, "for a country detective"—which made Blake feel the other way, and not only look it, but betray it in his voice—

"Yes, sir, I *have* got a reputation; and it's as good as anybody's in the profession, too, country or no country."

"Oh, I beg pardon; I didn't mean any offense. What I started out to ask was only about the old woman that raided the town—the stoop-shouldered old woman, you know, that you said you were going to catch; and I knew you would, too, because you have the reputation of never boasting, and—well, you—you've caught the old woman?"

"Damn the old woman!"

"Why, sho! you don't mean to say you haven't caught her?"

"No, I haven't caught her. If anybody could have caught her, I could; but nobody couldn't, I don't care who he is."

"I am sorry, real sorry—for your sake; because, when it gets around that a detective has expressed himself confidently, and then—"

"Don't you worry, that's all—don't you worry; and as for the town, the town needn't worry either. She's my meat—make yourself easy about that. I'm on her track; I've got clues that—"

"That's good! Now if you could get an old veteran detective down from St. Louis to help you find out what the clues mean, and where they lead to, and then—"

"I'm plenty veteran enough myself, and I don't need anybody's help. I'll have her inside of a we—inside of a month. That I'll swear to!"

Tom said carelessly:

"I suppose that will answer—yes, that will answer. But I reckon she is pretty old, and old people don't often outlive the cautious pace of the

---

2) a made man: 성공한 사람

professional detective when he has got his clues together and is out on his still-hunt."

Blake's dull face flushed under this gibe, but before he could set his retort in order Tom had turned to Wilson, and was saying, with placid indifference of manner and voice—

"Who got the reward, Pudd'nhead?"

Wilson winced slightly, and saw that his own turn was come.

"What reward?"

"Why, the reward for the thief, and the other one for the knife."

Wilson answered—and rather uncomfortably, to judge by his hesitating fashion of delivering himself—

"Well, the—well, in fact, nobody has claimed it yet."

Tom seemed surprised.

"Why, is that so?"

Wilson showed a trifle of irritation when he replied—

"Yes, it's so. And what of it?"[3)]

"Oh, nothing. Only I thought you had struck out a new idea, and invented a scheme that was going to revolutionize the timeworn and ineffectual methods of the—" He stopped, and turned to Blake, who was happy now that another had taken his place on the gridiron. "Blake, didn't you understand him to intimate that it wouldn't be necessary for you to hunt the old woman down?"

"B'George, he said he'd have thief and swag both inside of three days—he did, by hokey! and that's just about a week ago. Why, I said at the time that no thief and no thief's pal was going to try to pawn or sell a thing where he knowed the pawnbroker could get both rewards by taking *him* into camp *with* the swag. It was the blessedest idea that ever *I* struck!"

---

3) what of it?: 그래서 뭐?

"You'd change your mind," said Wilson, with irritated bluntness, "if you knew the entire scheme instead of only part of it."

"Well," said the constable, pensively, "I had the idea that it wouldn't work, and up to now I'm right anyway."

"Very well, then, let it stand at that, and give it a further show. It has worked at least as well as your own methods, you perceive."[4]

The constable hadn't anything handy to hit back with, so he discharged a discontented sniff, and said nothing.

After the night that Wilson had partly revealed his scheme at his house, Tom had tried for several days to guess out the secret of the rest of it, but had failed. Then it occurred to him to give Roxana's smarter head a chance at it. He made up a supposititious case,[5] and laid it before her. She thought it over, and delivered her verdict upon it. Tom said to himself, "She's hit it, sure!" He thought he would test that verdict now, and watch Wilson's face; so he said reflectively:

"Wilson, you're not a fool a fact of recent discovery. Whatever your scheme was, it had sense in it, Blake's opinion to the contrary notwithstanding. I don't ask you to reveal it, but I will suppose a case—a case which you will answer as a starting point for the real thing I am going to come at, and that's all I want. You offered five hundred dollars for the knife, and five hundred for the thief. We will suppose, for argument's sake, that the first reward is *advertised* and the second offered by *private letter* to pawnbrokers and—"

Blake slapped his thigh, and cried out—

"By Jackson, he's got you, Pudd'nhead! Now why couldn't I or any fool have thought of that?"

Wilson said to himself, "Anybody with a reasonably good head

---

4) It has worked at least as well as your own methods, you perceive: 당신도 알다시피, 이 방법도 적어도 당신 방법만큼의 성과를 올렸다 (두 방법 모두 실패했다는 말)

5) supposititious case: 가상의 상황

would have thought of it. I am not surprised that Blake didn't detect it; I am only surprised that Tom did. There is more to him than I supposed." He said nothing aloud, and Tom went on:

"Very well. The thief would not suspect that there was a trap, and he would bring or send the knife, and say he bought it for a song, or found it in the road, or something like that, and try to collect the reward, and be arrested—wouldn't he?"

"Yes," said Wilson.

"I think so," said Tom. "There can't be any doubt of it. Have you ever seen that knife?"

"No."

"Has any friend of yours?"

"Not that I know of."

"Well, I begin to think I understand why your scheme failed."

"What do you mean, Tom? What are you driving at?"[6] asked Wilson, with a dawning sense of discomfort.[7]

"Why, that there isn't any such knife."

"Look here, Wilson," said Blake, "Tom Driscoll's right, for a thousand dollars—if I had it."

Wilson's blood warmed a little,[8] and he wondered if he had been played upon by those strangers—it certainly had something of that look. But what could they gain by it? He threw out that suggestion. Tom replied:

"Gain? Oh, nothing that you would value, maybe. But they are strangers making their way in a new community. Is it nothing to them to appear as pets of an Oriental prince—at no expense? It is nothing to them to be able to dazzle this poor town with thousand-dollar

---

6) What are you driving at?: 무슨 말을 하는 것이지?
7) with a dawning sense of discomfort: 불안감을 느끼기 시작하며
8) Wilson's blood warmed a little: Wilson은 약간 화가 났다

rewards—at no expense? Wilson, there isn't any such knife, or your scheme would have fetched it to light.[9] Or if there is any such knife, they've got it yet. I believe, myself, that they've seen such a knife, for Angelo pictured it out with his pencil too swiftly and handily for him to have been inventing it, and of course I can't swear that they've never had it; but this I'll go bail for[10]—if they had it when they came to this town, they've got it yet."[11]

Blake said—

"It looks mighty reasonable, the way Tom puts it; it most certainly does."

Tom responded, turning to leave—

"You find the old woman, Blake, and if she can't furnish the knife, go and search the twins!"

Tom sauntered away. Wilson felt a good deal depressed. He hardly knew what to think. He was loath to withdraw his faith from the twins, and was resolved not to do it on the present indecisive evidence; but—well, he would think, and then decide how to act.

"Blake, what do you think of this matter?"

"Well, Pudd'nhead, I'm bound to say I put it up the way Tom does. They hadn't the knife; or if they had it, they've got it yet."

The men parted. Wilson said to himself:

"I believe they had it; if it had been stolen, the scheme would have restored it, that is certain. And so I believe they've got it."

Tom had no purpose in his mind when he encountered those two men. When he began his talk he hoped to be able to gall them a little and get a trifle of malicious entertainment out of it. But when he left,

---

9) your scheme would have fetched it to light: 당신의 계획이 그것(the knife)을 드러냈을 것이다

10) but this I'll go bail for: 이건 내가 보증 하겠다

11) they've got it yet: 그들이 아직 가지고 있다

he left in great spirits, for he perceived that just by pure luck and no troublesome labor he had accomplished several delightful things: he had touched both men on a raw spot[12] and seen them squirm; he had modified Wilson's sweetness for the twins with one small bitter taste that he wouldn't be able to get out of his mouth right away; and, best of all, he had taken the hated twins down a peg with the community;[13] for Blake would gossip around freely, after the manner of detectives, and within a week the town would be laughing at them in its sleeve[14] for offering a gaudy reward for a bauble which they either never possessed or hadn't lost. Tom was very well satisfied with himself.

Tom's behavior at home had been perfect during the entire week. His uncle and aunt had seen nothing like it before. They could find no fault with him anywhere.

On Saturday evening he said to the Judge—

"I've had something preying on my mind,[15] uncle, and as I am going away, and might never see you again, I can't bear it any longer. I made you believe I was afraid to fight that Italian adventurer. I had to get out of it on some pretext or other,[16] and maybe I chose badly, being taken unawares, but no honorable person could consent to meet him in the field, knowing what I knew about him."

"Indeed? What was that?"

"Count Luigi is a confessed assassin."

"Incredible!"

"It's perfectly true. Wilson detected it in his hand, by palmistry, and charged him with it, and cornered him up so close that he had to

---

12) touched both men on a raw spot: 둘의 아픈 데를 건드리다

13) taken the hated twins down a peg with the community: 증오스러운 쌍둥이를 마을에서 골탕 먹게 만들다

14) laughing at them in its sleeve: 뒤에서 그들을 비웃다

15) I've had something preying on my mind: 내 마음을 괴롭히는 것이 있었다

16) I had to get out of it on some pretext or other: 이런 저런 핑계로 그것(결투)을 피해야 했다

confess; but both twins begged us on their knees to keep the secret, and swore they would lead straight lives here; and it was all so pitiful that we gave our word of honor never to expose them while they kept the promise. You would have done it yourself, uncle."

"You are right, my boy; I would. A man's secret is still his own property, and sacred, when it has been surprised out of him like that. You did well, and I am proud of you." Then he added mournfully, "But I wish I could have been saved the shame of meeting an assassin on the field of honor."

"It couldn't be helped, uncle. If I had known you were going to challenge him, I should have felt obliged to sacrifice my pledged word in order to stop it, but Wilson couldn't be expected to do otherwise than keep silent."

"Oh, no, Wilson did right, and is in no way to blame. Tom, Tom, you have lifted a heavy load from my heart; I was stung to the very soul when I seemed to have discovered that I had a coward in my family."

"You may imagine what it cost *me* to assume such a part, uncle."

"Oh, I know it, poor boy, I know it. And I can understand how much it has cost you to remain under that unjust stigma to this time. But it is all right now, and no harm is done. You have restored my comfort of mind, and with it your own; and both of us had suffered enough."

The old man sat awhile plunged in thought; then he looked up with a satisfied light in his eye, and said: "That this assassin should have put the affront upon me[17] of letting me meet him on the field of honor as if he were a gentleman is a matter which I will presently settle—but not now. I will not shoot him until after election. I see a way to ruin

17) should have put the affront upon me: 나를 모욕하다

them both before; I will attend to that first. Neither of them shall be elected, that I promise. You are sure that the fact that he is an assassin has not got abroad?"[18]

"Perfectly certain of it, sir."

"It will be a good card. I will fling a hint at it from the stump on the polling day.[19] It will sweep the ground from under[20] both of them."

"There's not a doubt of it. It will finish them."

"That and outside work among the voters will, to a certainty. I want you to come down here by and by and work privately among the rag-tag and bobtail.[21] You shall spend money among them; I will furnish it."

Another point scored against the detested twins! Really it was a great day for Tom. He was encouraged to chance a parting shot, now, at the same target, and did it—

"You know that wonderful Indian knife that the twins have been making such a to-do about?[22] Well, there's no track or trace of it yet; so the town is beginning to sneer and gossip and laugh. Half the people believe they never had any such knife, the other half believe they had it and have got it still. I've heard twenty people talking like that today."

Yes, Tom's blemishless week had restored him to the favor of his aunt and uncle.

His mother was satisfied with him, too. Privately, she believed she was coming to love him, but she did not say so. She told him to go along to St. Louis now, and she would get ready and follow. Then she smashed her whisky bottle and said—

---

18) has not got abroad: 소문이 널리 퍼지지 않았다
19) from the stump on the polling day: 선거 날 연단에서
20) sweep the ground from under: 완패 시키다
21) the rag-tag and bobtail: 서민, 사회의 하층계급

"Dah now! I's a-gwyne to make you walk as straight as a string,[23] Chambers, en so I's boun,[24] you ain't gwyne to git no bad example out o' yo' mammy. I tole you you couldn't go into no bad comp'ny. Well, you's gwyne into my comp'ny, en I's gwyne to fill de bill.[25] Now, den, trot along, trot along!"

Tom went aboard one of the big transient boats that night with his heavy satchel of miscellaneous plunder, and slept the sleep of the unjust, which is serener and sounder than the other kind,[26] as we know by the hanging-eve history[27] of a million rascals. But when he got up in the morning, luck was against him again: a brother-thief had robbed him while he slept, and gone ashore at some intermediate landing.

---

22) making such a to-do about: 소동을 피우던
23) walk as straight as a string: 줄 하나 만큼 똑바로 걷다
24) I's boun: I am bound=~할 작정이다
25) fill de bill: 요구를 만족시키다
26) the other kind: 올바른 사람=the just
27) the hanging-eve history: 잡히기 전날 밤 이야기

CHAPTER 16

If you pick up a starving dog and make him prosperous, he will not bite you. This is the principal difference between a dog and a man.

- Pudd'nhead Wilson's Calendar

We all know about the habits of the ant, we know all about the habits of the bee, but we know nothing at all about the habits of the oyster. It seems almost certain that we have been choosing the wrong time for studying the oyster.

-Pudd'nhead Wilson's Calendar

When Roxana arrived, she found her son in such despair and misery that her heart was touched and her motherhood rose up strong in her. He was ruined past hope now; his destruction would be immediate and sure, and he would be an outcast and friendless—That was reason enough for a mother to love a child; so she loved him, and told him so. It made him wince, secretly—for she was a "nigger." That he was one himself was far from reconciling him to that despised race.

Roxana poured out endearments upon him, to which he responded uncomfortably, but as well as he could. And she tried to comfort him, but that was not possible. These intimacies quickly became horrible to him, and within the hour he began to try to get up courage enough to tell her so, and require that they be discontinued or very considerably modified. But he was afraid of her; and besides, there came a lull now, for she had begun to think. She was trying to invent a saving plan.

Finally she started up, and said she had found a way out. Tom was almost suffocated by the joy of this sudden good news. Roxana said—

"Here is de plan, en she'll win,[1] sure. I's a nigger, en nobody ain't gwyne to doubt it dat hears me talk. I's wuth six hund'd dollahs.[2] Take en sell me, en pay off dese gamblers."

Tom was dazed. He was not sure he had heard aright. He was dumb for a moment; then he said:

"Do you mean that you would be sold into slavery to save me?"

"Ain't you my chile? En does you know anything dat a mother won't do for her chile? Dey ain't nothin' a white mother won't do for her chile.[3] Who made 'em so? De Lord done it. En who made de niggers? De Lord made 'em. In de inside, mothers is all de same.[4] De good lord He made 'em so. I's gwyne to be sole into slavery, en in a year you's gwyne to buy yo' ole mammy free ag'in. I'll show you how. Dat's de plan."

Tom's hopes began to rise, and his spirits along with them. He said—

"It's lovely of you, Mammy—it's just—"

"Say it ag'in! En keep on sayin' it! It's all de pay a body kin want in dis worl',[5] en it's mo' den enough. Laws bless you, honey, when I's slavin' aroun', en dey 'buses me,[6] if I knows you's a-sayin' dat, 'way off yonder somers, it'll heal up all de sore places, en I kin stan' 'em."[7]

---

1) en she'll win: and she will win=그리고 그 계획은 성공할 것이다

2) I's wuth six hund'd dollahs: I am worth six hundred dollars

3) Dey ain't nothin' a white mother won't do for her chile: There is nothing a white mother won't do for her child=백인 엄마가 자기 아이를 위해 못할 것이 없다

4) In de inside, mothers is all de same: In the inside, mothers are all the same=엄마들의 본성은 다 똑같다

5) It's all de pay a body kin want in dis worl': It's all the pay a body can want in this world=그것(그렇게 말하는 것을 듣는 것)이 사람이 세상에서 바랄 수 있는 최상의 보상이다

6) when I's slav' aroun', en dey 'buses me: when I am slaving around, and they abuses me=내가 노예로 일하고 있고 그들이 나를 학대할 때

7) if I knows you's a-sayin' dat, 'way off yonder somers, it'll heal up all de sore places, en I kin stan' 'em: if I know you are saying that, away off yonder somewhere, it'll heal up all the sore

"I *do* say it again, Mammy, and I'll keep on saying it, too. But how am I going to sell you? You're free, you know."

"Much diff'rence dat make! White folks ain't partic'lar.[8] De law kin sell me now if dey tell me to leave de state in six months en I don't go.[9] You draw up a paper—bill o' sale—en put it 'way off yonder, down in de middle o' Kaintuck somers, en sign some names to it, en say you'll sell me cheap 'ca'se you's hard up;[10] you'll fine you ain't gwyne to have no trouble.[11] You take me up de country a piece, en sell me on a farm—dem people ain't gwyne to ask no questions if I's a bargain."[12]

Tom forged a bill of sale and sold him mother to an Arkansas cotton planter[13] for a trifle over six hundred dollars. He did not want to commit this treachery, but luck threw the man in his way, and this saved him the necessity of going up-country to hunt up a purchaser, with the added risk of having to answer a lot of questions, whereas this planter was so pleased with Roxy that he asked next to none at all. Besides, the planter insisted that Roxy wouldn't know where she was, at first, and that by the time she found out she would already have become contented. And Tom argued with himself that it was an

---

places, and I can stand them=만약 네가 어딘가 먼 곳에서 그렇게 말하는 것을 내가 안다면, 그것이 모든 아픈 곳들을 낫게 하고 내가 그것들을 참을 수 있을 것이다

8) White folks ain't partic'lar: White folks aren't particular=백인들은 관심갖지 않는다

9) De law kin sell me now if dey tell me to leave de state in six months en I don't go: The law can sell me now if they tell me to leave the state in six months and I don't go=그들이 나에게 이 주(Missouri)를 6개월 내에 떠나라고 하고 내가 떠나지 않는다면 법적으로 당장 나를 팔 수 가 있다. (Missouri주는 노예제도에 찬성하고 있었기 때문에 노예제가 없는 북부에서 온 흑인이라도 Missouri주에 6개월 이상 머물러 있으면 노예로 팔 수 가 있었다)

10) 'ca'se you's hard up: because you are hard up=네가 돈에 쪼들리기 때문에

11) you'll fine you ain't gwyne to have no trouble: you'll find you are not going to have any trouble=아무 문제도 없을 것이다

12) if I's a bargain: 날 싸게 판다면

13) an Arkansas cotton planter: Arkansas주의 목화농장주인 (Roxy의 뜻에 반해 down the river에 그녀를 팔아넘긴 것을 의미함)

immense advantage for Roxy to have a master who was so pleased with her, as this planter manifestly was. In almost no time his flowing reasonings[14] carried him to the point of even half believing he was doing Roxy a splendid surreptitious service in selling her "down the river." And then he kept diligently saying to himself all the time, "It's for only a year—In a year I buy her free again; she'll keep that in mind, and it'll reconcile her." Yes, the little deception could do no harm, and everything would come out right and pleasant in the end, anyway. By agreement, the conversation in Roxy's presence was all about the man's "up-country" farm,[15] and how pleasant a place it was, and how happy the slaves were there; so poor Roxy was entirely deceived; and easily, for she was not dreaming that her own son could be guilty of treason to a mother who, in voluntarily going into slavery—slavery of any kind, mild or severe, or of any duration, brief or long—was making a sacrifice for him compared with which[16] death would have been a poor and commonplace one. She lavished tears and loving caresses upon him, privately, and then went away with her owner; went away brokenhearted, and yet proud of what she was doing and glad that it was in her power to do it.

Tom squared his accounts,[17] and resolved to keep to the very letter of his reform, and never to put that will in jeopardy again. He had three hundred dollars left. According to his mother's plan, he was to put that safely away, and add her half of his pension to it monthly. In one year this fund would buy her free again.

For a whole week he was not able to sleep well, so much the villainy which he had played upon his trusting mother preyed upon his rag of

14) his flowing reasonings: 거침없는 논리들
15) "up-country" farm: (강) 위쪽 마을 농장
16) compared with which: 그것(Tom을 위해 자신을 다시 노예로 팔게 한 희생)과 비교해서
17) Tom squared his accounts: Tom은 빚을 갚았다

conscience; but after that he began to get comfortable again, and was presently able to sleep like any other miscreant.

The boat bore Roxy away from St. Louis at four in the afternoon, and she stood on the lower guard abaft the paddle-box and watched Tom through a blur of tears until he melted into the throng of people and disappeared; then she looked no more, but sat there on a coil of cable crying, till far into the night. When she went to her foul steerage bunk at last, between the clashing engines, it was not to sleep, but only to wait for the morning, and, waiting, grieve.

It had been imagined that she "would not know," and would think she was traveling upstream. She! why, she had been steamboating for years. At dawn she got up and went listlessly and sat down on the cable-coil again. She passed many a snag whose "break" could have told her a thing to break her heart,[18] for it showed a current moving in the same direction that the boat was going; but her thoughts were elsewhere, and she did not notice. But at last the roar of a bigger and nearer break than usual brought her out of her torpor, and she looked up, and her practiced eye fell upon that tell-tale rush of water.[19] For one moment her petrified gaze fixed itself there. Then her head dropped upon her breast, and she said—

"Oh, de good Lord God have mercy on po' sinful me—*I's sole down de river*!"[20]

---

18) She passed many a snag whose "break" could have told her a thing to break her heart: 그녀는 부딪쳐 깨지는 물결이 그녀의 가슴을 깰 이야기를 말해주었을 많은 나뭇가지를 지나갔다

19) that tell-tale rush of water: 물의 암시하는 거친 흐름

20) *I's sole down de river!:* I was sold down the river!

CHAPTER 17

Even popularity can be overdone. In Rome, along at first, you are full of regrets that Michelangelo died; but by and by, you only regret that you didn't see him do it.

- Pudd'nhead Wilson's CalendarJuly 4.

Statistics show that we lose more fools on this day than in all the other days of the year put together. This proves, by the number left in stock,[1] *that one Fourth of July per year is now inadequate, the country has grown so.*

- Pudd'nhead Wilson's Calendar

The summer weeks dragged by, and then the political campaign opened—opened in pretty warm fashion, and waxed hotter and hotter daily. The twins threw themselves into it with their whole heart, for their self-love was engaged. Their popularity, so general at first, had suffered afterward; mainly because they had been *too* popular, and so a natural reaction had followed. Besides, it had been diligently whispered around that it was curious—indeed, *very* curious that that wonderful knife of theirs did not turn up—*if* it was so valuable, or *if* it had ever existed. And with the whisperings went chucklings and nudgings and winks, and such things have an effect. The twins considered that success in the election would reinstate them, and that defeat would work them irreparable damage. Therefore they worked

1) by the number left in stock: (바보들이) 남아있는 숫자로 본다면

hard, but not harder than Judge Driscoll and Tom worked against them in the closing days of the canvass.[2] Tom's conduct had remained so letter-perfect during two whole months now, that his uncle not only trusted him with money with which to persuade voters, but trusted him to go and get himself out of the safe in the private sitting-room.

The closing speech of the campaign was made by Judge Driscoll, and he made it against both of the foreigners. It was disastrously effective. He poured out rivers of ridicule upon them, and forced the big mass meeting to laugh and applaud. He scoffed at them as adventures, mountebanks, sideshow riff-raff, dime-museum freaks;[3] he assailed their showy titles with measureless derision; he said they were back-alley barbers disguised as nobilities, peanut peddlers masquerading as gentlemen, organ-grinders bereft of their brother-monkey.[4] At last he stopped and stood still. He waited until the place had become absolutely silent and expectant, then he delivered his deadliest shot; delivered it with ice-cold seriousness and deliberation, with a significant emphasis upon the closing words: he said he believed that the reward offered for the lost knife was humbug and buncombe,[5] and that its owner would know where to find it whenever he should have occasion to *assassinate somebody*.

Then he stepped from the stand, leaving a startled and impressive hush behind him instead of the customary explosion of cheers and party cries.

The strange remark flew far and wide over the town and made an extraordinary sensation. Everybody was asking, "What could he mean

---

2) in the closing days of the canvass: 선거유세의 막바지에

3) adventures, mountebanks, sideshow riffraff, dime museum freaks: 투기꾼, 사기꾼, 서커스의 구경거리, 하찮은 쓰레기, 기형 싸구려 구경거리 (샴쌍둥이였던 첫 원고의 흔적)

4) organ-grinders bereft of their brother monkey: 형제 원숭이가 없는 손풍금 연주자 (길거리에서 구걸하는 손풍금 연주자들은 주로 원숭이를 구경거리로 데리고 다녔음)

5) humbug and buncombe: 새빨간 거짓말이고 허풍

by that?" And everybody went on asking that question, but in vain; for the judge only said he knew what he was talking about, and stopped there; Tom said he hadn't any idea what his uncle meant, and Wilson, whenever he was asked what he thought it meant, parried the question by asking the questioner what he thought it meant.

Wilson was elected, the twins were defeated—crushed, in fact, and left forlorn and substantially friendless. Tom went back to St. Louis happy.

Dawson's Landing had a week of repose now, and it needed it. But it was in an expectant state, for the air was full of rumors of a new duel. Judge Driscoll's election labors had prostrated him, but it was said that as soon as he was well enough to entertain a challenge he would get one from Count Luigi.

The brothers withdrew entirely from society, and nursed their humiliation in privacy. They avoided the people, and went out for exercise only late at night, when the streets were deserted.

CHAPTER 18

Gratitude and treachery are merely the two extremities of the same procession. You have seen all of it that is worth staying for when the band and the gaudy officials have gone by.

- Pudd'nhead Wilson's Calendar

THANKSGIVING DAY. Let us all give humble, hearty, and sincere thanks now, but the turkeys. In the island of Fiji they do not use turkeys; they use plumbers. It does not become you and me to sneer at Fiji.[1)]

- Pudd'nhead Wilson's Calendar

The Friday after the election was a rainy one in St. Louis. It rained all day long, and rained hard, apparently trying its best to wash that soot-blackened town white, but of course not succeeding. Toward midnight Tom Driscoll arrived at his lodgings from the theater in the heavy downpour, and closed his umbrella and let himself in; but when he would have shut the door, he found that there was another person entering—doubtless another lodger; this person closed the door and tramped upstairs behind Tom. Tom found his door in the dark, and entered it, and turned up the gas.[2)] When he faced about,[3)] lightly whistling, he saw the back of a man. The man was closing and locking his door for him. His whistle

---

1) It does not become you and me to sneer at Fiji: 여러분이나 나는 피지 사람들을 비웃지 않는다
2) turned up the gas: 가스등을 켰다
3) faced about: 뒤 돌았다

faded out and he felt uneasy. The man turned around, a wreck of shabby old clothes, sodden with rain and all a-drip, and showed a black face under an old slouch hat. Tom was frightened. He tried to order the man out, but the words refused to come, and the other man got the start.[4)] He said, in a low voice—

"Keep still—I's yo' mother!"

Tom sunk in a heap on a chair, and gasped out—

"It was mean of me, and base[5)]—I know it; but I meant it for the best, I did indeed—I can swear it."

Roxana stood awhile looking mutely down on him while he writhed in shame and went on incoherently babbling self-accusations mixed with pitiful attempts at explanation and palliation of his crime; then she seated herself and took off her hat, and her unkempt masses of long brown hair tumbled down about her shoulders.

"It ain't no fault o' yo'n dat dat ain't gray,"[6)] she said sadly, noticing the hair.

"I know it, I know it! I'm a scoundrel. But I swear I meant it for the best. It was a mistake, of course, but I thought it was for the best, I truly did."

Roxana began to cry softly, and presently words began to find their way out between her sobs. They were uttered lamentingly, rather than angrily—

"Sell a pusson down de river[7)]—*down de river*!—for de bes'! I wouldn't treat a dog so! I is all broke down and en wore out[8)] now, en

4) the other man got the start: 상대편 남자가 먼저 말했다

5) It was mean of me, and base: 내가 비겁하고 비열했다

6) It ain't no fault o' yo'n dat dat ain't gray: It is no fault of yours that that isn't gray=이게(자신의 머리카락) 희끗해지지 않은 건 네 잘못때문이 아니다 (네 탓이었으면 희끗해 졌을 것이라고 비꼬는 말)

7) Sell a pusson down de river: Sell a person down the river=사람을 강 밑 마을로 팔다니

8) wore out: worn out=기진맥진한

so I reckon it ain't in me to storm aroun' no mo', like I used to when I 'uz trompled on en 'bused.[9] I don't know—but maybe it's so. Leastways, I's suffered so much dat mournin' seem to come mo' handy to me now den stormin'."[10]

These words should have touched Tom Driscoll, but if they did, that effect was obliterated by a stronger one—one which removed the heavy weight of fear which lay upon him, and gave his crushed spirit a most grateful rebound, and filled all his small soul with a deep sense of relief. But he kept prudently still, and ventured no comment. There was a voiceless interval of some duration now, in which no sounds were heard but the beating of the rain upon the panes, the sighing and complaining of the winds, and now and then a muffled sob from Roxana. The sobs became more and more infrequent, and at least ceased. Then the refugee began to talk again.

"Shet down dat light a little.[11] More. More yit. A pusson dat is hunted don't like de light.[12] Dah—dat'll do. I kin see whah you is, en dat's enough. I's gwyne to tell you de tale, en cut it jes as short as I kin, en den I'll tell you what you's got to do. Dat man dat bought me ain't a bad man; he's good enough, as planters goes;[13] en if he could a had his way I'd a be'n a house servant in his fambly en be'n comfortable: but his wife she was a Yank, en not right down good lookin', en she riz up

---

9) it ain't in me to storm aroun' no mo', like I used to when I 'uz trompledon en 'bused: it isn't in me to storm around any more, like I used to when I was trampled on and abused=전에 짓밟히고 학대당할 때 그랬던 것처럼 날 뛸 힘도 더 이상 내게 없다

10) Leastways, I's suffered so much dat mournin' seem to come mo' handy to me now den stormin': Leastwise, I was suffered so much that mourning seems to come more handy to me now than storming=어쨌든 너무 고통을 받아 미친 듯 날뛰는 것보다 한탄하는 것이 더 도움이 되는 것 같다

11) Shet down dat light a little: Shut down that light a little=(가스등)불빛을 좀 줄여라

12) A pusson dat is hunted don't like de light: A person that is hunted doesn't like the light 쫓기는 사람은 불빛을 좋아하지 않는다

13) as planters goes: 농장주인들 중에서는

agin me straight off;[14] so den dey sent me out to de quarter 'mongst de common fiel' han's.[15] Dat woman warn't satisfied even wid dat, but she worked up de overseer agin' me,[16] she 'uz dat jealous en hateful; so de overseer he had me out befo' day in de mawnin's en worked me de whole long day as long as dey' uz any light to see by;[17] en many's de lashin' I got 'ca'se I couldn't come up to de work o' de stronges'.[18] Dat overseer 'uz a Yank too, outen New Englan',[19] en anybody down South kin tell you what dat mean. Dey knows how to work a nigger to death, en dey knows how to whale 'em[20] too—whale 'em till dey backs is welted like a washboard.[21] 'Long at fust[22] my marster say de good word for me to de overseer, but dat 'uz bad for me; for de mistis she fine it out, en arter dat I jist ketched it at every turn[23]—dey warn't no mercy for me no mo'."

Tom's heart was fired—with fury against the planter's wife; and he

---

14) she was a Yank, en not right down good lookin', en she riz up agin me straight off: she was a Yankee, and not right down good looking, and she rose up against me straight off=그녀는 북부 출신이었고, 완전히 못생겼다, 그리고 그녀는 나를 싫어해 당장 들고 일어났다

15) so den dey sent me out to de quarter 'mongst de common fiel' han's: so then they sent me out to the quarter amongst the common field hands=그래서 그들은 밭에서 일하는 노예들이 머무는 숙소를 나를 내 보냈다

16) she worked up de overseer ag'in' me: 그녀는 농장 관리인을 부추겨 나에게 적대적으로 만들었다.

17) so de overseer he had me out befo' day in de mawnin's en worked me de whole long day as long as dey' uz any light to see by: so the overseer had me out before day in the mornings and worked me the whole long day as long as there was any light to see by

18) many's de lashin' I got 'ca'se I couldn't come up to de work o' de stronges': many is the lashings I got because I couldn't come up to the work of the strongest=가장 힘 센 사람들만큼 일할 수가 없었기에 많은 채찍질을 당했다

19) outen New Englan': out of New England (New England는 노예폐지운동의 중심지였음)

20) to whale 'em: to whale them=그들(흑인 노예들)을 채찍질하다

21) whale 'em till dey backs is welted like a washboard: 그들의 등이 빨래판처럼 울퉁불퉁 부풀어 오를 때 까지 채찍질하다

22) 'Long at fust: Along at first=처음엔

23) for de mistis she fine it out, en arter dat I jist ketched it at every turn: for the mistress she found it out, and after that I just caught it at every turn=왜냐하면 안주인이 그것을 알아냈고, 그 이후엔 기회가 있을 때마다 채찍질을 당했다

said to himself, "But for that meddlesome fool, everything would have gone all right." He added a deep and bitter curse against her.

The expression of this sentiment was fiercely written in his face, and stood thus revealed to Roxana by a white glare of lightning which turned the somber dusk of the room into dazzling day at that moment. She was pleased—pleased and grateful; for did not that expression show that her child was capable of grieving for his mother's wrongs and of feeling resentment toward her persecutors?—a thing which she had been doubting. But her flash of happiness was only a flash, and went out again and left her spirit dark; for she said to herself, "He sole me down de river—he can't feel for a body long; dis'll pass en go."[24] Then she took up her tale again.

"'Bout ten days ago I 'uz sayin' to myself dat I couldn't las' many mo' weeks I 'uz so wore out wid de awful work en de lashin', en so downhearted en misable.[25] En I didn't care no mo', nuthe—life warn't wuth noth'n' to me,[26] if I got to go on like dat. Well, when a body is in a frame o' mine like dat, what do a body care what a body do? Dey was a little sickly nigger wench 'bout ten year ole dat 'uz good to me, en hadn't no mammy, po' thing, en I loved her en she loved me; en she come out whah I 'uz workin', en she had a roasted tater,[27] en tried to slip it to me robbin' herself,[28] you see, 'ca'se she knowed de overseer didn't give me enough to eat—en he ketched her at it,[29] en giver her a

24) he can't feel for a body long; dis'll pass en go: 그는 사람에게 감동을 오랫동안 느끼지 못해; 이것도 지나가 버릴거야

25) so downhearted en misable: so downhearted and miserable

26) En I didn't care no mo', nuther life warn't wuth noth'n' to me: And I didn't care any more, neither life wasn't worth anything to me=그리고 난 더 이상 관심이 없었다 삶이 나에게 가치가 없었다

27) whah I 'uz workin', en she had a roasted tater: where I was working and she had a roasted tater (potato)

28) robbin' herself: 자신 것을 줄여서

29) he ketched her at it: he caught her at it=그(농장 관리인)는 그녀(10살짜리 소녀)가 그렇

lick acrost de back wid his stick, which 'uz as thick as a broom handle, en she drop' screamin' on de groun', en squirmin' en wallerin' aroun' in de dust like a spider dat's got crippled. I couldn't stan' it.[30] All de hellfire dat 'uz ever in my heart flame' up,[31] en I snatch de stick outen his han' en laid him flat.[32] He laid dah moanin' en cussin', en all out of his head,[33] you know, en de niggers 'uz plumb sk'yred to death.[34] Dey gathered roun' him to he'p him, en I jumped on his hoss35) en took out for de river as tight as I could go. I knowed what dey would do wid me. Soon as he got well he would start in en work me to death if marster let him; en if dey didn't do dat, they'd sell me furder down de river,[36] en dat's de same thing, so I 'lowed to drown myself en git out o' my troubles.[37] It 'uz gitt'n' towards dark. I 'uz at de river in two minutes. Den I see a canoe, en I says dey ain't no use to drown myself tell I got to;[38] so I ties de hoss in de edge o' de timber en shove out[39] down de river, keepin' in under de shelter o' de bluff bank en prayin' for de dark to shet down quick.[40] I had a pow'ful good start,[41] 'ca'se de

---

게 하는 것(Roxy에게 roasted potato를 주는 것)을 잡았다

30) I couldn't stan' it: I couldn't stand it=나는 참을 수가 없었다

31) All de hellfire dat 'uz ever in my heart flame' up: All the hellfire that was ever in my heart flamed up=내 가슴에 있었던 모든 분노가 타 올랐다

32) laid him flat: 그를 때려 눕혔다

33) all out of his head: 완전히 정신이 나가서

34) de niggers 'uz plumb sk'yred to death: the niggers were all scared to death=그리고 흑인들은 완전히 두려워 죽으려고 했다

35) hoss: horse

36) they'd sell me furder down de river: they'd sell me further down the river=그들은 나를 강의 더 아랫 마을로 팔아버릴 것이다

37) so I 'lowed to drown myself en git out o' my troubles: so I allowed to drown myself and get out of my troubles=그래서 나는 강에 빠져 나의 고난으로부터 벗어나려고 했다

38) tell I got to: till I got to=내가 그렇게 해야만 할 때까지

39) shove out: 배를 저어 떠나다

40) keepin' in under de shelter o' de bluff bank en prayin' for de dark to shet down quick: keeping it under the shelter of the bluff bank and praying for the dark to shut down quick=그것(배)를 깎아지른 듯한 제방 아래 숨겨놓고 어둠이 빨리 내려 깔리기를 기도하고 있었다

41) a pow'ful good start: 먼저 출발했다

big house 'uz three mile back f'um de river en on'y de work mules to ride dah on,[42] en on'y niggers ride 'em, en *dey* warn't gwyne to hurry[43]—dey'd gimme all de chance dey could. Befo' a body could go to de house en back it would be long pas' dark, en dey couldn't track de hoss en fine out which way I went tell mawnin', en de niggers would tell 'em all de lies dey could 'bout it.

"Well, de dark come, en I went on a-spinnin' down de river. I paddled mo'n two hours,[44] den I warn't worried no mo'; so I quit paddlin' en floated down de current, considerin' what I 'uz gwyne to do if I didn't have to drown myself. I made up some plans, en floated along, turnin' 'em over in my mine.[45] Well, when it 'uz a little pas' midnight, as I reckoned, en I had come fifteen or twenty mile, I see de lights o' a steamboat layin' at de bank, whah dey warn't no town en no woodyard, en putty soon I ketched de shape o' de chimbly-tops agin de stars,[46] en den good gracious me,[47] I 'most jumped out o' my skin for joy![48] It 'uz de Gran' Mogul—I 'uz chambermaid on her for eight seasons in de Cincinnati en Orleans trade. I slid 'long pas'—don't see nobody stirrin' nowhah—hear 'em a-hammerin' away in de engine room,[49] den I knowed what de matter was some

---

42) on'y de work mules to ride dah on: only the work mules to ride there on=거기까진 일하는 노새만을 타고 갈 수 있었다

43) dey warn't gwyne to hurry: They weren't going to hurry=그들(흑인들)은 서두르지 않았을 것이다

44) I paddled mo'n two hours: I paddled more than two hours=나는 두시간이상 노를 저었다

45) turnin' 'em over in my mine: turning them over in my mind=마음속으로 그것(계획)들을 곰곰이 생각하며

46) putty soon I ketched de shape o' de chimbly-tops agin de stars: pretty soon I caught the shape of the chimney tops against the stars

47) good gracious me: 어라!

48) I 'most jumped out o' my skin for joy!: I almost jumped out of my skin for joy!=기뻐서 펄쩍 뛸 뻔 했다

49) hear 'em a-hammerin' away in de engine room: hear them hammering away in the engine room=기관실에서 그들이 망치질하는 소리를 들었다

o' de machinery's broke. I got asho' below de boat and turn' de canoe loose, den I goes 'long up, en dey 'uz jes one plank out,[50] en I step 'board de boat. It 'uz pow'ful hot, deckhan's en roustabouts 'uz sprawled aroun' asleep on de fo'cas'l,[51] de second mate, Jim Bangs, he sot dah on de bitts wid his head down, asleep[52]—'ca'se dat's de way de second mate stan' de cap'n's watch!—en de ole watchman, Billy Hatch, he 'uz a-noddin' on de companionway;—en I knowed 'em all; en, lan', but dey did look good! I says to myself, I wished old marster'd come along *now* en try to take me—bless yo' heart, I's 'mong frien's,[53] I is. So I tromped right along 'mongst 'em, en went up on de b'iler deck[54] en 'way back aft to de ladies' cabin guard, en sot down dah in de same cheer dat I'd sot in mos' a hund'd million times, I reckon; en it 'uz jist home ag'in,[55] I tell you!

"In 'bout an hour I heard de ready-bell jingle, en den de racket begin. Putty soon I hear de gong strike. 'Set her back on de outside,' I says to myself 'I reckon I knows dat music!' I hear de gong ag'in. 'Come ahead on de inside,' I says. Gong ag'in. 'Stop de outside.' gong ag'in. 'Come ahead on de outside—now we's pinted for Sent Louis,[56] en I's outer de woods en ain't got to drown myself at all.' I knowed de Mogul 'uz in de Sent Louis trade now, you see. It 'uz jes fair daylight when we passed our plantation, en I seed a gang o' niggers en white folks huntin'

---

50) dey 'uz jes one plank out: There was just one plank out=널판 지지대가 하나 나와 있었다

51) deckhan's en roustabouts 'uz sprawled aroun' asleep on de fo'cas'l: deckhands and roustabouts was sprawled around asleep on the forecastle=갑판 선원과 부두 인부는 앞 상갑판에서 대자로 누워 잠들어 있었다

52) he sot dah on de bitts wid his head down, asleep: he sat there on the bitts with his head down, asleep=그는 밧줄을 감는 계주에 고개를 숙이고 앉아 있었다, 잠든 채

53) I's 'mong frien's: I was among friends

54) de b'iler deck: the boiler deck=기관실 갑판

55) it 'uz jist home ag'in: it was just home again=다시 집에 돌아온 것 이었다

56) now we's pinted for Sent Louis: now we were pointed for Saint Louis=이제 우린 Saint Louis를 향해 가고 있었다

up en down de sho', en troublin' deyselves a good deal 'bout me;[57] but I warn't troublin' myself none 'bout dem.

"'Bout dat time[58] Sally Jackson, dat used to be my second chambermaid en 'uz head chambermaid now, she come out on de guard, en 'uz pow'ful glad to see me, en so 'uz all de officers; en I tole 'em I'd got kidnapped en sole down de river, en dey made me up twenty dollahs en give it to me,[59] en Sally she rigged me out wid good clo'es, en when I got here I went straight to whah you used to wuz,[60] en den I come to dis house, en dey say you's away but 'spected back every day;[61] so I didn't dast[62] to go down de river to Dawson's, 'ca'se I might miss you.

"Well, las' Monday I 'uz pass'n by one o' dem places[63] in Fourth street whah dey sticks up runaway-nigger bills, en he'ps to ketch 'em, en I seed my marster![64] I 'mos' flopped down on de groun', I felt so gone.[65] He had his back to me, en 'uz talkin' to de man en givin' him some bills—nigger bills, I reckon, en I's de nigger. He's offerin' a reward—dat's it. Ain't I right, don't you reckon?"

Tom had been gradually sinking into a state of ghastly terror, and he

---

57) I seed a gang o' niggers en white folks huntin' up en down de sho', en troublin' deyselves a good deal 'bout me: I saw a gang of niggers and white folks hunting up and down the shore, and troubling themselves a good deal about me (=나 때문에 많이 고생하고 있는 것)

58) 'Bout dat time: About that time=그때 쯤

59) en sole down de river, en dey made me up twenty dollahs en give it to me: and sold down the river, and they made me up twenty dollars and gave it to me

60) whah you used to wuz: where you used to be=네가 종종 있었던 곳

61) 'spected back every day: expected back every day=곧 돌아올 것으로 기대한다

62) dast: dare

63) I 'uz pass'n by one o' dem places: I was passing by one of those places

64) whah dey sticks up runaway nigger bills, en he'ps to ketch 'em, en I seed my marster: where they sticks up runaway nigger bills, and help to catch them, and I saw my master (=그들이 도망친 노예 전단을 붙이고 그들을 잡도록 돕는 곳에서)

65) I 'mos' flopped down on de groun', I felt so gone: I almost flopped down on the ground, I felt so gone=나는 땅바닥에 거의 털썩 주저앉을 뻔 했다, 나는 완전히 끝났다고 생각했다.

said to himself, now: "I'm lost, no matter what turn things take![66] This man has said to me that he thinks there was something suspicious about that sale; he said he had a letter from a passenger on the Grand Mogul saying that Roxy came here on that boat and that everybody on board knew all about the case; so he says that her coming here instead of flying to a free state looks bad for me, and that if I don't find her for him, and that pretty soon,[67] he will make trouble for me. I never believed that story; I couldn't believe she would be so dead to[68] all motherly instincts as to come here, knowing the risk she would run of getting me into irremediable trouble. And after all, here she is! And I stupidly swore I would help find her, thinking it was a perfectly safe thing to promise. If I venture to deliver her up,[69] she—she—but how can I help myself? I've got to do that or pay the money, and where's the money to come from? I—I—well, I should think that if he would swear to treat her kindly hereafter—and she says, herself, that he is a good man—and if he would swear to never allow her to be overworked, or ill fed, or—"

A flash of lightning exposed Tom's pallid face, drawn and rigid with these worrying thoughts.[70] Roxana spoke up sharply now, and there was apprehension in her voice—

"Turn up dat light! I want to see yo' face better. Dah now—lemme look at you. Chambers, you's as white as yo' shirt! Has you see dat man? Has he be'n to see you?"

"Ye-s."

"When?"

"Monday noon."

---

66) no matter what turn things take: 어떻게 일이 결말나던 간에
67) that pretty soon: 곧 그렇게 하지 (Roxy를 찾지) 않는다면. that은 문장 앞부분을 말함
68) so dead to: 그렇게 무감각해지다
69) venture to deliver her up: 그녀를 (주인에게) 넘기려고 시도하다

"Monday noon! Was he on my track?"

"He—well, he thought he was. That is, he hoped he was. This is the bill you saw." He took it out of his pocket.

"Read it to me!"

She was panting with excitement, and there was a dusky glow in her eyes that Tom could not translate with certainty, but there seemed to be something threatening about it. The handbill had the usual rude woodcut of a turbaned Negro woman running, with the customary bundle on a stick over her shoulder, and the heading, in bold type, "***$100 Reward.***" Tom read the bill aloud—at least the part that described Roxana and named the master and his St. Louis address and the address of the Fourth-street agency; but he left out the item that applicants for the reward might also apply to Mr. Thomas Driscoll.

"Gimme de bill!"

Tom had folded it and was putting it in his pocket. He felt a chilly streak creeping down his back, but said as carelessly as he could—

"The bill? Why, it isn't any use to you, you can't read it. What do you want with it?"

"Gimme de bill!" Tom gave it to her, but with a reluctance which he could not entirely disguise. "Did you read it all to me?"

"Certainly I did."

"Hole up yo' han' en swah to it."[71)]

Tom did it. Roxana put the bill carefully away in her pocket, with her eyes fixed upon Tom's face all the while; then she said—

"Yo's lyin'!"

"What would I want to lie about it for?"

"I don't know—but you is. Dat's my opinion, anyways. But nemmine 'bout dat. When I seed dat man I 'uz dat sk'yerd dat I could sca'cely

---

70) drawn and rigid with these worrying thoughts: 걱정으로 일그러지고 굳은

wobble home.[72] Den I give a nigger man a dollar for dese clo'es,[73] en I ain't ben in a house sence, night ner day, till now.[74] I blacked my face en laid hid in de cellar of a ole house dat's burnt down, daytimes, en robbed de sugar hogsheads en grain sacks on de wharf, nights, to git somethin' to eat, en never dast to try to buy noth'n', en I's mos' starved. En I never dast to come near dis place till dis rainy night, when dey ain't no people roun' sca'cely. But tonight I be'n a-stanin' in de dark alley ever sence night come,[75] waitin' for you to go by. En here I is."

She fell to thinking. Presently she said—

"You seed dat man at noon, las' Monday?"

"Yes."

"I seed him de middle o' dat arternoon. He hunted you up, didn't he?"

"Yes."

"Did he give you de bill dat time?"

"No, he hadn't got it printed yet."

Roxana darted a suspicious glance at him.

"Did you he'p him fix up de bill?"[76]

Tom cursed himself for making that stupid blunder, and tried to rectify it by saying he remember now that it *was* at noon Monday that the man gave him the bill. Roxana said—

"You's lyin' ag'in, sho." Then she straightened up and raised her finger:

---

71) Hole up yo' han' en swah to it: Hold up your hand and swear to it=손을 들고 맹세해라

72) I 'uz dat sk'yerd dat I could sca'cely wobble home: I was so scared that I could scarcely wobble home=나는 너무 두려워서 거의 집으로 올 수가 없었다

73) for dese clo'es: for these clothes

74) I ain't ben in a house sence, night ner day, till now: I haven't been in a house since, night nor day, till now=지금까지 밤이든 낮이든 집 안에 들어간 적이 없었다

75) I be'n a-stanin' in de dark alley ever sence night come: I have been standing in the dark alley ever since night had come=해가 진 때부터 여태 어두운 뒷골목에 서 있었다

76) fix up de bill: 전단 만드는 것

"Now den! I's gwyne to ask you a question, en I wants to know how you's gwyne to git aroun' it.[77] You knowed he 'uz arter me;[78] en if you run off, 'stid o' stayin' here to he'p him,[79] he'd know dey 'uz somethin' wrong 'bout dis business, en den he would inquire 'bout you, en dat would take him to yo' uncle, en yo' uncle would read de bill en see dat you be'n sellin' a free nigger down de river, en you know *him*, I reckon! He'd t'ar up de will en kick you outen de house.[80] Now, den, you answer me dis question: hain't you tole dat man[81] dat I would be sho' to come here, en den you would fix it so he could set a trap en ketch me?"

Tom recognized that neither lies nor arguments could help him any longer—he was in a vise, with the screw turned on, and out of it there was no budging.[82] His face began to take on an ugly look, and presently he said, with a snarl—

"Well, what could I do? You see, yourself, that I was in his grip and couldn't get out."

Roxy scorched him with a scornful gaze awhile, then she said:

"What could you do? You could be Judas to yo' own mother to save yo' wuthless hide![83] Would anybody b'lieve it? No—a dog couldn't![84] You is de low-downest orneriest hound dat was ever pup'd into dis

---

77) I wants to know how you's gwyne to git aroun' it: I want to know how you are going to get around it=네가 이 문제를 어떻게 해결하려고 하는지 알고 싶다

78) he 'uz arter me: he was after me

79) 'stid o' stayin' here to he'p him: instead of staying here to help him=여기 머무르며 그를 도와주는 대신

80) He'd t'ar up de will en kick you outen de house: He would tear up the will and kick you out of the house=그는 유언장을 찢어버리고 너를 집에서 내 을 것이다

81) hain't you tole dat man: haven't you told that man=그자에게 이야기 하지 않았니

82) he was in a vise, with the screw turned on, and out of it there was no budging: 그는 나사가 돌고 있는 바이스에 끼어 있었고 여기서 움직여 빠져 나올수가 없었다

83) You could be Judas to yo' own mother to save yo' wuthless hide: You could be Judas to your mother to save your worthless hide=가치없는 네 한 몸을 지키기 위해 네 엄마에게 유다 같은 배반자가 되다니

84) a dog couldn't!: 개도 그럴 순 없다!

worl' en I's 'sponsible for it!"[85]—and she spat on him.

He made no effort to resent this. Roxy reflected a moment, then she said—

"Now I'll tell you what you's gwyne to do. You's gwyne to give dat man de money dat you's got laid up,[86] en make him wait till you kin go to de judge en git de res' en buy me free agin."

"Thunder![87] What are you thinking of? Go and ask him for three hundred dollars and odd? What would I tell him I want it for, pray?"

Roxy's answer was delivered in a serene and level voice.

"You'll tell him you's sole me to pay yo' gamblin' debts, en dat you lied to me en was a villain, en dat I 'quires[88] you to git dat money en buy me back ag'in."

"Why, you've gone stark mad! He would tear the will to shreds in a minute—don't you know that?"

"Yes, I does."

"Then you don't believe I'm idiot enough to go to him, do you?" "I don't b'lieve nothin' 'bout it[89]—I *knows* you's a-goin'. I knows it 'ca'se you knows dat if you don't raise dat money I'll go to him myself, en

---

85) You is de low-downest orneriest hound dat was ever pup'd into dis worl' en I's 'sponsible for it!=You are the low-downest orneriest hound that was ever pupped into this world—and I am responsible for it!=넌 세상에 태어난 가장 비열하고 천한 개다 그리고 그것은 (그런 개가 태어난 것은) 내 책임이다

86) you's got laid up: 네가 모은, 네가 준비한

87) Thunder!=무슨 그런 말을!

88) I 'quires: I require

89) I don't b'lieve nothin' 'bout it: I believe nothing about it=난 그것에 대해 아무것도 믿지 않아 (Tom이 갈 것을 알기 때문에 믿음의 문제가 아니라는 것)

den he'll sell you down de river, en you kin see how you like it!"

Tom rose, trembling and excited, and there was an evil light in his eye. He strode to the door and said he must get out of this suffocating place for a moment and clear his brain in the fresh air so that he could determine what to do. The door wouldn't open. Roxy smiled grimly, and said—

"I's got the key, honey—set down. You needn't cle'r up yo' brain none to fine out what you gwyne to do—*I* knows what you's gwyne to do." Tom sat down and began to pass his hands through his hair with a helpless and desperate air. Roxy said, "Is dat man in dis house?"

Tom glanced up with a surprised expression, and asked—

"What gave you such an idea?"

"You done it. Gwyne out to cle'r yo' brain![90] In de fust place you ain't got none to cle'r,[91] en in de second place yo' ornery eye tole on you.[92] You's de low-downest hound dat ever—but I done told you dat befo'. Now den, dis is Friday. You kin fix it up wid dat man, en tell him you's gwyne away to git de res' o' de money, en dat you'll be back wid it nex' Tuesday, or maybe Wednesday. You understan'?"

Tom answered sullenly—

"Yes."

"En when you gits de new bill o' sale dat sells me to my own self, take en send it in de mail to Mr. Pudd'nhead Wilson, en write on de back dat he's to keep it tell I come. You understan'?"

"Yes."

"Dat's all, den. Take yo' umbreller, en put on yo' hat."

---

90) gwyne out to cle'r yo' brain!: Going out to clear your brain!=머리를 식히기 위해 밖으로 나간다고!

91) In de fust place you ain't got none to cle'r: In the first place, you have got none to clear=첫째, 넌 식힐 머리도 없고

92) in de second place yo' ornery eye tole on you: 둘째, 너의 비열한 눈빛이 네 생각을 말해 주고 있다

"Why?"

"Beca'se you's gwyne to see me home to de wharf. You see dis knife? I's toted it aroun' sence de day I seed dat man en bought dese clo'es en it. If he ketched me, I'uz gwyne to kill myself wid it. Now start along, en go sof', en lead de way; en if you gives a sign in dis house, or if anybody comes up to you in de street, I's gwyne to jam it right into you. Chambers, does you b'lieve me when I says dat?"

"It's no use to bother me with that question. I know your word's good."

"Yes, it's diff'rent from yo'n! Shet de light out en move along—here's de key."

They were not followed. Tom trembled every time a late straggler brushed by them on the street, and half expected to feel the cold steel in his back. Roxy was right at his heels and always in reach. After tramping a mile they reached a wide vacancy on the deserted wharves, and in this dark and rainy desert they parted.

As Tom trudged home, his mind was full of dreary thoughts and wild plans; but at last he said to himself, wearily—

"There is but the one way out. I must follow her plan. But with a variation—I will not ask for the money and ruin myself; I will *rob* the old skinflint."

CHAPTER 19

Few things are harder to put up with than the annoyance of a good example.

– Pudd'nhead Wilson's Calendar

It were not best that we should all think alike; it is difference of opinion that makes horse-races.

- Pudd'nhead Wilson's Calendar

Dawson's Landing was comfortably finishing its season of dull repose and waiting patiently for the duel. Count Luigi was waiting, too; but not patiently, rumor said. Sunday came, and Luigi insisted on having his challenge conveyed. Wilson carried it. Judge Driscoll declined to fight with an assassin—"that is,"[1] he added significantly, "in the field of honor."

Elsewhere, of course, he would be ready. Wilson tried to convince him that if he had been present himself when Angelo told about the homicide committed by Luigi, he would not have considered the act discreditable to Luigi; but the obstinate old man was not to be moved.

Wilson went back to his principal and reported the failure of his mission. Luigi was incensed, and asked how it could be that the old gentleman, who was by no means dull-witted, held his trifling nephew's evidence in inferences to be of more value than Wilson's. But Wilson laughed, and said:

---

1) that is: 다시 말하자면

"That is quite simple; that is easily explicable. I am not his doll his baby—his infatuation: his nephew is. The judge and his late wife never had any children. The judge and his wife were past middle age when this treasure fell into their lap. One must make allowances for a parental instinct that has been starving for twenty-five or thirty years. It is famished, it is crazed with hunger by that time, and will be entirely satisfied with anything that comes handy; its taste is atrophied, it can't tell mud-cat from shad. A devil born to a young couple is measurably recognizable by them as a devil before long, but a devil adopted by an old couple is an angel to them, and remains so, through thick and thin.[2] Tom is this old man's angel; he is infatuated with him. Tom can persuade him into things which other people can't—not all things; I don't mean that, but a good many—particularly one class of things: the things that create or abolish personal partialities or prejudices in the old man's mind. The old man liked both of you. Tom conceived a hatred for you. That was enough; it turned the old man around at once. The oldest and strongest friendship must go to the ground[3] when one of these late-adopted darlings throws a brick at it."

"It's a curious philosophy," said Luigi.

"It ain't philosophy at all,—it's a fact. And there is something pathetic and beautiful about it, too. I think there is nothing more pathetic than to see one of these poor old childless couples taking a menagerie of yelping little worthless dogs to their hearts; and then adding some cursing and squawking parrots and a jackass-voiced macaw; and next a couple of hundred screeching songbirds, and presently some fetid guinea-pigs and rabbits, and a howling colony of cats. It is all a groping and ignorant effort to construct out of base metal and brass filings, so to speak, something to take the place of that

---

2) through thick and thin: 언제나 변함없이

golden treasure denied them by Nature, a child. But this is a digression. The unwritten law of this region requires you to kill Judge Driscoll on sight, and he and the community will expect that attention at your hands—though of course your own death by his bullet will answer every purpose.[4] Look out for him! Are you healed—that is, fixed?"[5]

"Yes, he shall have his opportunity. If he attacks me, I will respond."

As Wilson was leaving, he said—

"The judge is still a little used up by his campaign work, and will not get out for a day or so; but when he does get out, you want to be on the alert."

About eleven at night the twins went out for exercise, and started on a long stroll in the veiled moonlight.

Tom Driscoll had landed at Hackett's Store, two miles below Dawson's, just about half an hour earlier, the only passenger for that lonely spot, and had walked up the shore road and entered Judge Driscoll's house without having encountered anyone either on the road or under the roof.

He pulled down his window blinds and lighted his candle. He laid off his coat and hat and began his preparations. He unlocked his trunk and got his suit of girl's clothes out from under the male attire in it, and laid it by. Then he blacked his face with burnt cork and put the cork in his pocket. His plan was to slip down to his uncle's private sitting room below, pass into the bedroom, steal the safe key from the old gentleman's clothes, and then go back and rob the safe. He took up his candle to start. His courage and confidence were high, up to this point, but both began to waver a little now. Suppose he should make a noise,

---

3) go to the ground: 지다, 땅에 떨어지다

4) your own death by his bullet will answer every purpose: 그의 총탄에 의한 당신의 죽음도 (이 지역 불문율의) 목적에 알맞을 것이다

5) Are you healed that is, fixed?: 다 나았는가, 다시 말하자면, 준비는 되었나?

by some accident, and get caught—say, in the act of opening the safe? Perhaps it would be well to go armed. He took the Indian knife from its hiding place, and felt a pleasant return of his waning courage. He slipped stealthily down the narrow stair, his hair rising and his pulses halting at the slightest creak. When he was halfway down, he was disturbed to perceive that the landing below was touched by a faint glow of light. What could that mean? Was his uncle still up? No, that was not likely; he must have left his night taper there when he went to bed. Tom crept on down, pausing at every step to listen. He found the door standing open, and glanced in. What he saw pleased him beyond measure. His uncle was asleep on the sofa; on a small table at the head of the sofa a lamp was burning low, and by it stood the old man's small tin cashbox, closed. Near the box was a pile of bank notes and a piece of paper covered with figures in pencil. The safe door was not open. Evidently the sleeper had wearied himself with work upon his finances, and was taking a rest.

Tom set his candle on the stairs, and began to make his way toward the pile of notes, stooping low as he went. When he was passing his uncle, the old man stirred in his sleep, and Tom stopped instantly—stopped, and softly drew the knife from its sheath, with his heart thumping, and his eyes fastened upon his benefactor's face. After a moment or two he ventured forward again—one step—reached for his prize and seized it, dropping the knife sheath. Then he felt the old man's strong grip upon him, and a wild cry of "Help! help!" rang in his ear. Without hesitation he drove the knife home[6)]—and was free. Some of the notes escaped from his left hand and fell in the blood on the floor. He dropped the knife and snatched them up and started to fly; transferred them to his left hand, and seized the knife again, in his fright and confusion, but

---

6) Without hesitation he drove the knife home: 주저없이 그는 칼로 (Judge Driscoll을) 깊숙이 찔렀다

remembered himself and flung it from him, as being a dangerous witness to carry away with him.

He jumped for the stair-foot, and closed the door behind him; and as he snatched his candle and fled upward, the stillness of the night was broken by the sound of urgent footsteps approaching the house. In another moment he was in his room, and the twins were standing aghast over the body of the murdered man!

Tom put on his coat, buttoned his hat under it, threw on his suit of girl's clothes, dropped the veil, blew out his light, locked the room door by which he had just entered, taking the key, passed through his other door into the back hall, locked that door and kept the key, then worked his way along in the dark and descended the back stairs. He was not expecting to meet anybody, for all interest was centered in the other part of the house now; his calculation proved correct. By the time he was passing through the backyard, Mrs. Pratt, her servants, and a dozen half-dressed neighbors had joined the twins and the dead, and accessions were still arriving at the front door.

As Tom, quaking as with a palsy, passed out at the gate, three women came flying from the house on the opposite side of the lane. They rushed by him and in at the gate, asking him what the trouble was there, but not waiting for an answer. Tom said to himself, "Those old maids waited to dress they did the same thing the night Stevens's house burned down next door." In a few minutes he was in the haunted house. He lighted a candle and took off his girl-clothes. There was blood on him all down his left side, and his right hand was red with the stains of the blood-soaked notes which he has crushed in it; but otherwise he was free from this sort of evidence. He cleansed his hand on the straw, and cleaned most of the smut from his face. Then he burned the male and female attire to ashes, scattered the ashes, and put on a disguise proper for a tramp. He blew out his light, went below, and was soon loafing down the river road with the intent to borrow and use one of Roxy's devices. He found a canoe and paddled off downstream, setting the canoe adrift as dawn approached, and making his way by land to the next village, where he kept out of sight till a transient steamer came along, and then took deck passage for St. Louis. He was ill at ease until Dawson's Landing was behind him; then he said to himself, "All the detectives on earth couldn't trace me now; there's not a vestige of a clue left in the world; that homicide will take its place with the permanent mysteries, and people won't get done trying to guess out the secret of it for fifty years."

In St. Louis, next morning, he read this brief telegram in the papers—dated at Dawson's Landing:

"Judge Driscoll, an old and respected citizen, was assassinated here about midnight by a profligate Italian nobleman or a barber on account of a quarrel growing out of the recent election. The assassin will probably be lynched."

"One of the twins!" soliloquized Tom. "How lucky! It is the knife that has done him this grace. We never know when fortune is trying to favor us. I actually cursed Pudd'nhead Wilson in my heart for putting it out of my power to sell that knife. I take it back now."[7)]

7) I take it back now: 이제 그걸 (Wilson을 저주한 던 것) 취소한다

Tom was now rich and independent. He arranged with the planter, and mailed to Wilson the new bill of sale which sold Roxana to herself; then he telegraphed his Aunt Pratt: "Have seen the awful news in the papers and am almost prostrated with grief. Shall start by packet today. Try to bear up8) till I come."

When Wilson reached the house of mourning and had gathered such details as Mrs. Pratt and the rest of the crowd could tell him, he took command as mayor, and gave orders that nothing should be touched, but everything left as it was until Justice Robinson should arrive and take the proper measures as coroner. He cleared everybody out of the room but the twins and himself. The sheriff soon arrived and took the twins away to jail. Wilson told them to keep heart,[9)] and promised to do his best in their defense when the case should come to trial. Justice Robinson came presently, and with him Constable Blake. They examined the room thoroughly. They found the knife and the sheath. Wilson noticed that there were fingerprints on the knife-handle. That pleased him, for the twins had required the earliest comers to make a scrutiny of their hands and clothes, and neither these people nor Wilson himself had found any bloodstains upon them. Could there be a possibility that the twins had spoken the truth when they said they found the man dead when they ran into the house in answer to the cry for help? He thought of that mysterious girl at once. But this was not the sort of work for a girl to be engaged in. No matter; Tom Driscoll's room must be examined.

After the coroner's jury[10)] had viewed the body and its surroundings, Wilson suggested a search upstairs, and he went along. The jury forced an entrance to Tom's room, but found nothing, of course.

---

8) to bear up: 견디다
9) to keep heart: 용기를 잃지 않다
10) the coroner's jury: 검시 배심원

The coroner's jury found that the homicide was committed by Luigi, and that Angelo was accessory to it.

The town was bitter against the misfortunates, and for the first few days after the murder they were in constant danger of being lynched. The grand jury presently indicted Luigi for murder in the first degree, and Angelo as accessory before the fact. The twins were transferred from the city jail to the county prison to await trial.

Wilson examined the finger-marks on the knife handle and said to himself, "Neither of the twins made those marks." Then manifestly there was another person concerned, either in his own interest or as hired assassin.

But who could it be? That, he must try to find out. The safe was not opened, the cashbox was closed, and had three thousand dollars in it. Then robbery was not the motive, and revenge was. Where had the murdered man an enemy except Luigi? There was but that one person in the world with a deep grudge against him.

The mysterious girl! The girl was a great trial to Wilson. If the motive had been robbery, the girl might answer; but there wasn't any girl that would want to take this old man's life for revenge. He had no quarrels with girls; he was a gentleman.

Wilson had perfect tracings of the finger-marks of the knife handle; and among his glass records he had a great array of finger prints of women and girls, collected during the last fifteen or eighteen years, but he scanned them in vain, they successfully withstood every test; among them were no duplicates of the prints on the knife.

The presence of the knife on the stage of the murder was a worrying circumstance for Wilson. A week previously he had as good as admitted to himself that he believed Luigi had possessed such a knife, and that he still possessed it notwithstanding his pretense that it had been stolen. And now here was the knife, and with it the twins. Half the town had said the twins were humbugging when they claimed they had lost their knife, and now these people were joyful, and said, "I told you so!"

If their finger-prints had been on the handle—but it was useless to bother any further about that; the finger-prints on the handle were *not* theirs—that he knew perfectly.

Wilson refused to suspect Tom; for, firstly, Tom couldn't murder anybody he hadn't character enough;[11] secondly, if he could murder a person he wouldn't select his doting benefactor and nearest relative; thirdly, self-interest was in the way; for while the uncle lived, Tom was sure of a free support and a chance to get the destroyed will revived again, but with the uncle gone, that chance was gone too. It was true the will had really been revived, as was now discovered, but Tom could not have been aware of it, or he would have spoken of it, in his native talky, unsecretive way. Finally, Tom was in St. Louis when the murder was done, and got the news out of the morning journals, as was shown by his telegram to his aunt. These speculations were

11) he hadn't character enough: 그럴만한 인물이 못 되었다

umemphasized sensations rather than articulated thoughts,[12] for Wilson would have laughed at the idea of seriously connecting Tom with the murder.

Wilson regarded the case of the twins as desperate—in fact, about hopeless. For he argued that if a confederate was not found, an enlightened Missouri jury would hang them; sure; if a confederate was found, that would not improve the matter, but simply furnish one more person for the sheriff to hang. Nothing could save the twins but the discovery of a person who did the murder on his sole personal account an undertaking which had all the aspect of the impossible. Still, the person who made the finger-prints must be sought. The twins might have no case *with* him, but they certainly would have none without him.[13]

So Wilson mooned around,[14] thinking, thinking, guessing, guessing, day and night, and arriving nowhere. Whenever he ran across a girl or a woman he was not acquainted with, he got her finger-prints, on one pretext or another; and they always cost him a sigh when he got home, for they never tallied with the finger-marks on the knife handle.

As to the mysterious girl, Tom swore he knew no such girl, and did not remember ever seeing a girl wearing a dress like the one described by Wilson. He admitted that he did not always lock his room, and that sometimes the servants forgot to lock the house doors; still, in his opinion the girl must have made but few visits or she would have been discovered. When Wilson tried to connect her with the stealing-raid, and thought she might have been the old woman's confederate, if not

12) These speculations were umemphasized sensations rather than articulated thoughts: 이런 추측들은 조리있는 생각이기보다 약한 정도였다

13) The twins might have no case *with* him, but they certainly would have none without him: 그 쌍둥이들이 그 (지문을 남긴 자)와 아무 관계가 없을 수도 있다, 하지만 그가 없이는 아무런 변호도 할 수 없을 것이다

14) mooned around: 부질없이 멍하니 돌아다녔다

the very thief disguised as an old woman, Tom seemed stuck, and also much interested, and said he would keep a sharp eye out for this person or persons, although he was afraid that she or they would be too smart to venture again into a town where everybody would now be on the watch for a good while to come.

Everybody was pitying Tom, he looked so quiet and sorrowful, and seemed to feel his great loss so deeply. He was playing a part, but it was not all a part.[15] The picture of his alleged uncle, as he had last seen him, was before him in the dark pretty frequently, when he was awake, and called again in his dreams, when he was asleep. He wouldn't go into the room where the tragedy had happened. This charmed the doting Mrs. Pratt, who "realized now, as she had never done before," she said, what a sensitive and delicate nature her darling had, and how he adored his poor uncle.

---

15) He was playing a part, but it was not all a part: 그는 가장하고 있었으나, 모두가 다 가장은 아니었다

CHAPTER 20

Even the clearest and most perfect circumstantial evidence is likely to be at fault, after all, and therefore ought to be received with great caution. Take the case of any pencil, sharpened by any woman; if you have witnesses, you will find she did it with a knife; but if you take simply the aspect of the pencil, you will say she did it with her teeth.

- Pudd'nhead Wilson's Calendar

The weeks dragged along, no friend visiting the jailed twins but their counsel and Aunt Patsy Cooper, and the day of trial came at last—the heaviest day in Wilson's life; for with all his tireless diligence he had discovered no sign or trace of the missing confederate. "Confederate" was the term he had long ago privately accepted for that person not as being unquestionably the right term, but as being at least possibly the right one, though he was never able to understand why the twins did not vanish and escape, as the confederate had done, instead of remaining by the murdered man and getting caught there.

The courthouse was crowded, of course, and would remain so to the finish, for not only in the town itself, but in the country for miles around, the trial was the one topic of conversation among the people. Mrs. Pratt, in deep mourning, and Tom with a weed on his hat, had seats near Pembroke Howard, the public prosecutor, and back of them sat a great array of friends of the family. The twins had but one friend present to keep their counsel in countenance, their poor old sorrowing landlady. She sat near Wilson, and looked her friendliest. In the "nigger corner" sat Chambers; also Roxy, with good clothes on, and her bill of sale in her pocket. It was her most precious possession, and she never parted with it, day or night. Tom had allowed her thirty-five dollars a month ever since he came into his property,[1] and had said that he and she ought to be grateful to the twins for making them rich; but had roused such a temper in her by this speech that he did not repeat the argument afterward. She said the old judge had treated her child a thousand times better than he deserved, and had never done her an unkindness in his life; so she hated these outlandish devils for killing him, and shouldn't ever sleep satisfied till she saw them hanged for it. She was here to watch the trial now, and was going to lift up just one "hooraw"[2] over it if the county judge put her in jail a year for it. She gave her turbaned head a toss and said, "When dat verdic' comes, I's gwyne to lif' dat *roof*, now, I *tell* you."[3]

Pembroke Howard briefly sketched the state's case. He said he would show by a chain of circumstantial evidence without break or fault in it anywhere, that the principal prisoner at the bar committed the murder; that the motive was partly revenge, and partly a desire to take his own life out of jeopardy, and that his brother, by his presence, was a consenting accessory to the crime; a crime which was the basest known to the calendar of human misdeeds—assassination; that it was conceived by the blackest of hearts and consummated by the cowardliest of hands; a crime which had broken a loving sister's heart, blighted the happiness of a young nephew who was as dear as a son, brought inconsolable grief to many friends, and sorrow and loss to the whole community. The utmost penalty of the outraged law would be exacted, and upon the accused, now present at the bar, that penalty

---

1) ever since he came into his property: 재산을 얻은 (상속받은) 이후 내내

2) hooraw: hurrah=만세!

3) When dat verdic' comes, I's gwyne to lif' dat *roof*, now, I tell you: When that verdict comes, I am going to lift that roof, now, I *tell* you=판결이 내려질 때, 내가 지붕을 들썩거리게 할거야. 정말로.

would unquestionably be executed. He would reserve further remark until his closing speech.

He was strongly moved, and so also was the whole house; Mrs. Pratt and several other women were weeping when he sat down, and many an eye that was full of hate was riveted upon the unhappy prisoners.

Witness after witness was called by the state, and questioned at length; but the cross-questioning was brief. Wilson knew they could furnish nothing valuable for his side. People were sorry for Pudd'nhead Wilson; his budding career would get hurt by this trial.

Several witnesses swore they heard Judge Driscoll say in his public speech that the twins would be able to find their lost knife again when they needed it to assassinate somebody with. This was not news, but now it was seen to have been sorrowfully prophetic, and a profound sensation quivered through the hushed courtroom when those dismal words were repeated.

The public prosecutor rose and said that it was within his knowledge, through a conversation held with Judge Driscoll on the last day of his life, that counsel for the defense had brought him a challenge from the person charged at the bar with murder; that he had refused to fight with a confessed assassin—"that is, on the field of honor," but had added significantly, that he would be ready for him elsewhere. Presumably the person here charged with murder was warned that he must kill or be killed the first time he should meet Judge Driscoll. If counsel for the defense chose to let the statement stand so, he would not call him to the witness stand. Mr. Wilson said he would offer no denial. [Murmurs, in the house—"It is getting worse and worse for Wilson's case."]

Mrs. Pratt testified that she heard no outcry, and did not know what woke her up, unless it was the sound of rapid footsteps approaching the front door. She jumped up and ran out in the hall just as she was, and heard the footsteps flying up the front steps and then following behind her as she ran to the sitting room. There she found the accused standing over her murdered brother—[Here she broke down and sobbed. Sensation in the court.] Resuming, she said the persons entered behind her were Mr. Rogers and Mr. Buckstone.

Cross-examined by Wilson, she said the twins proclaimed their innocence; declared that they had been taking a walk, and had hurried to the house in response to a cry for help which was so loud and strong that they had heard it at a considerable distance; that they begged her and the gentlemen just mentioned to examine their hands and clothes—which was done, and no blood stains found.

Confirmatory evidence followed from Rogers and Buckstone.

The finding of the knife was verified, the advertisement minutely describing it and offering a reward for it was put in evidence, and its exact correspondence with that description proven. Then followed a few minor details, and the case for the state was closed.

Wilson said that he had three witnesses, the Misses Clarkson, who would testify that they met a veiled young woman leaving Judge Driscoll's premises by the back gate a few minutes after the cries for help were heard, and that their evidence, taken with certain circumstantial evidence which he would call to the court's attention to, would in his opinion convince the court that there was still one person concerned in this crime who had not yet been found, and also that a stay of proceedings[4] ought to be granted, in justice to his clients, until that person should be discovered. As it was late, he would ask leave to defer the examination of his three witnesses until the next morning.

The crowd poured out of the place and went flocking away in excited groups and couples, talking the events of the session over with

---

4) a stay of proceedings: 재판을 연기하다

vivacity and consuming interest, and everybody seemed to have had a satisfactory and enjoyable day except the accused, their counsel, and their old lady friend. There was no cheer among these, and no substantial hope.

In parting with the twins Aunt Patsy did attempt a good-night with a gay pretense of hope and cheer in it, but broke down without finishing.

Absolutely secure as Tom considered himself to be, the opening solemnities of the trial had nevertheless oppressed him with a vague uneasiness, his being a nature sensitive to even the smallest alarms; but from the moment that the poverty and weakness of Wilson's case lay exposed to the court, he was comfortable once more, even jubilant. He left the courtroom sarcastically sorry for Wilson. "The Clarksons met an unknown woman in the back lane," he said to himself, "*that* is his case! I'll give him a century to find her in—a couple of them if he likes. A woman who doesn't exist any longer, and the clothes that gave her her sex burnt up and the ashes thrown away—oh, certainly, he'll find her easy enough!" This reflection set him to admiring, for the hundredth time, the shrewd ingenuities by which he had insured himself against detection—more, against even suspicion.

"Nearly always in cases like this there is some little detail or other overlooked, some wee little track or trace left behind, and detection follows; but here there's not even the faintest suggestion of a trace left. No more than a bird leaves when it flies through the air—yes, through the night, you may say. The man that can track a bird through the air in the dark and find that bird is the man to track me out and find the judge's assassin—no other need apply. And that is the job that has been laid out for poor Pudd'nhead Wilson, of all people in the world! Lord, it will be pathetically funny to see him grubbing and groping after that woman that don't exist, and the right person sitting under his very nose all the time!" The more he thought the situation over, the more the humor of it struck him. Finally he said, "I'll never let him hear the last of that woman.[5] Every time I catch him in company, to his dying day, I'll ask him in the guileless affectionate way that used to gravel him so when I inquired how his unborn law business was coming along, 'Got on her track yet—hey, Pudd'nhead?'" He wanted to laugh, but that would not have answered; there were people about, and he was mourning for his uncle. He made up his mind that it would be good entertainment to look in on Wilson that night and watch him worry over his barren law case and goad him with an exasperating word or two of sympathy and commiseration now and then.

Wilson wanted no supper, he had no appetite. He got out all the finger-prints of girls and women in his collection of records and pored gloomily over them an hour or more, trying to convince himself that that troublesome girl's marks were there somewhere and had been overlooked. But it was not so. He drew back his chair, clasped his hands over his head, and gave himself up to dull and arid musings.

Tom Driscoll dropped in, an hour after dark, and said with a pleasant laugh as he took a seat

"Hello, we've gone back to the amusements of our days of neglect and obscurity for consolation, have we?" and he took up one of the glass strips and held it against the light to inspect it.

"Come, cheer up, old man; there's no use in losing your grip[6] and going back to this child's play merely because this big sun-spot is

---

5) I'll never let him hear the last of that woman: 그 여자 이야기를 그에게 끝없이 듣게 할 것이다

6) losing your grip: 열정을 잃다

drifting across your shiny new disk.[7] It'll pass, and you'll be all right again" and he laid the glass down. "Did you think you could win always?"

"Oh, no," said Wilson, with a sigh, "I didn't expect that, but I can't believe Luigi killed your uncle, and I feel very sorry for him. It makes me blue. And you would feel as I do, Tom, if you were not prejudiced against those young fellows."

"I don't know about that," and Tom's countenance darkened, for his memory reverted to his kicking. "I owe them no good will, considering the brunette one's treatment of me that night. Prejudice or no prejudice, Pudd'nhead, I don't like them, and when they get their deserts[8] you're not going to find me sitting on the mourner's bench."

He took up another strip of glass, and exclaimed—

"Why, here's old Roxy's label! Are you going to ornament the royal palaces with nigger paw-marks, too? By the date here, I was seven months old when this was done, and she was nursing me and her little nigger cub. There's a line straight across her thumb-print. How comes that?" and Tom held out the piece of glass to Wilson.

"That is common," said the bored man, wearily. "Scar of a cut or a scratch, usually"—and he took the strip of glass indifferently, and raised it toward the lamp.

All the blood sank suddenly out of his face; his hand quaked, and he gazed at the polished surface before him with the glassy stare of a corpse.[9]

"Great heavens, what's the matter with you, Wilson? Are you going to faint?"

---

7) this big sunspot is drifting across your shiny new disk: 당신의 빛나는 태양 표면에 이 큰 흑점이 흘러간다고

8) deserts: 응분의 벌

9) with the glassy stare of a corpse: 죽은 사람의 눈같이 멍한 시선으로

Tom sprang for a glass of water and offered it, but Wilson shrank shuddering from him and said—

"No, no!—take it away!" His breast was rising and falling, and he moved his head about in a dull and wandering way, like a person who had been stunned. Presently he said, "I shall feel better when I get to bed; I have been overwrought today; yes, and overworked for many days."

"Then I'll leave you and let you get to your rest. Good night, old man." But as Tom went out he couldn't deny himself a small parting gibe: "Don't take it so hard; a body can't win every time; you'll hang somebody yet."[10]

Wilson muttered to himself, "It is no lie to say I am sorry I have to begin with you, miserable dog though you are!"

He braced himself up[11] with a glass of cold whisky, and went to work again. He did not compare the new finger-marks unintentionally left by Tom a few minutes before on Roxy's glass with the tracings of the marks left on the knife handle, there being no need for that for his trained eye—but busied himself with another matter, muttering from time to time, "Idiot that I was!—Nothing but a *girl* would do me—a man in girl's clothes never occurred to me." First, he hunted out the plate containing the finger-prints made by Tom when he was twelve years old, and laid it by itself; then he brought forth the marks made by Tom's baby fingers when he was a suckling of seven months, and placed these two plates with the one containing this subject's newly (and unconsciously) made record.

"Now the series is complete," he said with satisfaction, and sat down to inspect these things and enjoy them.

But his enjoyment was brief. He stared a considerable time at the three strips, and seemed stupefied with astonishment. At last he put

10) you'll hang somebody yet: 언제가 당신도 누굴 교수형에 처할 것이다 (=이길 것이다)

them down and said, "I can't make it out at all hang it,[12] the baby's don't tally with the others!"

He walked the floor for half an hour puzzling over his enigma, then he hunted out two other glass plates.

He sat down and puzzled over these things a good while, but kept muttering, "It's no use; I can't understand it. They don't tally right, and yet I'll swear the names and dates are right, and so of course they *ought* to tally. I never labeled one of these thing carelessly in my life. There is a most extraordinary mystery here."

He was tired out now, and his brains were beginning to clog. He said he would sleep himself fresh, and then see what he could do with this riddle. He slept through a troubled and unrestful hour, then unconsciousness began to shred away, and presently he rose drowsily to a sitting posture. "Now what was that dream?" he said, trying to recall it. "What was that dream?—it seemed to unravel that puz—"

He landed in the middle of the floor at a bound, without finishing the sentence, and ran and turned up his light and seized his "records." He took a single swift glance at them and cried out—

"It's so! Heavens, what a revelation! And for twenty-three years no man has ever suspected it!"

---

11) braced himself up: 마음을 가다듬다
12) hang it: 제기랄!

CHAPTER 21

He is useless on top of the ground; he ought to be under it, inspiring the cabbages.

- Pudd'nhead Wilson's Calendar

April 1. This is the day upon which we are reminded of what we are on the other three hundred and sixty-four.

- Pudd'nhead Wilson's Calendar

Wilson put on enough clothes for business purposes and went to work under a high pressure of steam.[1] He was awake all over. All sense of weariness had been swept away by the invigorating refreshment of the great and hopeful discovery which he had made. He made fine and accurate reproductions of a number of his "records," and then enlarged them on a scale of ten to one with his pantograph. He did these pantograph enlargements on sheets of white cardboard, and made each individual line of the bewildering maze of whorls or curves or loops which constituted the "pattern" of a "record" stand out bold and black by reinforcing it with ink. To the untrained eye the collection of delicate originals made by the human finger on the glass plates looked about alike; but when enlarged ten times they resembled the markings of a block of wood

1) under a high pressure of steam: 힘차게 기운을 내서

that has been sawed across the grain, and the dullest eye could detect at a glance, and at a distance of many feet, that no two of the patterns were alike. When Wilson had at last finished his tedious and difficult work, he arranged its results according to a plan in which a progressive order and sequence was a principal feature; then he added to the batch several pantograph enlargements which he had made from time to time in bygone years.

The night was spent and the day well advanced now. By the time he had snatched a trifle of breakfast, it was nine o'clock, and the court was ready to begin its sitting.[2) He was in his place twelve minutes later, with his "records."

Tom Driscoll caught a slight glimpse of the records, and nudged his nearest friend and said, with a wink, "Pudd'nhead's got a rare eye to business—thinks that as long as he can't win his case it's at least a noble good chance to advertise his palace-window decorations without any expense." Wilson was informed that his witnesses had been delayed, but would arrive presently; but he rose and said he should probably not have occasion to make use of their testimony. [An amused murmur ran through the room—"It's a clean backdown!] he gives up without hitting a lick!"] Wilson continued—

"I have other testimony,—and better. [This compelled interest, and evoked murmurs of surprise that had a detectable ingredient of disappointment in them.] "If I seem to be springing this evidence upon the court, I offer as my justification for this, that I did not discover its existence until late last night, and have been engaged in examining and classifying it ever since until half an hour ago. I shall offer it presently; but first I with to say a few preliminary words.

---

2) begin its sitting: 재판을 개정(시작)하다

"May it please the court[3], the claim given the front place, the claim most persistently urged, the claim most strenuously and I may even say, aggressively and defiantly insisted upon by the prosecution is this—that the person whose hand left the bloodstained finger prints upon the handle of the Indian knife is the person who committed the murder." Wilson paused, during several moments, to give impressiveness to what he was about to say, and then added tranquilly, "We grant that claim."

It was an electrical surprise. No one was prepared for such an admission. A buzz of astonishment rose on all sides, and people were heard to intimate that the overworked lawyer had lost his mind. Even the veteran judge, accustomed as he was to legal ambushes and masked batteries in criminal procedure, was not sure that his ears were not deceiving him, and asked counsel what it was he had said. Howard's impassive face betrayed no sign, but his attitude and bearing lost something of their careless confidence for a moment. Wilson resumed:

"We not only grant that claim, but we welcome it and strongly endorse it. Leaving that matter for the present, we will now proceed to consider other points in the case which we propose to establish by evidence, and shall include that one in the chain in its proper place."[4)]

He had made up his mind to try a few hardy guesses, in mapping out his theory of the origin and motive of the murder—guesses designed to fill up gaps in it—guesses which could help if they hit, and would probably do no harm if they didn't.

"To my mind, certain circumstances of the case before the court seem to suggest a motive for the homicide quite different from the one insisted on by the state. It is my conviction that the motive was not revenge, but robbery. It has been urged that the presence of the

---

3) May it please the court: 존경하는 재판관님. 법정에서 변론할 때 관용적으로 쓰는 말
4) shall include that one in the chain in its proper place: 그것을 고리의 적절한 위치에 끼워 넣겠다

accused brothers in that fatal room, just after notification that one of them must take the life of Judge Driscoll or lose his own the moment the parties should meet, clearly signifies that the natural instinct of self-preservation moved my clients to go there secretly and save Count Luigi by destroying his adversary.

"Then why did they stay there, after the deed was done? Mrs. Pratt had time, although she did not hear the cry for help, but woke up some moments later, to run to that room—and there she found these men standing and making no effort to escape. If they were guilty, they ought to have been running out of the house at the same time that she was running to that room. If they had had such a strong instinct toward self-preservation as to move them to kill that unarmed man, what had become of it now, when it should have been more alert than ever. Would any of us have remained there? Let us not slander our intelligence to that degree.[5]

"Much stress has been laid upon the fact that the accused offered a very large reward for the knife with which this murder was done; that no thief came forward to claim that extraordinary reward; that the latter fact was good circumstantial evidence that the claim that the knife had been stolen was a vanity and a fraud; that these details taken in connection with the memorable and apparently prophetic speech of the deceased concerning that knife, and the final discovery of that very knife in the fatal room where no living person was found present with the slaughtered man but the owner of the knife and his brother, form an indestructible chain of evidence which fixed the crime upon those unfortunate strangers.

"But I shall presently ask to be sworn, and shall testify that there was a large reward offered for the thief, also; that it was offered secretly

---

5) Let us not slander our intelligence to that degree: 우리들의 지성을 그만큼이나 비하하지 맙시다

and not advertised; that this fact was indiscreetly mentioned—or at least tacitly admitted in what was supposed to be safe circumstances, but may not have been. The thief may have been present himself." [Tom Driscoll had been looking at the speaker, but dropped his eyes at this point.]" "In that case he would retain the knife in his possession, not daring to offer it for sale, or for pledge in a pawn shop." [There was a nodding of heads among the audience by way of admission that this was not a bad stroke.] "I shall prove to the satisfaction of the jury that there was a person in Judge Driscoll's room several minutes before the accused entered it." [This produced a strong sensation; the last drowsy-head in the courtroom roused up now, and made preparation to listen.] "If it shall seem necessary, I will prove by the Misses Clarkson that they met a veiled person—ostensibly a woman coming out of the back gate a few minutes after the cry for help was heard. This person was not a woman, but a man dressed in woman's clothes." Another sensation. Wilson had his eye on Tom when he hazarded this guess,[6] to see what effect it would produce. He was satisfied with the result, and said to himself, "It was a success—he's hit!"

"The object of that person in that house was robbery, not murder. It is true that the safe was not open, but there was an ordinary tin cashbox on the table, with three thousand dollars in it. It is easily supposable that the thief was concealed in the house; that he knew of this box, and of its owner's habit of counting its contents and arranging his accounts at night—if he had that habit, which I do not assert, of course—that he tried to take the box while its owner slept, but made a noise and was seized, and had to use the knife to save himself from capture; and that he fled without his booty because he heard help coming.

---

6) when he hazarded this guess: 그의 추측을 과감히 말했을 때

"I have now done with my theory, and will proceed to the evidences by which I propose to try to prove its soundness." Wilson took up several of his strips of glass. When the audience recognized these familiar mementoes of Pudd'nhead's old-time childish "puttering"[8] and folly, the tense and funereal interest vanished out of their faces, and the house burst into volleys of relieving and refreshing laughter, and Tom chirked up and joined in the fun himself; but Wilson was apparently not disturbed. He arranged his records on the table before him, and said—

"I beg the indulgence of the court while I make a few remarks in explanation of some evidence which I am about to introduce, and which I shall presently ask to be allowed to verify under oath on the witness stand. Every human being carries with him from his cradle to his grave certain physical marks which do not change their character, and by which he can always be identified—and that without shade of doubt or question. These marks are his signature, his physiological autograph, so to speak, and this autograph can not be counterfeited, nor can he disguise it or hide it away, nor can it become illegible by the wear and mutations of time. This signature is not his face—age can change that beyond recognition; it is not his hair, for that can fall out; it is not his height, for duplicates of that exist; it is not his form, for duplicates of that exist also, whereas this signature is each man's very own there is no duplicate of it among the swarming populations of the globe!" [The audience were interested once more.]

"This autograph consists of the delicate lines or corrugations with which Nature marks the insides of the hands and the soles of the feet. If you will look at the balls of your fingers—you that have very sharp eyesight—you will observe that these dainty, curving lines lie close

7) puttering: 빈둥거림

together, like those that indicate the borders of oceans in maps, and that they form various clearly defined patterns, such as arches, circles, long curves, whorls, etc., and that these patters differ on the different fingers." [Every man in the room had his hand up to the light now, and his head canted to one side, and was minutely scrutinizing the balls of his fingers; there were whispered ejaculations of, 'Why, it's so—I never noticed that before!'] "The patterns on the right hand are not the same as those on the left." [Ejaculations of 'Why, that's so, too!'] Taken finger for finger,[8] your patterns differ from your neighbor's." [Comparisons were made all over the house—even the judge and jury were absorbed in this curious work.] "The patterns of a twin's right hand are not the same as those on his left. One twin's patterns are never the same as his fellow twin's patters—the jury will find that the patterns upon the finger-balls of the twins' hands follow this rule." [An examination of the twins' hands was begun at once.] "You have often heard of twins who were so exactly alike that when dressed alike their own parents could not tell them apart. Yet there was never a twin born into this world that did not carry from birth to death a sure identifier in this mysterious and marvelous natal autograph. That once known to you, his fellow twin could never personate him and deceive you."

Wilson stopped and stood silent. Inattention dies a quick and sure death[9] when a speaker does that. The stillness gives warning that something is coming. All palms and finger-balls went down now, all slouching forms straightened, all heads came up, all eyes were fastened upon Wilson's face. He waited yet one, two, three moments, to let his pause complete and perfect its spell upon the house; then, when

---

8) Taken finger for finger: 손가락 한개 한개를 비교해 보면

9) Inattention dies a quick and sure death: 부주의는 즉각 완전히 사라졌다=즉각 완전히 주의를 기울였다

through the profound hush he could hear the ticking of the clock on the wall, he put out his hand and took the Indian knife by the blade and held it aloft where all could see the sinister spots upon its ivory handle; then he said, in a level and passionless voice—

"Upon this haft stands the assassin's natal autograph, written in the blood of that helpless and unoffending old man who loved you and whom you all loved. There is but one man in the whole earth whose hand can duplicate that crimson sign"—he paused and raised his eyes to the pendulum swinging back and forth "and please God we will produce that man in this room before the clock strikes noon!"

Stunned, distraught, unconscious of its own movement, the house half rose, as if expecting to see the murderer appear at the door, and a breeze of muttered ejaculations swept the place. "Order in the court! —sit down!" This from the sheriff. He was obeyed, and quiet reigned again. Wilson stole a glance at Tom, and said to himself, "He is flying signals of distress now;[10] even people who despise him are pitying him; they think this is a hard ordeal for a young fellow who has lost his benefactor by so cruel a stroke—and they are right." He resumed his speech:

"For more than twenty years I have amused my compulsory leisure with collecting these curious physical signatures in this town. At my house I have hundreds upon hundreds of them. Each and every one is labeled with name and date; not labeled the next day or even the next hour, but in the very minute that the impression was taken. When I go upon the witness stand I will repeat under oath the things which I am now saying. I have the finger-prints of the court, the sheriff, and every member of the jury. There is hardly a person in this room, white or black, whose natal signature I cannot produce, and not one of them

---

10) He is flying signals of distress now: 그는 이제 괴롭다는 신호를 보내고 있군

can so disguise himself that I cannot pick him out from a multitude of his fellow creatures and unerringly identify him by his hands. And if he and I should live to be a hundred[11] I could still do it." [The interest of the audience was steadily deepening now.]

"I have studied some of these signatures so much that I know them as well as the bank cashier knows the autograph of his oldest customer. While I turn my back now, I beg that several persons will be so good as to pass their fingers through their hair, and then press them upon one of the panes of the window near the jury, and that among them the accused may set *their* finger-marks. Also, I beg that these experimenters, or others, will set their finger-marks upon another pane, and add again the marks of the accused, but not placing them in the same order or relation to the other signatures as before—for, by one chance in a million, a person might happen upon the right marks by pure guesswork, once, therefore I wish to be tested twice."

He turned his back, and the two panes were quickly covered with delicately lined oval spots, but visible only to such persons as could get a dark background for them—the foliage of a tree, outside, for instance. Then, upon call, Wilson went to the window, made his examination, and said—

"This is Count Luigi's right hand; this one, three signatures below, is his left. Here is Count Angelo's right; down here is his left. Now for the other pane: here and here are Count Luigi's, here and here are his brother's." He faced about. "Am I right?"

A deafening explosion of applause was the answer. The bench said—

"This certainly approaches the miraculous!"

Wilson turned to the window again and remarked, pointing with his finger—

---

11) if he and I should live to be a hundred: 그와 내가 100살까지 살더라도

"This is the signature of Mr. Justice Robinson." [Applause.] This, of Constable Blake." [Applause.] "This of John Mason, juryman." [Applause.] "This, of the sheriff." [Applause.] "I cannot name the others, but I have them all at home, named and dated, and could identify them all by my finger print records."

He moved to his place through a storm of applause—which the sheriff stopped, and also made the people sit down, for they were all standing and struggling to see, of course. Court, jury, sheriff, and everybody had been too absorbed in observing Wilson's performance to attend to the audience earlier.

"Now then," said Wilson, "I have here the natal autographs of the two children—thrown up to ten times the natural size[12)] by the pantograph, so that anyone who can see at all can tell the markings apart at a glance. We will call the children A and B. Here are A's finger-marks, taken at the age of five months. Here they are again taken at seven months." [Tom started[13)]] "They are alike, you see. Here are B's at five months, and also at seven months. They, too, exactly copy each other, but the patterns are quite different from A's, you observe. I shall refer to these again presently, but we will turn them face down now.

"Here, thrown up ten sizes, are the natal autographs of the two persons who are here before you accused of murdering Judge Driscoll. I made these pantograph copies last night, and will so swear when I go upon the witness stand. I ask the jury to compare them with the finger-marks of the accused upon the window panes, and tell the court if they are the same."

He passed a powerful magnifying glass to the foreman. One jury man after another took the cardboard and the glass and made the

12) thrown up to ten times the natural size: 10배로 확대된

comparison. Then the foreman said to the judge:

"Your honor, we are all agreed that they are identical."

Wilson said to the foreman—

"Please turn that cardboard face down, and take this one, and compare it searchingly, by the magnifier, with the fatal signature upon the knife handle, and report your finding to the court."

Again the jury made minute examinations, and again reported—

"We find them to be exactly identical, your honor."

Wilson turned toward the counsel for the prosecution, and there was a clearly recognizable note of warning in his voice when he said—

"May it please the court, the state has claimed, strenuously and persistently, that the blood-stained finger-prints upon that knife handle were left there by the assassin of Judge Driscoll. You have heard us grant that claim, and welcome it." He turned to the jury: "Compare the finger-prints of the accused with the finger-prints left by the assassin—and report."

The comparison began. As it proceeded, all movement and all sound ceased, and the deep silence of an absorbed and waiting suspense settled upon the house; and when at last the words came—

"They do not even resemble," a thunder crash of applause followed and the house sprang to its feet, but was quickly repressed by official force and brought to order again. Tom was altering his position every few minutes now, but none of his changes brought repose nor any small trifle of comfort. When the house's attention was become fixed once more, Wilson said gravely, indicating the twins with a gesture—

"These men are innocent—I have no further concern with them." [Another outbreak of applause began, but was promptly checked.][14) "We will now proceed to find the guilty. [Tom's eyes were starting

---

13) started: 움찔하다.

from their sockets—yes, it was a cruel day for the bereaved youth, everybody thought.] "We will return to the infant autographs of A and B. I will ask the jury to take these large pantograph facsimilies of A's, marked five months and seven months. Do they tally?"

The foreman responded—

"Perfectly."

"Now examine this pantograph, taken at eight months, and also marked A. Does it tally with the other two?"

The surprised response was—

"*No—They differ widely*!"

"You are quite right. Now take these two pantographs of B's autograph, marked five months and seven months. Do they tally with each other?"

"Yes—perfectly."

"Take this third pantograph marked B, eight months'. Does it tally with B's other two?"

"*By no means*!"

"Do you know how to account for those strange discrepancies? I will tell you. For a purpose unknown to us, but probably a selfish one, somebody changed those children in the cradle."

This produced a vast sensation, naturally; Roxana was astonished at this admirable guess, but not disturbed by it. To guess the exchange was one thing, to guess who did it quite another. Pudd'nhead Wilson could do wonderful things, no doubt, but he couldn't do impossible ones. Safe? She was perfectly safe. She smiled privately.

"Between the ages of seven months and eight months those children were changed in the cradle"—he made one of this effect-collecting pauses, and added—"and the person who did it is in this house!"

---

14) was promptly checked: 즉시 제지받았다

Roxy's pulses stood still! The house was thrilled as with an electric shock, and the people half rose as if to seek a glimpse of the person who had made that exchange. Tom was growing limp; the life seemed oozing out of him. Wilson resumed:

"A was put into B's cradle in the nursery; B was transferred to the kitchen and became a negro and a slave"—[Sensation—confusion of angry ejaculations]—"but within a quarter of an hour he will stand before you white and free!" [Burst of applause, checked by the officers.] "From seven months onward until now, A has still been a usurper, and in my finger-record he bears B's name. Here is his pantograph at the age of twelve. Compare it with the assassin's signature upon the knife handle. Do they tally?"

The foreman answered—

"*To the minutest detail!*"

Wilson said, solemnly—

"The murderer of your friend and mine—York Driscoll, of the generous hand and the kindly spirit—sits among you. Valet de Chambre, negro and slave—falsely called Thomas à Becket Driscoll—make upon the window the finger-prints that will hang you!"

Tom turned his ashen face imploring toward the speaker, made some impotent movements with his white lips, then slid limp and lifeless to the floor.

Wilson broke the awed silence with the words—

"There is no need. He has confessed."

Roxy flung herself upon her knees, covered her face with her hands, and out through her sobs the words struggled—

"De Lord have mercy on me, po' misasble sinner dat I is!"

The clock struck twelve.

The court rose; the new prisoner, handcuffed, was removed.

CONCLUSION

It is often the case that the man who can't tell a lie thinks he is the best judge of one.

- Pudd'nhead Wilson's Calendar

October 12, the Discovery.. It was wonderful to find America, but it would have been more wonderful to miss it.

- Pudd'nhead Wilson's Calendar

The town sat up all night[1] to discuss the amazing events of the day and swap guesses as to when Tom's trial would begin. Troop after troop of citizens came to serenade Wilson, and require a speech, and shout themselves hoarse over every sentence that fell from his lips for all his sentences were golden, now, all were marvelous. His long fight against hard luck and prejudice was ended; he was a made man

1) sat up all night: 밤을 샜다

for good.[2] And as each of these roaring gangs of enthusiasts marched away, some remorseful member of it was quite sure to raise his voice and say—

"And this is the man the likes of us[3] have called a pudd'nhead for more than twenty years. He has resigned from that position, friends."

"Yes, but it isn't vacant   we're elected."[4]

The twins were heroes of romance, now, and with rehabilitated reputations. But they were weary of Western adventure, and straightway retired to Europe.

Roxy's heart was broken. The young fellow upon whom she had inflicted twenty-three years of slavery continued the false heir's pension of thirty-five dollars a month to her, but her hurts were too deep for money to heal; the spirit in her eye was quenched, her martial bearing departed with it, and the voice of her laughter ceased in the land. In her church and its affairs she found her only solace.

The real heir suddenly found himself rich and free, but in a most embarrassing situation. He could neither read nor write, and his speech was the basest dialect of the negro quarter.[5] His gait, his attitudes, his gestures, his bearing, his laugh—all were vulgar and uncouth; his manners were the manners of a slave. Money and fine clothes could not mend these defects or cover them up; they only made them the more glaring and the more pathetic. The poor fellow could not endure the terrors of the white man's parlor, and felt at home and at peace nowhere but in the kitchen. The family pew[6] was a misery to him, yet he could nevermore enter into the solacing refuge

---

2) he was a made man for good: 그는 완전히 성공한 사람이 되었다
3) the likes of us: 우리같은 사람들
4) we're elected: 우리가 (멍청이 자리에) 당선되었다
5) the basest dialect of the negro quarter: 흑인 구역의 가장 천한 언어
6) The family pew: (교회의) 가족석

of the "nigger gallery"[7]—that was closed to him for good and all. But we cannot follow his curious fate further that would be a long story.

The false heir made a full confession and was sentenced to imprisonment for life. But now a complication came up. The Percy Driscoll estate was in such a crippled shape when its owner died that it could pay only sixty percent of its great indebtedness, and was settled at that rate. But the creditors came forward now, and complained that inasmuch as through an error for which *they* were in no way to blame the false heir was not inventoried at the time with the rest of the property, great wrong and loss had thereby been inflicted upon them. They rightly claimed that "Tom" was lawfully their property and had been so for eight years; that they had already lost sufficiently in being deprived of his services during that long period, and ought not to be required to add anything to that loss; that if he had been delivered up to them in the first place, they would have sold him and he could not have murdered Judge Driscoll; therefore it was not he that had really committed the murder, the guilt lay with the erroneous inventory. Everybody saw that there was reason in this.[8] Everybody granted that if "Tom" were white and free it would be unquestionably right to punish him—it would be no loss to anybody; but to shut up a valuable slave for life—that was quite another matter.

7) nigger gallery: (교회의) 흑인석
8) Everybody saw that there was reason in this: 모두 그 주장에 일리가 있다고 생각했다

As soon as the Governor understood the case, he pardoned Tom at once, and the creditors sold him down the river.

Those Extraordinary Twins

A man who is not born with the novel-writing gift has a troublesome time of it when he tries to build a novel. I know this from experience. He has no clear idea of his story; in fact he has no story. He merely has some people in his mind, and an incident or two, also a locality. He knows these people, he knows the selected locality, and he trusts that he can plunge those people into those incidents with interesting results. So he goes to work. To write a novel? No—that is a thought which comes later; in the beginning he is only proposing to tell a little tale; a very little tale; a six-page tale. But as it is a tale which he is not acquainted with, and can only find out what it is by listening as it goes along telling itself, it is more than apt to go on and on and on till it spreads itself into a book. I know about this, because it has happened to me so many times.

And I have noticed another thing: that as the short tale grows into the long tale, the original intention (or motif) is apt to get abolished and find itself superseded by a quite different one. It was so in the case of a magazine sketch which I once started to write—a funny and fantastic sketch about a prince and a pauper; it presently assumed a grave cast of its own accord, and in that new shape spread itself out into a book. Much the same thing happened with "Pudd'nhead Wilson." I had a sufficiently hard time with that tale, because it changed itself from a farce to tragedy while I was going along with it—a most embarrassing circumstance. But what was a great deal worse was, that it was not one story, but two stories tangled together; and they obstructed and interrupted each other at every turn and created no end of confusion and annoyance. I could not offer the book for publication, for I was afraid it would unseat the reader's reason. I did not know what was the matter with it, for I had not noticed, as yet, that it was two stories in one. It took me months to make that discovery. I carried the manuscript back and forth across the Atlantic two or three times, and read it and studied over it on shipboard; and at last I saw where the difficulty lay. I had no further trouble. I pulled one of the stories out by the roots, and left the other one—a kind of literary Caesarean operation.

Would the reader care to know something about the story which I pulled out? He has been told many a time how the born-and-trained novelist works. Won't he let me round and complete his knowledge by telling him how the jack-leg does it?

Originally the story was called "Those Extraordinary Twins." I meant to make it very short. I had seen a picture of a youthful Italian "freak" or "freaks" which was—or which were—on exhibition in our cities—a combination consisting of two heads and four arms joined to a single body and a single pair of legs—and I thought I would write an extravagantly fantastic little story with this freak of nature for hero—or heroes—a silly young Miss for heroine, and two old ladies and two boys for the minor parts. I lavishly elaborated these people and their doings, of course. But the tale kept spreading along, and spreading along, and other people got to intruding themselves and taking up more and more room with their talk and their affairs.

Among them came a stranger named Pudd'nhead Wilson, and a woman named Roxana; and presently the doings of these two pushed up into prominence a young fellow named Tom Driscoll, whose proper place was away in the obscure background. Before the book was half finished those three were taking things almost entirely into their own hands and working the whole tale as a private venture of their own—a tale which they had nothing at all to do with, by rights.

When the book was finished and I came to look around to see what had become of the team I had originally started out with—Aunt Patsy Cooper, Aunt Betsy Hale, the two boys, and Rowena the light-weight heroine—they were nowhere to be seen; they had disappeared from the story some time or other. I hunted about and found them—found them stranded, idle, forgotten, and permanently useless. It was very awkward. It was awkward all around; but more particularly in the case of Rowena, because there was a love-match on, between her and one of the twins that constituted the freak, and I had worked it up to a blistering heat and thrown in a quite dramatic love-quarrel, wherein Rowena scathingly denounced her betrothed for getting drunk, and scoffed at his explanation of how it had happened, and wouldn't listen to it, and had driven him from her in the usual "forever" way; and now here she sat crying and broken-hearted; for she had found that he had spoken only the truth; that it was not he, but the other half of the freak, that had drunk the liquor that made him drunk; that her half was a prohibitionist and had never drunk a drop in his life, and, although tight as a brick three days in the week, was wholly innocent of blame; and indeed, when sober, was constantly doing all he could to reform his brother, the other half, who never got any satisfaction out of drinking, anyway, because liquor never affected him. Yes, here she was, stranded with that deep injustice of hers torturing her poor torn heart.

I didn't know what to do with her. I was as sorry for her as anybody could be, but the campaign was over, the book was finished, she was sidetracked, and there was no possible way of crowding her in, anywhere. I could not leave her there, of course; it would not do. After spreading her out so, and making such a to-do over her affairs, it would be absolutely necessary to account to the reader for her. I thought and thought and studied and studied; but I arrived at nothing. I finally saw plainly that there was really no way but one—I must simply give her the grand bounce. It grieved me to do it, for after associating with her so much I had come to kind of like her after a fashion, notwithstanding she was such an ass and said such stupid irritating things and was so nauseatingly sentimental. Still it had to be done. So, at the top of Chapter XVII, I put in a "Calendar" remark concerning July Fourth, and began the chapter with this statistic:

"Rowena went out in the back yard after supper to see the fireworks and fell down the well and got drowned."

It seemed abrupt, but I thought maybe the reader wouldn't notice it, because I changed the subject right away to something else. Anyway it loosened up Rowena from where she was stuck and got her out of the way, and that was the main thing. It seemed a prompt good way of weeding out people that had got stalled, and a plenty good enough way for those others; so I hunted up the two boys and said "they went out back one night to stone the cat and fell down the well and got drowned." Next I searched around and found old Aunt Patsy Cooper and Aunt Betsy Hale where they were aground, and said "they went out back one night to visit the sick and fell down the well and got drowned." I was going to drown some of the others, but I gave up the idea, partly because I believed that if I kept that up it would arouse attention, and perhaps sympathy with those people, and partly because it was not a large well and would not hold any more anyway.

Still the story was unsatisfactory. Here was a set of new characters who were become inordinately prominent and who persisted in remaining so to the end; and back yonder was an older set who made a large noise and a great to-do for a little while and then suddenly played out utterly and fell down the well. There was a radical defect somewhere, and I must search it out and cure it.

The defect turned out to be the one already spoken of—two stories in one, a farce and a tragedy. So I pulled out the farce and left the tragedy. This left the original team in, but only as mere names, not as characters. Their prominence was wholly gone; they were not even worth drowning; so I removed that detail. Also I took those twins apart and made two separate men of them. They had no occasion to have foreign names now, but it was too much trouble to remove them all through, so I left them christened as they were and made no explanation.

The Suppresed Farce

CHAPTER 1

The conglomerate twins were brought on the the stage in Chapter I of the original extravaganza. Aunt Patsy Cooper has received their letter applying for board and lodging, and Rowena, her daughter, insane with joy, is begging for a hearing of it:

"Well, set down then, and be quiet a minute and don't fly around so; it fairly makes me tired to see you. It starts off so: 'HONORED MADAM'—"

"I like that, ma, don't you? It shows they're high-bred."

"Yes, I noticed that when I first read it. 'My brother and I have seen your advertisement, by chance, in a copy of your local journal—'"

"It's so beautiful and smooth, ma—don't you think so?"

"Yes, seems so to me—'and beg leave to take the room you offer. We are twenty-four years of age, and twins—'"

"Twins! How sweet! I do hope they are handsome, and I just know they are! Don't you hope they are, ma?"

"Land, I ain't particular. 'We are Italians by birth—'"

"It's so romantic! Just think there's never been one in this town, and everybody will want to see them, and they're all ours! Think of that!"

"—'but have lived long in the various countries of Europe, and several years in the United States.'"

"Oh, just think what wonders they've seen, ma! Won't it be good to hear them talk?"

"I reckon so; yes, I reckon so. 'Our names are Luigi and Angelo

Capello—'"

"Beautiful, perfectly beautiful! Not like Jones and Robinson and those horrible names."

"'You desire but one guest, but dear madam, if you will allow us to pay for two we will not discommode you. We will sleep together in the same bed. We have always been used to this, and prefer it.' And then he goes on to say they will be down Thursday."

"And this is Tuesday—I don't know how I'm ever going to wait, ma! The time does drag along so, and I'm so dying to see them! Which of them do you reckon is the tallest, ma?"

"How do you s'pose I can tell, child? Mostly they are the same size—twins are."

"'Well then, which do you reckon is the best looking?"

"Goodness knows—I don't."

"I think Angelo is; it's the prettiest name, anyway. Don't you think it's a sweet name, ma?"

"Yes, it's well enough. I'd like both of them better if I knew the way to pronounce them—the Eyetalian way, I mean. The Missouri way and the Eyetalian way is different, I judge."

"Maybe—yes. It's Luigi that writes the letter. What do you reckon is the reason Angelo didn't write it?"

"Why, how can I tell? What's the difference who writes it, so long as it's done?"

"Oh, I hope it wasn't because he is sick! You don't think he is sick, do you, ma?"

"Sick your granny; what's to make him sick?"

"Oh, there's never any telling. These foreigners with that kind of names are so delicate, and of course that kind of names are not suited to our climate—you wouldn't expect it."

[And so-on and so-on, no end. The time drags along; Thursday comes; the boat arrives in a pouring storm toward midnight.]

At last there was a knock at the door and the anxious family jumped to open it. Two negro men entered, each carrying a trunk, and proceeded upstairs toward the guest-room. Then followed a stupefying apparition—a double-headed human creature with four arms, one body, and a single pair of legs!

It—or they, as you please—bowed with elaborate foreign formality, but the Coopers could not respond immediately; they were paralyzed. At this moment there came from the rear of the group a fervent ejaculation—"My lan'!"—followed by a crash of crockery, and the slave-wench Nancy stood petrified and staring, with a tray of wrecked tea-things at her feet. The incident broke the spell, and brought the family to consciousness. The beautiful heads of the new-comer bowed again, and one of them said with easy grace and dignity:

"I crave the honor, Madam and Miss, to introduce to you my brother, Count Luigi Capello," (the other head bowed), "and myself—Count Angelo; and at the same time offer sincere apologies for the lateness of our coming, which was unavoidable," and both heads bowed again.

The poor old lady was in a whirl of amazement and confusion, but she managed to stammer out:

"I'm sure I'm glad to make your acquaintance, sir—I mean, gentlemen. As for the delay, it is nothing, don't mention it. This is my daughter Rowena, sir—gentlemen. Please step into the parlor and sit down and have a bite and sup; you are dreadful wet and must be uncomfortable—both of you, I mean."

But to the old lady's relief they courteously excused themselves, saying it would be wrong to keep the family out of their beds longer; then each head bowed in turn and uttered a friendly good night, and the singular figure moved away in the wake of Rowena's small brothers, who bore candles, and disappeared up the stairs.

The widow tottered into the parlor and sank into a chair with a gasp, and Rowena followed, tongue-tied and dazed. The two sat silent in the throbbing summer heat, unconscious of the million-voiced music of the mosquitoes, unconscious of the roaring gale, the lashing and thrashing of the rain along the windows and the roof, the white glare of the lightnings, the tumultuous booming and bellowing of the thunder, conscious of nothing but that prodigy, that uncanny apparition that had come and gone so suddenly—that weird strange thing that was so soft-spoken and so gentle of manner and yet had shaken them up like an earthquake with the shock of its gruesome aspect. At last a cold little shudder quivered along down the widow's meager frame and she said in a weak voice:

"Ugh, it was awful—just the mere look of that phillipena!" Rowena did not answer. Her faculties were still caked; she had not yet found her voice. Presently the widow said, a little resentfully:

"Always been used to sleeping together—in fact, *prefer* it. And I was thinking it was to accommodate me. I thought it was very good of them, whereas a person situated as that young man is—"

"Ma, you oughtn't to begin by getting up a prejudice against him.

I'm sure he is good-hearted and means well. Both of his faces show it."

"I'm not so certain about that. The one on the left—I mean the one on *its* left—hasn't near as good a face, in my opinion, as its brother."

"That's Luigi."

"Yes, Luigi; anyway it's the dark-skinned one; the one that was west of his brother when they stood in the door. Up to all kinds of mischief and disobedience when he was a boy, I'll be bound. I lay his mother had trouble to lay her hand on him when she wanted him. But the one on the right is as good as gold, I can see that."

"That's Angelo."

"Yes, Angelo, I reckon, though I can't tell t'other from which by their names, yet awhile. But it's the right-hand one—the blonde one. He has such kind blue eyes, and curly copper hair and fresh complexion—"

"And such a noble face!—oh, it *is* a noble face, ma, just royal, you may say! And beautiful—deary me, how beautiful! But both are that; the dark one's as beautiful as a picture. There's no such wonderful faces and handsome heads in this town—none that even begin. And such hands!—especially Angelo's—so shapely and—"

"Stuff, how could you tell which they belonged to?—they had gloves on."

"Why, didn't I see them take off their hats?"

"That don't signify. They might have taken off each other's hats. Nobody could tell. There was just a wormy squirming of arms in the air—seemed to be a couple of dozen of them, all writhing at once, and it just made me dizzy to see them go."

"Why, ma, I hadn't any difficulty. There's two arms on each shoulder—"

"There, now. One arm on each shoulder belongs to each of the creatures, don't it? For a person to have two arms on one shoulder wouldn't do him any good, would it? Of course not. Each has an arm on each shoulder. Now then, you tell me which of them belongs to which, if you can. *They* don't know, themselves—they just work whichever arm comes handy. Of course they do; especially if they are in a hurry and can't stop to think which belongs to which."

The mother seemed to have the rights of the argument, so the daughter abandoned the struggle. Presently the widow rose with a yawn and said: "Poor thing, I hope it won't catch cold; it was powerful wet, just drenched, you may say. I hope it has left its boots outside, so they can be dried." Then she gave a little start, and looked perplexed.

"Now I remember I heard one of them ask Joe to call him at half after seven—I think it was the one on the left—no, it was the one to the east of the other one—but I didn't hear the other one say any thing. I wonder if he wants to be called too. Do you reckon it's too late to ask?"

"Why, ma, it's not necessary. Calling one is calling both. If one gets up, the other's *got* to."

"Sho, of course; I never thought of that. Well, come along, maybe we can get some sleep, but I don't know, I'm so shook up with what we've been through."

The stranger had made an impression on the boys, too. They had a word of talk as they were getting to bed. Henry, the gentle, the humane, said:

"I feel ever so sorry for it, don't you, Joe?"

But Joe was a boy of this world, active, enterprising, and had a theatrical side to him:

"Sorry? Why, how you talk! It can't stir a step without attracting attention. It's just grand!"

Henry said, reproachfully:

"Instead of pitying it, Joe, you talk as if—"

"Talk as if *what*? I know one thing mighty certain: if you can fix me so I can eat for two and only have to stub toes for one, I ain't going to fool away no such chance just for sentiment."

The twins were wet and tired, and they proceeded to undress without any preliminary remarks. The abundance of sleeve made the partnership coat hard to get off, for it was like skinning a tarantula; but it came at last, after much tugging and perspiring. The mutual vest followed. Then the brothers stood up before the glass, and each took off his own cravat and collar. The collars were of the standing kind, and came high up under the ears, like the sides of a wheelbarrow, as required by the fashion of the day. The cravats were as broad as a bank-bill, with fringed ends which stood far out to right and left like the wings of a dragon-fly, and this also was strictly in accordance with the fashion of the time. Each cravat, as to color, was in perfect taste, so far as its owner's complexion was concerned—a delicate pink, in the case of the blonde brother, a violent scarlet in the case of the brunette—but as a combination they broke all the laws of taste known to civilization. Nothing more fiendish and irreconcilable than those shrieking and blaspheming colors could have been contrived, The wet boots gave no end of trouble—to Luigi. When they were off at last, Angelo said, with bitterness:

"I wish you wouldn't wear such tight boots, they hurt my feet." Luigi answered with indifference:

"My friend, when I am in command of our body, I choose my apparel according to my own convenience, as I have remarked more than several times already. When you are in command, I beg you will do as you please."

Angelo was hurt, and the tears came into his eyes. There was gentle reproach in his voice, but, not anger, when he replied:

"Luigi, I often consult your wishes, but you never consult mine.

When I am in command I treat you as a guest; I try to make you feel at home; when you are in command you treat me as an intruder, you make me feel unwelcome. It embarrasses me cruelly in company, for I can see that people notice it and comment on it."

"Oh, damn the people," responded the brother languidly, and with the air of one who is tired of the subject.

A slight shudder shook the frame of Angelo, but he said nothing and the conversation ceased. Each buttoned his own share of the night shirt in silence; then Luigi, with Paine's "Age of Reason" in his hand, sat down in one chair and put his feet in another and lit his pipe, while Angelo took his "Whole Duty of Man", and both began to read. Angelo presently began to cough; his coughing increased and became mixed with gaspings for breath, and he was finally obliged to make an appeal to his brother's humanity:

"Luigi, if you would only smoke a little milder tobacco, I am sure I could learn not to mind it in time, but this is so strong, and the pipe is so rank that—"

"Angelo, I wouldn't be such a baby! I have learned to smoke in a week, and the trouble is already over with me; if you would try, you could learn too, and then you would stop spoiling my comfort with your everlasting complaints."

"Ah, brother, that is a strong word—everlasting—and isn't quite fair. I only complain when I suffocate; you know I don't complain when we are in the open air."

"Well, anyway, you could learn to smoke yourself."

"But my *principles*, Luigi, you forget my principles. You would not have me do a thing which I regard as a sin?"

"Oh, d-bosh!"

The conversation ceased again, for Angelo was sick and discouraged and strangling; but after some time he closed his book and asked

Luigi to sing "From Greenland's Icy Mountains" with him, but he would not, and when he tried to sing by himself Luigi did his best to drown his plaintive tenor with a rude and rollicking song delivered in a thundering bass.

After the singing there was silence, and neither brother was happy. Before blowing the light out Luigi swallowed half a tumbler of whisky, and Angelo, whose sensitive organization could not endure intoxicants of any kind, took a pill to keep it from giving him the headache.

CHAPTER 2

The family sat in the breakfast room waiting for the twins to come down. The widow was quiet, the daughter was alive with happy excitement. She said:

"Ah, they're a boon, ma, just a boon! don't you think so?"

"Laws, I hope so, I don't know."

"Why, ma, yes you do. They're so fine, and handsome, and high-bred, and polite, so every way superior to our gawks here in this village; why, they'll make life different from what it was—so humdrum and commonplace, you know—oh, you may be sure they're full of accomplishments, and knowledge of the world, and all that, that will be an immense advantage to society here. Don't you think so, ma?"

"Mercy on me, how should I know, and I've hardly set eyes on them yet." After a pause she added, "They made considerable noise after they went up."

"Noise? Why, ma, they were singing! And it was beautiful, too."

"Oh, it was well enough, but too mixed-up, seemed to me."

"Now, ma, honor bright, did you ever hear 'Greenland's Icy Mountains' sung sweeter—now did you?"

"If it had been sung by itself, it would have been uncommon sweet, I don't deny it; but what they wanted to mix it up with 'Old Bob Ridley' for, I can't make out. Why, they don't go together, at all. They are not of the same nature. 'Bob Ridley' is a common rackety slam-bang secular song, one of the rippingest and rantingest and noisiest there is. I am no judge of music, and I don't claim it, but in my opinion nobody can make those two songs go together right."

"Why, ma, I thought—"

"It don't make any difference what you thought, it can't be done. They tried it, and to my mind it was a failure. I never heard such a crazy uproar; seemed to me, sometimes, the roof would come off; and as for the cats—well, I've lived a many a year, and seen cats aggravated in more ways than one, but I've never seen cats take on the way they took on last night."

"Well, I don't think that that goes for anything, ma, because it is the nature of cats that any sound that is unusual—"

"Unusual! You may well call it so. Now if they are going to sing duets every night, I do hope they will both sing the same tune at the same time, for in my opinion a duet that is made up of two different tunes is a mistake; especially when the tunes ain't any kin to one another, that way."

"But, ma, I think it must be a foreign custom; and it must be right too; and the best way, because they have had every opportunity to know what is right, and it don't stand to reason that with their education they would do anything but what the highest musical authorities have sanctioned. You can't help but admit that, ma."

The argument was formidably strong; the old lady could not find any way around it; so, after thinking it over awhile she gave in with a sigh of discontent, and admitted that the daughter's position was probably correct. Being vanquished, she had no mind to continue the topic at that disadvantage, and was about to seek a change when a change came of itself. A footstep was heard on the stairs, and she said:

"There—he's coming!"

"*They*, ma—you ought to say *they*—it's nearer right."

The new lodger, rather shoutingly dressed but looking superbly handsome, stepped with courtly carnage into the trim little breakfast room and put out all his cordial arms at once, like one of those pocket-knives with a multiplicity of blades, and shook hands with the whole family simultaneously. He was so easy and pleasant and hearty that all embarrassment presently thawed away and disappeared, and a cheery feeling of friendliness and comradeship took its place. He—or preferably they—were asked to occupy the seat of honor at the foot of the table. They consented with thanks, and carved the beefsteak with one set of their hands while they distributed it at the same time with the other set.

"Will you have coffee, gentlemen, or tea?"

"Coffee for Luigi, if you please, madam, tea for me."

"Cream and sugar?"

"For me, yes, madam; Luigi takes his coffee black. Our natures differ a good deal from each other, and our tastes also."

The first time the negro girl Nancy appeared in the door and saw the two heads turned in opposite directions and both talking at once, then saw the commingling arms feed potatoes into one mouth and coffee into the other at the same time, she had to pause and pull herself out of a faintness that came over her; but after that she held her grip and was able to wait on the table with fair courage.

Conversation fell naturally into the customary grooves. It was a little jerky, at first, because none of the family could get smoothly through a sentence without a wabble in it here and a break there, caused by some new surprise in the way of attitude or gesture on the part of the twins. The weather suffered the most. The weather was all finished up and disposed of, as a subject, before the simple Missourians had gotten sufficiently wonted to the spectacle of one body feeding two heads to feel composed and reconciled in the presence of so bizarre a miracle.

And even after everybody's mind became tranquilized there was still one slight distraction left: the hand that picked up a biscuit carried it to the wrong head, as often as any other way, and the wrong mouth devoured it. This was a puzzling thing, and marred the talk a little. It bothered the widow to such a degree that she presently dropped out of the conversation without knowing it, and fell to watching and guessing and talking to herself:

"Now that hand is going to take that coffee—to no, it's gone to the other mouth; I can't understand it; and now, here is the dark-complected hand with a potato in its fork, I'll see what goes with it—there, the light-complected head's got it, as sure as I live!"

Finally Rowena said:

"Ma, what is the matter with you? Are you dreaming about something?"

The old lady came to herself and blushed; then she explained with the first random thing that came into her mind:

"I saw Mr. Angelo take up Mr. Luigi's coffee, and I thought maybe he—shan't I give *you* a cup, Mr. Angelo?"

"Oh no, madam, I am very much obliged, but I never drink coffee, much as I would like to. You did see me take up Luigi's cup, it is true, but if you noticed, I didn't carry it to my mouth, but to his."

"Y-es, I thought you did: Did you mean to?"

"How?"

The widow was a little embarrassed again. She said:

"I don't know but what I'm foolish, and you mustn't mind; but you see, he got the coffee I was expecting to see you drink, and you got a potato that I thought he was going to get. So I thought it might be a mistake all around, and everybody getting what wasn't intended for him."

Both twins laughed and Luigi said:

"Dear madam, there wasn't any mistake. We are always helping each other that way. It is a great economy for us both; it saves time and labor. We have a system of signs which nobody can notice or understand but ourselves. If I am using both my hands and want some coffee, I make the sign and Angelo furnishes it to me; and you saw that when he needed a potato I delivered it."

"How convenient!"

"Yes, and often of the extremest value. Take these Mississippi boats, for instance. They are always overcrowded. There is table-room for only half of the passengers, therefore they have to set a second table for the second half. The stewards rush both parties, they give them no time to eat a satisfying meal, both divisions leave the table hungry. It isn't so with us. Angelo books himself for the one table, I book myself for the other. Neither of us eats anything at the other's table, but just simply works—works. Thus, you see there are four hands to feed Angelo, and the same four to feed me. Each of us eats two meals."

The old lady was dazed with admiration, and kept saying, "It is perfectly wonderful, perfectly wonderful!" and the boy Joe licked his chops enviously, but said nothing—at least aloud.

"Yes," continued Luigi, "our construction may have its disadvantages—in fact, *has*—but it also has its compensations, of one sort and another. Take travel, for instance. Travel is enormously expensive, in all countries; we have been obliged to do a vast deal of it—come, Angelo, don't put any more sugar in your tea, I'm just over one indigestion and don't want another right away—been obliged to do a deal of it, as I was saying. Well, we always travel as one person, since we occupy but one seat; so we save half the fare."

"How romantic!" interjected Rowena, with effusion.

"Yes, my dear young lady, and how practical too, and economical. In Europe, beds in the hotels are not charged with the board, but separately—another saving, for we stood to our rights and paid for the one bed only. The landlords often insisted that as both of us occupied the bed we ought—"

"No, they didn't," said Angelo. "They did it only twice, and in both cases it was a double bed—a rare thing in Europe—and the double bed gave them some excuse. Be fair to the landlords; twice doesn't constitute 'often.'"

"Well, that depends—that depends. I knew a man who fell down a well twice. He said he didn't mind the first time, but he thought the second time was once too often. Have I misused that word, Mrs. Cooper?"

"To tell the truth, I was afraid you had, but it seems to look, now, like you hadn't." She stopped, and was evidently struggling with the difficult problem a moment, then she added in the tone of one who is convinced without being converted, "It seems so, but I can't somehow tell why."

Rowena thought Luigi's retort was wonderfully quick and bright, and she remarked to herself with satisfaction that there wasn't any young native of Dawson's Landing that could have risen to the occasion like that. Luigi detected the applause in her face, and expressed his pleasure and his thanks with his eyes; and so eloquently withal, that the girl was proud and pleased, and hung out the delicate sign of it on her cheeks.

Luigi went on, with animation:

"Both of us get a bath for one ticket, theater seat for one ticket, pew-rent is on the same basis, but at peep-shows we pay double."

"We have much to be thankful for," said Angelo, impressively, with a reverent light in his eye and a reminiscent tone in his voice, "we have been greatly blessed. As a rule, what one of us has lacked, the other, by the bounty of Providence, has been able to supply. My brother is hardy, I am not; he is very masculine, assertive, aggressive; I am much less so. I am subject to illness, he is never ill. I cannot abide medicines, and cannot take them, but he has no prejudice against them, and—"

"Why, goodness gracious," interrupted the widow, "when you are sick, does he take the medicine for you?"

"Always, madam."

"Why, I never heard such a thing in my life! I think it's beautiful of you."

"Oh, madam, it's nothing, don't mention it, it's really nothing at all."

"But I say it's beautiful, and I stick to it!" cried the widow, with a speaking moisture in her eye. "A well brother to take the medicine for his poor sick brother—I wish I had such a son," and she glanced reproachfully at her boys. "I declare I'll never rest till I've shook you by the hand," and she scrambled out of her chair in a fever of generous enthusiasm, and made for the twins, blind with her tears, and began to shake. The boy Joe corrected her:

"You're shaking the wrong one, ma."

This flurried her, but she made a swift change and went on shaking.

"Got the wrong one again, ma," said the boy.

"Oh, shut up, can't you!" said the widow, embarrassed and irritated. "Give me *all* your hands, I want to shake them all; for I know you are both just as good as you can be."

It was a victorious thought, a master-stroke of diplomacy, though that never occurred to her and she cared nothing for diplomacy. She shook the four hands in turn cordially, and went back to her place in a state of high and fine exultation that made her look young and handsome.

"Indeed I owe everything to Luigi," said Angelo, affectionately. "But for him I could not have survived our boyhood days, when we were friendless and poor—ah, so poor! We lived from hand to mouth—lived on the coarse fare of unwilling charity, and for weeks and weeks together not a morsel of food passed my lips, for its character revolted me and I could not eat it. But for Luigi I should have died. He ate for us both."

"How noble!" sighed Rowena.

"Do you hear that?" said the widow, severely, to her boys. "Let it be an example to you—I mean you, Joe."

Joe gave his head a barely perceptible disparaging toss and said:

"Et for both. It ain't anything—I'd a done it."

"Hush, if you haven't got any better manners than that. You don't see the point at all. It wasn't good food."

"I don't care—it was food, and I'd a et it if it was rotten."

"Shame! Such language! Can't you understand? They were starving—actually starving—and he ate for both, and—"

"Shucks! you gimme a chance and I'll—"

"There, now—close your head! and don't you open it again till you're asked."

[Angelo goes on and tells how his parents the Count and Countess had to fly from Florence for political reasons, and died poor in Berlin bereft of their great property by confiscation; and how he and Luigi had to travel with a freak-show during two years and suffer semi-starvation.]

"That hateful black-bread; but I seldom ate anything during that time; that was poor Luigi's affair—"

"I'll never Mister him again!" cried the widow, with strong emotion, "he's Luigi to me, from this out!"

"Thank you a thousand times, madam, a thousand times! though in truth I don't deserve it."

"Ah, Luigi is always the fortunate one when honors are showering," said Angelo, plaintively; "now what have I done, Mrs. Cooper, that you leave me out? Come, you must strain a point in my favor."

"Call you Angelo? Why, certainly I will; what are you thinking of! In the case of twins, why—"

"But, ma, you're breaking up the story—do let him go on."

"You keep still, Rowena Cooper, and he can go on all the better, I reckon. One interruption don't hurt, it's two that makes the trouble."

"But you've added one, now, and that is three."

"Rowena! I will not allow you to talk back at me when you have got nothing rational to say."

CHAPTER 3

[After breakfast the whole village crowded in, and there was a grand reception in honor of the twins; and at the close of it the gifted "freak" captured everybody's admiration by sitting down at the piano and knocking out a classic four-handed piece in great style. Then the judge took it—or them—driving in his buggy and showed off his village.]

All along the streets the people crowded the windows and stared at the amazing twins. Troops of small boys flocked after the buggy, excited and yelling. At first the dogs showed no interest. They thought they merely saw three men in a buggy—a matter of no consequence; but when they found out the facts of the case, they altered their opinion pretty radically, and joined the boys, expressing their minds as they came. Other dogs got interested; indeed, all the dogs. It was a spirited sight to see them come leaping fences, tearing around corners, swarming out of every bystreet and alley. The noise they made was something beyond belief—or praise. They did not seem to be moved by malice but only by prejudice, the common human prejudice against lack of conformity. If the twins turned their heads, they broke and fled in every direction, but stopped at a safe distance and faced about; and then formed and came on again as soon as the strangers showed them their back. Negroes and farmers' wives took to the woods when the buggy came upon them suddenly, and altogether the drive was pleasant and animated, and a refreshment all around.

[It was a long and lively drive. Angelo was a Methodist, Luigi was a Freethinker. The judge was very proud of his Freethinkers' Society, which was flourishing along in a most prosperous way and already had two members—himself and the obscure and neglected Pudd'nhead Wilson. It was to meet that evening, and he invited Luigi to join; a thing which Luigi was glad to do, partly because it would please himself, and partly because it would gravel Angelo.]

They had now arrived at the widow's gate, and the excursion was ended. The twins politely expressed their obligations for the pleasant outing which had been afforded them; to which the judge bowed his thanks, and then said he would now go and arrange for the freethinkers' meeting, and would call for Count Luigi in the evening.

"For you also, dear sir," he added hastily, turning to Angelo and bowing. "In addressing myself particularly to your brother, I was not meaning to leave you out. It was an unintentional rudeness, I assure you, and due wholly to accident—accident and preoccupation. I beg you to forgive me."

His quick eye had seen the sensitive blood mount into Angelo's face, betraying the wound that had been inflicted. The sting of the slight had gone deep, but the apology was so prompt, and so evidently sincere, that the hurt was almost immediately healed, and a forgiving smile testified to the kindly judge that all was well again.

Concealed behind Angelo's modest and unassuming exterior, and unsuspected by any but his intimates, was a lofty pride, a pride of almost abnormal proportions, indeed, and this rendered him ever the prey of slights; and although they were almost always imaginary ones, they hurt none the less on that account. By ill fortune Judge Driscoll had happened to touch his sorest point, *i.e.*, his conviction that his brother's presence was welcomer everywhere than his own; that he was often invited, out of mere courtesy, where only his brother was wanted, and that in a majority of cases he would not be included in an invitation if he could be left out without offense. A sensitive nature like this is necessarily subject to moods; moods which traverse the whole gamut of feeling; moods which know all the climes of emotion, from the sunny heights of joy to the black abysses of despair. At times, in his seasons of deepest depressions, Angelo almost wished that he and his brother might become segregated from each other and be separate individuals, like other men. But of course as soon as his mind cleared and these diseased imaginings passed away, he shuddered at the repulsive thought, and earnestly prayed that it might visit him no more. To be separate, and as other men are! How awkward it would seem; how unendurable. What would he do with his hands, his arms? How would his legs feel? How odd, and strange, and grotesque every action, attitude, movement, gesture would be. To sleep by himself, eat by himself, walk by himself—how lonely, how unspeakably lonely! No, no, any fate but that. In every way and from every point, the idea was revolting.

This was of course natural; to have felt otherwise would have been unnatural. He had known no life but a combined one; he had been familiar with it from his birth; he was not able to conceive of any other as being agreeable, or even bearable. To him, in the privacy of his secret thoughts, all other men were monsters, deformities: and during three-fourths of his life their aspect had filled him with what promised to be an unconquerable aversion. But at eighteen his eye began to take note of female beauty; and little by little, undefined longings grew up in his heart, under whose softening influences the old stubborn aversion gradually diminished, and finally disappeared. Men were still monstrosities to him, still deformities, and in his sober moments he had no desire to be like them, but their strange and unsocial and uncanny construction was no longer offensive to him.

This had been a hard day for him, physically and mentally. He had been called in the morning before he had quite slept off the effects of the liquor which Luigi had drunk; and so, for the first half hour had had the seedy feeling, and languor, the brooding depression, the cobwebby mouth and druggy taste that come of dissipation and are so ill a preparation for bodily or intellectual activities; the long violent strain of the reception had followed; and this had been followed, in turn, by the dreary sight-seeing, the judge's wearying explanations and laudations of the sights, and the stupefying clamor of the dogs. As a congruous conclusion, a fitting end, his feelings had been hurt, a slight had been put upon him. He would have been glad to forego dinner and betake himself to rest and sleep, but he held his peace and said no word, for he knew his brother, Luigi, was fresh, unweary, full of life, spirit, energy; he would have scoffed at the idea of wasting valuable time on a bed or a sofa, and would have refused permission.

CHAPTER 4

Rowena was dining out, Joe and Harry were belated at play, there were but three chairs and four persons that noon at the home dinner-table—the twins, the widow, and her chum, Aunt Betsy Hale. The widow soon perceived that Angelo's spirits were as low as Luigi's were high, and also that he had a jaded look. Her motherly solicitude was aroused, and she tried to get him interested in the talk and win him to a happier frame of mind, but the cloud of sadness remained on his countenance. Luigi lent his help, too. He used a form and a phrase which he was always accustomed to employ in these circumstances. He gave his brother an affectionate slap on the shoulder and said, encouragingly:

"Cheer up, the worst is yet to come!"

But this did no good. It never did. If anything, it made the matter worse, as a rule, because it irritated Angelo. This made it a favorite with Luigi. By and by the widow said:

"Angelo, you are tired, you've overdone yourself; you go right to bed after dinner, and get a good nap and a rest, then you'll be all right."

"Indeed, I would give anything if I could do that, madam."

"And what's to hender, I'd like to know? Land, the room's yours to do what you please with! The idea that you can't do what you like with your own!"

"But, you see, there's one prime essential—an essential of the very first importance—which isn't my own."

"What is that?"

"My body."

The old ladies looked puzzled, and Aunt Betsy Hale said:

"Why bless your heart, how is that?"

"It's my brother's."

"Your brother's! I don't quite understand. I supposed it belonged to both of you."

"So it does. But not to both at the same time."

"That is mighty curious; I don't see how it can be. I shouldn't think it could be managed that way."

"Oh, it's a good enough arrangement, and goes very well; in fact, it wouldn't do to have it otherwise. I find that the Teetotalers and the Anti-Teetotalers hire the use of the same hall for their meetings. Both parties don't use it at the same time, do they?"

"You bet they don't!" said both old ladies in a breath.

"And, moreover," said Aunt Betsy, "the Freethinkers and the Baptist Bible class use the same room over the Market house, but you can take my word for it they don't mush up together and use it at the same time."

"Very well," said Angelo, "you understand it now. And it stands to reason that the arrangement couldn't be improved. I'll prove it to you. If our legs tried to obey two wills, how could we ever get anywhere? I would start one way, Luigi would start another, at the same moment—the result would be a standstill, wouldn't it?"

"As sure as you are born! Now ain't that wonderful! A body would never have thought of it."

"We should always be arguing and fussing and disputing over the merest trifles. We should lose worlds of time, for we couldn't go down-stairs or up, couldn't go to bed, couldn't rise, couldn't wash, couldn't dress, couldn't stand up, couldn't sit down, couldn't even cross our legs, without calling a meeting first and explaining the case and passing resolutions, and getting consent. It wouldn't ever do—now would it?"

"Do? Why, it would wear a person out in a week! Did you ever hear anything like it, Patsy Cooper?"

"Oh, you'll find there's more than one thing about them that ain't commonplace," said the widow, with the complacent air of a person with a property right in a novelty that is under admiring scrutiny.

"Well, now, how ever do you manage it? I don't mind saying I'm suffering to know."

"He who made us," said Angelo reverently, "and with us this difficulty, also provided a way out of it. By a mysterious law of our being, each of us has utter and indisputable command of our body a week at a time, turn and turn about."

"Well, I never! Now ain't that beautiful!"

"Yes, it is beautiful and infinitely wise and just. The week ends every Saturday at midnight to the minute, to the second, to the last shade of a fraction of a second, infallibly, unerringly, and in that instant the one brother's power over the body vanishes and the other brother takes possession, asleep or awake."

"How marvelous are His ways, and past finding out!"

Luigi said:

"So exactly to the instant does the change come, that during our stay in many of the great cities of the world, the public clocks were regulated by it; and as hundreds of thousands of private clocks and watches were set and corrected in accordance with the public clocks, we really furnished the standard time for the entire city."

"Don't tell me that He don't do miracles any more! Blowing down the walls of Jericho with rams' horns warn't as difficult, in my opinion."

"And that is not all," said Angelo. "A thing that is even more marvelous, perhaps, is the fact that the change takes note of longitude and fits itself to the meridian we are on. Luigi is in command this week. Now, if on Saturday night at a moment before midnight we could fly in an instant to a point fifteen degrees west of here, he would hold possession of the power another hour, for the change observes local time and no other."

Betsy Hale was deeply impressed, and said with solemnity:

"Patsy Cooper, for *de*tail it lays over the Passage of the Red Sea."

"No, I shouldn't go as far as that," said Aunt Patsy, "but if you've a mind to say Sodom and Gomorrah, I am with you, Betsy Hale."

"I am agreeable, then, though I do think I was right, and I believe parson Maltby would say the same. Well, now, there's another thing. Suppose one of you wants to borrow the legs a minute from the one that's got them, could he let him?"

"Yes, but we hardly ever do that. There were disagreeable results, several times, and so we very seldom ask or grant the privilege, nowadays, and we never even think of such a thing unless the case is extremely urgent. Besides, a week's possession at a time seems so little that we can't bear to spare a minute of it. People who have the use of their legs all the time never think of what a blessing it is, of course. It never occurs to them; it's just their natural ordinary condition, and so it does not excite them at all. But when I wake up, on Sunday morning, and it's my week and I feel the power all through me, oh, such a wave of exultation and thanksgiving goes surging over me, and I want to shout 'I can walk! I can walk!' Madam, do you ever, at your uprising, want to shout 'I can walk! I can walk!'"

"No, you poor unfortunate cretur, but I'll never get out of my bed again without *doing* it! Laws, to think I've had this unspeakable blessing all my long life and never had the grace to thank the good Lord that gave it to me!"

Tears stood in the eyes of both the old ladies, and the widow said, softly:

"Betsy Hale, we have learned something, you and me."

The conversation now drifted wide, but by and by floated back once more to that admired detail, the rigid and beautiful impartiality with which the possession of power had been distributed, between the twins. Aunt Betsy saw in it a far finer justice than human law exhibits in related cases. She said:

"In my opinion it ain't right now, and never has been right, the way a twin born a quarter of a minute sooner than the other one gets all the land and grandeurs and nobilities in the old countries and his brother has to go bare and be a nobody. Which of you was born first?"

Angelo's head was resting against Luigi's; weariness had overcome him, and for the past five minutes he had been peacefully sleeping. The old ladies had dropped their voices to a lulling drone, to help him to steal the rest his brother wouldn't take him up-stairs to get. Luigi listened a moment to Angelo's regular breathing, then said in a voice barely audible:

"We were both born at the same time, but I am six months older than he is."

"For the land's sake!"

"'Sh! don't wake him up; he wouldn't like my telling this. It has always been kept secret till now."

"But how in the world can it be? If you were both born at the same time, how can one of you be older than the other?"

"It is very simple, and I assure you it is true. I was born with a full crop of hair, he was as bald as an egg for six months. I could walk six months before he could make a step. I finished teething six months ahead of him. I began to take solids six months before he left the breast. I began to talk six months before he could say a word. Last, and absolutely unassailable proof, *the sutures in my skull closed six months ahead of his*. Always just that six months' difference to a day. Was that accident? Nobody is going to claim that, I'm sure. It was ordained—it was law—it had its meaning, and we know what that meaning was. Now what does this overwhelming body of evidence establish? It establishes just one thing, and that thing it establishes beyond any peradventure whatever. Friends, we would not have it known for the world, and I must beg you to keep it strictly to yourselves, but the truth is, *we are no more twins than you are*."

The two old ladies were stunned, paralyzed—petrified, one may almost say—and could only sit and gaze vacantly at each other for some moments; then Aunt Betsy Hale said impressively:

"There's no getting around proof like that. I do believe it's the most amazing thing I ever heard of." She sat silent a moment or two and breathing hard with excitement, then she looked up and surveyed the strangers steadfastly a little while, and added: "Well, it does beat me, but I would have took you for twins anywhere."

"So would I, so would I," said Aunt Patsy with the emphasis of a certainty that is not impaired by any shade of doubt.

"*Any*body would—anybody in the world, I don't care who he is," said Aunt Betsy with decision.

"You won't tell," said Luigi, appealingly.

"Oh, dear no!" answered both ladies promptly, "you can trust us, don't you be afraid."

"That is good of you, and kind. Never let on; treat us always as if we were twins."

"You can depend on us," said Aunt Betsy, "but it won't be easy, because now that I know you ain't, you don't *seem* so."

Luigi muttered to himself with satisfaction: "That swindle has gone through without change of cars."

It was not very kind of him to load the poor things up with a secret like that, which would be always flying to their tongues' ends every time they heard any one speak of the strangers as twins, and would become harder and harder to hang on to with every recurrence of the temptation to tell it, while the torture of retaining it would increase with every new strain that was applied; but he never thought of that, and probably would not have worried much about it if he had.

A visitor was announced—some one to see the twins. They withdrew to the parlor, and the two old ladies began to discuss with interest the strange things which they had been listening to. When they had finished the matter to their satisfaction, and Aunt Betsy rose to go, she stopped to ask a question:

"How does things come on between Roweny and Tom Driscoll?"

"Well, about the same. He writes tolerable often, and she answers tolerable seldom."

"Where is he?"

"In St. Louis, I believe, though he's such a gad-about that a body can't be very certain of him, I reckon."

"Don't Roweny know?"

"Oh, yes, like enough. I haven't asked her lately."

"Do you know how him and the judge are getting along now?"

"First rate, I believe. Mrs. Pratt says so; and being right in the house, and sister to the one and aunt to t'other, of course she ought to know. She says the judge is real fond of him when he's away; but frets when he's around and is vexed with his ways, and not sorry to have him go again. He has been gone three weeks this time—a pleasant thing for both of them, I reckon."

"Tom's rather harum-scarum, but there ain't anything bad in him, I guess."

"Oh, no, he's just young, that's all. Still, twenty-three is old, in one way. A young man ought to be earning his living by that time. If Tom were doing that, or was even trying to do it, the judge would be a heap better satisfied with him. Tom's always going to begin, but somehow he can't seem to find just the opening he likes."

"Well, now, it's partly the judge's own fault. Promising the boy his property wasn't the way to set him to earning a fortune of his own. But what do you think is Roweny beginning to lean any toward him, or ain't she?"

Aunt Patsy had a secret in her bosom; she wanted to keep it there, but nature was too strong for her. She drew Aunt Betsy aside, and said in her most confidential and mysterious manner:

"Don't you breathe a syllable to a soul—I'm going to tell you something. In my opinion Tom Driscoll's chances were considerable better yesterday than they are to-day."

"Patsy Cooper, what *do* you mean?"

"It's so, as sure as you're born. I wish you could a been at breakfast and seen for yourself."

"You don't mean it!"

"Well, if I'm any judge, there's a leaning—there's a leaning, sure."

"My land! Which one of 'em is it?"

"I can't say for certain, but I think it's the youngest one—Anjy."

Then there were hand-shakings, and congratulations, and hopes, and so on, and the old ladies parted, perfectly happy—the one in knowing something which the rest of the town didn't, and the other in having been the sole person able to furnish that knowledge.

The visitor who had called to see the twins was the Rev. Mr. Hotchkiss, pastor of the Baptist church. At the reception Angelo had told him he had lately experienced a change in his religious views, and was now desirous of becoming a Baptist, and would immediately join Mr. Hotchkiss's church. There was no time to say more, and the brief talk ended at that point. The minister was much gratified, and had dropped in for a moment now, to invite the twins to attend his Bible class at eight that evening. Angelo accepted, and was expecting Luigi to decline, but he did not, because he knew that the Bible class and the Freethinkers met in the same room, and he wanted to treat his brother to the embarrassment of being caught in freethinking company

CHAPTER 5

[A long and vigorous quarrel follows, between the twins. And there is plenty to quarrel about, for Angelo was always seeking truth, and this obliged him to change and improve his religion with frequency, which wearied Luigi, and annoyed him too; for he had to be present at each new enlistment—which placed him in the false position of seeming to indorse and approve his brother's fickleness; moreover, he had to go to Angelo's prohibition meetings, and he hated them. On the other hand, when it was his week to command the legs he gave Angelo just cause of complaint, for he took him to circuses and horse-races and fandangoes, exposing him to all sorts of censure and criticism; and he drank, too; and whatever he drank went to Angelo's head instead of his own and made him act disgracefully. When the evening was come, the two attended the Freethinkers' meeting, where Angelo was sad and silent; then came the Bible class and looked upon him coldly, finding him in such company. Then they went to Wilson's house and Chapter XI of "Pudd'nhead Wilson" follows, which tells of the girl seen in Tom Driscoll's room; and closes with the kicking of Tom by Luigi at the anti-temperance mass-meeting of the Sons of Liberty; with the addition of some account of Roxy's adventures as a chambermaid on a Mississippi boat. Her exchange of the children had been flippantly and farcically described in an earlier chapter.]

Next morning all the town was a-buzz with great new: Pudd'head Wilson had a law-case!

The public astonishment was so great and the public curiosity so intense, that when the justice of the peace opened his court, the place was packed with people and even the windows were full. Everybody was flushed and perspiring; the summer heat was almost unendurable.

Tom Driscoll had brought a charge of assault and battery against the twins. Robert Allen was retained by Driscoll, David Wilson by the defense. Tom, his native cheerfulness unannihilated by his back-breaking and bone-bruising passage across the massed heads of the Sons of Liberty the previous night, laughed his little customary laugh, and said to Wilson:

"I've kept my promise, you see; I'm throwing my business your way. Sooner than I was expecting, too."

"It's very good of you—particularly if you mean to keep it up."

"Well, I can't tell about that yet. But we'll see. If I find you deserve it I'll take you under my protection and make your fame and fortune for you."

"I'll try to deserve it, Tom."

A jury was sworn in; then Mr. Allen said:

"We will detain your honor but a moment with this case. It is not one where any doubt of the fact of the assault can enter in. These gentlemen—the accused—kicked my client at the Market Hall last night; they kicked him with violence; with extraordinary violence; with even unprecedented violence, I may say; insomuch that he was lifted entirely off his feet and discharged into the midst of the audience. We can prove this by four hundred witnesses—we shall call but three. Mr. Harkness will take the stand."

Mr. Harkness, being sworn, testified that he was chairman upon the occasion mentioned; that he was close at hand and saw the defendants in this action kick the plaintiff into the air and saw him descend among the audience.

"Take the witness," said Allen.

"Mr. Harkness," said Wilson, "you say you saw these gentlemen, my clients, kick the plaintiff. Are you sure—and please remember that you are on oath—are you perfectly sure that you saw *both* of them kick him, or only one? Now be careful."

A bewildered look began to spread itself over the witness's face. He hesitated, stammered, but got out nothing. His eyes wandered to the twins and fixed themselves there with a vacant gaze.

"Please answer, Mr. Harkness, you are keeping the court waiting. It is a very simple question."

Counsel for the prosecution broke in with impatience:

"Your honor, the question is an irrelevant triviality. Necessarily, they both kicked him, for they have but the one pair of legs, and both are responsible for them."

Wilson said, sarcastically:

"Will your honor permit this new witness to be sworn? He seems to possess knowledge which can be of the utmost value just at this moment—knowledge which would at once dispose of what every one must see is a very difficult question in this case. Brother Allen, will you take the stand?"

"Go on with your case!" said Allen, petulantly. The audience laughed, and got a warning from the court.

"Now, Mr. Harkness," said Wilson, insinuatingly, "We shall have to insist upon an answer to that question."

"I—er—well, of course, I do not absolutely know, but in my opinion—"

"Never mind your opinion, sir—answer the question."

"I—why, I can't answer it."

"That will do, Mr. Harkness. Stand down."

The audience tittered, and the discomfited witness retired in a state of great embarrassment.

Mr. Wakeman took the stand and swore that he saw the twins kick the plaintiff off the platform.

The defense took the witness.

"Mr. Wakeman, you have sworn that you saw these gentlemen kick the plaintiff. Do I understand you to swear that you saw them both do it?"

"Yes, sir,"—with derision.

"How do you know that both did it?"

"Because I *saw* them do it."

The audience laughed, and got another warning from the court.

"But by what means do you know that both, and not one, did it?"

"Well, in the first place, the insult was given to both of them equally, for they were called a pair of scissors. Of course they would both want to resent it, and so—"

"Wait! You are theorizing now. Stick to facts—counsel will attend to the arguments. Go on."

"Well, they both went over there—*that* I saw."

"Very good. Go on."

"And they both kicked him—I swear to it."

"Mr. Wakeman, was Count Luigi, here, willing to join the Sons of Liberty last night?"

"Yes, sir, he was. He did join, too, and drank a glass or two of whisky, like a man."

"Was his brother willing to join?"

"No, sir, he wasn't. He is a teetotaler, and was elected through a mistake."

"Was he given a glass of whisky?"

"Yes, sir, but of course that was another mistake, and not intentional. He wouldn't drink it. He set it down." A slight pause, then he added, casually and quite simply: "The plaintiff reached for it and hogged it."

There was a fine outburst of laughter, but as the justice was caught out, himself, his reprimand was not very vigorous.

Mr. Allen jumped up and exclaimed:

"I protest against these foolish irrelevancies. What have they to do with the case?"

Wilson said:

"Calm yourself, brother, it was only an experiment. Now, Mr. Wakeman, if one of these gentlemen chooses to join an association and the other doesn't; and if one of them enjoys whisky and the other doesn't, but sets it aside and leaves it unprotected" [titter from the audience], "it seems to show that they have independent minds, and tastes, and preferences, and that one of them is able to approve of a thing at the very moment that the other is heartily disapproving of it. Doesn't it seem so to you?"

"Certainly it does. It's perfectly plain."

"Now, then, it might be—I only say it might be—that one of these brothers wanted to kick the plaintiff last night, and that the other didn't want that humiliating punishment inflicted upon him in that public way and before all those people. Isn't that possible?"

"Of course it is. It's more than possible. I don't believe the blond one would kick anybody. It was the other one that—"

"Silence!" shouted the plaintiff's counsel, and went on with an angry sentence which was lost in the wave of laughter that swept the house.

"That will do, Mr. Wakeman," said Wilson, "you may stand down."

The third witness was called. He had seen the twins kick the plaintiff. Mr. Wilson took the witness.

"Mr. Rogers, you say you saw these accused gentlemen kick the plaintiff?"

"Yes, sir."

"Both of them?"

"Yes, sir."

"Which of them kicked him first?"

"Why—they—they both kicked him at the same time.

"Are you perfectly sure of that?"

"Yes, sir."

"What makes you sure of it?"

"Why, I stood right behind them, and saw them do it."

"How many kicks were delivered?"

"Only one."

"If two men kick, the result should be two kicks, shouldn't it?"

"Why—why yes, as a rule."

"Then what do you think went with the other kick?"

"I—well—the fact is, I wasn't thinking of two being necessary, this time."

"What do you think now?"

"Well, I—I'm sure I don't quite know what to think, but I reckon that one of them did half of the kick and the other one did the other half."

Somebody in the crowd sung out:

"It's the first sane thing that any of them has said."

The audience applauded. The judge said:

"Silence! or I will clear the court."

Mr. Allen looked pleased, but Wilson did not seem disturbed. He said:

"Mr. Rogers, you have favored us with what you think and what you reckon, but as thinking and reckoning are not evidence, I will now give you a chance to come out with something positive, one way or the other, and shall require you to produce it. I will ask the accused to stand up and repeat the phenomenal kick of last night." The twins stood up. "Now, Mr. Rogers, please stand behind them."

A Voice: "No, stand in front!" [Laughter. Silenced by the court.]

Another Voice: "No, give Tommy another highst!" [Laughter. Sharply rebuked by the court.]

"Now, then, Mr. Rogers, two kicks shall be delivered, one after the other, and I give you my word that at least one of the two shall be delivered by one of the twins alone, without the slightest assistance from his brother. Watch sharply, for you have got to render a decision without any ifs or ands in it." Rogers bent himself behind the twins with palms just above his knees, in the modern attitude of the catcher at a baseball match, and riveted eyes on the pair of legs in front of him. "Are you ready, Mr. Rogers?"

"Ready, sir."

"Kick!!"

The kick was launched.

"Have you got that one classified, Mr. Rogers?"

"Let me study a minute, sir."

"Take as much time as you please. Let me know when you are ready."

For as much as a minute Rogers pondered, with all eyes and a breathless interest fastened upon him. Then he gave the word:

"Ready, sir."

"Kick!"

The kick that followed was an exact duplicate of the first one.

"Now, then, Mr. Rogers, one of those kicks was an individual kick, not a mutual one. You will now state positively which was the mutual one."

The witness said, with a crestfallen look:

"I've got to give it up. There ain't any man in the world that could tell t'other from which, sir."

"Do you still assert that last night's kick was a mutual kick?"

"Indeed I don't, sir."

"That will do, Mr. Rogers. If my brother Allen desires to address the court, your honor, very well; but as far as I am concerned I am ready to let the case be at once delivered into the hands of this intelligent jury without comment."

Mr. Justice Robinson had been in office only two months, and in that short time had not had many cases to try, of course. He had no knowledge of laws and courts except what he had picked up since he came into office. He was a sore trouble to the lawyers, for his rulings were pretty eccentric sometimes, and he stood by them with Roman simplicity and fortitude; but the people were well satisfied with him, for they saw that his intentions were always right, that he was entirely impartial, and that he usually made up in good sense what he lacked in technique, so to speak. He now perceived that there was likely to be a miscarriage of justice here, and he rose to the occasion.

"Wait a moment, gentlemen," he said, "it is plain that an assault has been committed—it is plain to anybody; but the way things are going, the guilty will certainly escape conviction. I can not allow this. Now—"

"But, your honor!" said Wilson, interrupting him, earnestly but respectfully, "you are deciding the case yourself, whereas the jury—"

"Never mind the jury, Mr. Wilson; the jury will have a chance when there is a reasonable doubt for them to take hold of—which there isn't, so far. There is no doubt whatever that an assault has been committed. The attempt to show that both of the accused committed it has failed. Are they both to escape justice on that account? Not in this court, if I can prevent it. It appears to have been a mistake to bring the charge against them as a corporation; each should have been charged in his capacity as an individual, and—"

"But, your honor!" said Wilson, "in fairness to my clients I must insist that inasmuch as the prosecution did not separate the—"

"No wrong will be done your clients, sir—they will be protected; also the public and the offended law. Mr. Allen, you will amend your pleadings, and put one of the accused on trial at a time."

Wilson broke in:

"But, your honor! This is wholly unprecedented! To imperil an accused person by arbitrarily altering and widening the charge against him in order to compass his conviction when the charge as originally brought promises to fail to convict, is a thing unheard of before."

"Unheard of *where*?"

"In the courts of this or any other State."

The judge said, with dignity:

"I am not acquainted with the customs of other courts, and am not concerned to know what they are. I am responsible for this court, and I cannot conscientiously allow my judgment to be warped and my judicial liberty hampered by trying to conform to the caprices of other courts, be they—"

"But, your honor, the oldest and highest courts in Europe—"

"This court is not run on the European plan, Mr. Wilson; it is not run on any plan but its own. It has a plan of its own; and that plan is, to find justice for both State and accused, no matter what happens to be practice and custom in Europe or anywhere else." [Great applause.] "Silence! It has not been the custom of this court to imitate other courts; it has not been the custom of this court to take shelter behind the decisions of other courts, and we will not begin now. We will do the best we can by the light that God has given us, and while this court continues to have His approval, it will remain indifferent to what other organizations may think of it." [Applause.] "Gentlemen, I *must* have order!—quiet yourselves! Mr. Allen, you will now proceed against the prisoners one at a time. Go on with the case."

Allen was not at his ease. However, after whispering a moment with his client and with one or two other people, he rose and said:

"Your honor, I find it to be reported and believed that the accused are able to act independently in many ways, but that this independence does not extend to their legs, authority over their legs being vested exclusively in the one brother during a specific term of days, and then passing to the other brother for a like term, and so on, by regular alternation. I could call witnesses who would prove that the accused had revealed to them the existence of this extraordinary fact, and had also made known which of them was in possession of the legs yesterday—and this would, of course, indicate where the guilt of the assault belongs—but as this would be mere hearsay evidence, these revelations not having been made under oath—"

"Never mind about that, Mr. Allen. It may not all be hearsay. We shall see. It may at least help to put us on the right track. Call the witnesses."

"Then I will call Mr. John Buckstone, who is now present, and I beg that Mrs. Patsy Cooper may be sent for. Take the stand, Mr. Buckstone."

Buckstone took the oath, and then testified that on the previous evening the Count Angelo Capello had protested against going to the hall, and had called all present to witness that he was going by compulsion and would not go if he could help himself. Also, that the Count Luigi had replied sharply that he would go, just the same, and that he, Count Luigi, would see to that himself. Also, that upon Count Angelo's complaining about being kept on his legs so long, Count Luigi retorted with apparent surprise, "*Your* legs!—I like your impudence!"

"*Now* we are getting at the kernel of the thing," observed the judge, with grave and earnest satisfaction. "It looks as if the Count Luigi was in possession of the battery at the time of the assault."

Nothing further was elicited from Mr. Buckstone on direct examination. Mr. Wilson took the witness.

"Mr. Buckstone, about what time was it that that conversation took place?"

"Toward nine yesterday evening, sir."

"Did you then proceed directly to the hall?"

"Yes, sir."

"How long did it take you to go there?"

"Well, we walked; and as it was from the extreme edge of the town, and there was no hurry, I judge it took us about twenty minutes, maybe a trifle more."

"About what hour was the kick delivered?"

"About thirteen minutes and a half to ten."

"Admirable! You are a pattern witness, Mr. Buckstone. How did you happen to look at your watch at that particular moment?"

"I always do it when I see an assault. It's likely I shall be called as a witness, and it's a good point to have."

"It would be well if others were as thoughtful. Was anything said, between the conversation at my house and the assault, upon the detail which we are now examining into?"

"No, sir."

"If power over the mutual legs was in the possession of one brother at nine, and passed into the possession of the other one during the next thirty or forty minutes, do you think you could have detected the change?"

"By no means!"

"That is all, Mr. Buckstone."

Mrs. Patsy Cooper was called. The crowd made way for her, and she came smiling and bowing through the narrow human lane, with Betsy Hale, as escort and support, smiling and bowing in her wake, the audience breaking into welcoming cheers as the old favorites filed along. The judge did not check this kindly demonstration of homage and affection, but let it run its course unrebuked.

The old ladies stopped and shook hands with the twins with effusion, then gave the judge a friendly nod, and bustled into the seats provided for them. They immediately began to deliver a volley of eager questions at the friends around them: "What is this thing for?" "What is that thing for?" "Who is that young man that's writing at the desk?

Why, I declare, it's Jack Bunce! I thought he was sick." "Which is the jury? Why, is *that* the jury? Billy Price and Job Turner, and Jack Lounsbury, and—well, I never!" "Now who would ever a thought—"

But they were gently called to order at this point, and asked not to talk in court. Their tongues fell silent, but the radiant interest in their faces remained, and their gratitude for the blessing of a new sensation and a novel experience still beamed undimmed from their eyes. Aunt Patsy stood up and took the oath, and Mr. Allen explained the point in issue, and asked her to go on now, in her own way, and throw as much light upon it as she could. She toyed with her reticule a moment or two, as if considering where to begin, then she said:

"Well, the way of it is this. They are Luigi's legs a week at a time, and then they are Angelo's, and he can do whatever he wants to with them."

"You are making a mistake, Aunt Patsy Cooper," said the judge. "You shouldn't state that as a *fact*, because you don't know it to be a fact."

"What's the reason I don't?" said Aunt Patsy, bridling a little.

"What is the reason that you do know it?"

"The best in the world because they told me."

"That isn't a reason."

"Well, for the land's sake! Betsy Hale, do you hear that?"

"*Hear* it?—I should think so," said Aunt Betsy, rising and facing the court. "Why, Judge, I was there and heard it myself. Luigi says to Angelo—no, it was Angelo said it to—"

"Come, come, Mrs. Hale, pray sit down, and—"

"Certainly, it's all right, I'm going to sit down presently, but not until I've—"

"But you *must* sit down!"

"*Must*! Well, upon my word if things ain't getting to a pretty pass when—"

The house broke into laughter, but was promptly brought to order, and meantime Mr. Allen persuaded the old lady to take her seat. Aunt Patsy continued:

"Yes, they told me that, and I know it's true. They're Luigi's legs this week, but—"

"Ah, they told you that, did they?" said the Justice, with interest.

"Well, no, I don't know that they told me, but that's neither here nor there. I know, without that, that at dinner yesterday, Angelo was as tired as a dog, and yet Luigi wouldn't lend him the legs to go up-stairs and take a nap with."

"Did he ask for them?"

"Let me see—it seems to me, somehow, that—that—Aunt Betsy, do you remember whether he—"

"Never mind about what Aunt Betsy remembers—she is not a witness; we only want to know what you remember yourself," said the judge.

"Well, it does seem to me that you are most cantankerously particular about a little thing, Sim Robinson. Why, when I can't remember a thing myself, I always—"

"Ah, *please* go on!"

"Now how can she when you keep fussing at her all the time?" said Aunt Betsy. "Why, with a person pecking at me that way, I should get that fuzzled and fuddled that—"

She was on her feet again, but Allen coaxed her into her seat once more, while the court squelched the mirth of the house. Then the judge said:

"Madam, do you know—do you absolutely know, independently of anything these gentlemen have told you—that the power over their legs passes from the one to the other regularly every week?"

"Regularly? Bless your heart, regularly ain't any name for the exactness of it! All the big cities in Europe used to set the clocks by it." [Laughter, *suppressed by the court.*]

"How do you *know*? That is the question. Please answer it plainly and squarely."

"Don't you talk to me like that, Sim Robinson—I won't have it. How do I know, indeed! How do you know what you know? Because somebody told you. You didn't invent it out of your own head, did you? Why, these twins are the truthfulest people in the world; and I don't think it becomes you to sit up there and throw slurs at them when they haven't been doing anything to you. And they are orphans besides—both of them. All—"

But Aunt Betsy was up again now, and both old ladies were talking at once and with all their might; but as the house was weltering in a storm of laughter, and the judge was hammering his desk with an iron paper-weight, one could only see them talk, not hear them. At last, when quiet was restored, the court said:

"Let the ladies retire."

"But, your honor, I have the right, in the interest of my clients, to cross-exam—"

"You'll not need to exercise it, Mr. Wilson—the evidence is thrown out."

"Thrown out!" said Aunt Patsy, ruffled; "and what's it thrown out for, I'd like to know."

"And so would I, Patsy Cooper. It seems to me that if we can save these poor persecuted strangers, it is our bounden duty to stand up here and talk for them till—"

"There, there, there, do sit down!"

It cost some trouble and a good deal of coaxing, but they were got into their seats at last. The trial was soon ended now. The twins themselves became witnesses in their own defense. They established the fact, upon oath, that the leg-power passed from one to the other every Saturday night at twelve o'clock sharp. But on cross-examination their counsel would not allow them to tell whose week of power the current week was. The judge insisted upon their answering, and proposed to compel them, but even the prosecution took fright and came to the rescue then, and helped stay the sturdy jurist's revolutionary hand. So the case had to go to the jury with that important point hanging in the air. They were out an hour and brought in this verdict:

"We the jury do find: 1, that an assault was committed, as charged; 2, that it was committed by one of the persons accused, he having been seen to do it by several credible witnesses; 3, but that his identity is so merged in his brother's that we have not been able to tell which was him. We cannot convict both, for only one is guilty. We cannot acquit both, for only one is innocent. Our verdict is that justice has been defeated by the dispensation of God, and ask to be discharged from further duty."

This was read aloud in court and brought out a burst of hearty applause. The old ladies made a spring at the twins, to shake and congratulate, but were gently disengaged by Mr. Wilson and softly crowded back into their places.

The judge rose in his little tribune, laid aside his silver-bowed spectacles, roached his gray hair up with his fingers, and said, with dignity and solemnity, and even with a certain pathos:

"In all my experience on the bench, I have not seen justice bow her head in shame in this court until this day. You little realize what far-reaching harm has just been wrought here under the fickle forms of law. Imitation is the bane of courts—I thank God that this one is free from the contamination of that vice—and in no long time you will see the fatal work of this hour seized upon by profligate so-called guardians of justice in all the wide circumstance of this planet and perpetuated in their pernicious decisions. I wash my hands of this iniquity. I would have compelled these culprits to expose their guilt, but support failed me where I had most right to expect aid and encouragement. And I was confronted by a law made in the interest of crime, which protects the criminal from testifying against himself. Yet I had precedents of my own whereby I had set aside that law on two different occasions and thus succeeded in convicting criminals to whose crimes there were no witnesses but themselves. What have you accomplished this day? Do you realize it? You have set adrift, unadmonished, in this community, two men endowed with an awful and mysterious gift, a hidden and grisly power for evil—a power by which each in his turn may commit crime after crime of the most heinous character, and no man be able to tell which is the guilty or which the innocent party in any case of them all. Look to your homes—look to your property—look to your lives—for you have need!

"Prisoners at the bar, stand up. Through suppression of evidence, a jury of your—our—countrymen have been obliged to deliver a verdict concerning your case which stinks to heaven with the rankness of its injustice. By its terms you, the guilty one, go free with the innocent. Depart in peace, and come no more! The costs devolve upon the outraged plaintiff—another iniquity. The court stands dissolved."

Almost everybody crowded forward to overwhelm the twins and their counsel with congratulations; but presently the two old aunties dug the duplicates out and bore them away in triumph through the hurrahing crowd, while lots of new friends carried Pudd'nhead Wilson off tavernward to feast him and "wet down" his great and victorious entry into the legal arena. To Wilson, so long familiar with neglect and depreciation, this strange new incense of popularity and admiration was as a fragrance blown from the fields of paradise. A happy man was Wilson.

CHAPTER 6

[A deputation came in the evening and conferred upon Wilson the welcome honor of a nomination for mayor; for the village has just been converted into a city by charter. Tom skulks out of challenging the twins. Judge Driscoll thereupon challenges Angelo (accused by Tom of doing the kicking); he declines, but Luigi accepts in his place against Angelo's timid protest.]

It was late Saturday night—nearing eleven.

The judge and his second found the rest of the war party at the further end of the vacant ground, near the haunted house. Pudd'nhead Wilson advanced to meet them, and said anxiously:

"I must say a word in behalf of my principal's proxy, Count Luigi, to whom you have kindly granted the privilege of fighting my principal's battle for him. It is growing late, and Count Luigi is in great trouble lest midnight shall strike before the finish."

"It is another testimony," said Howard, approvingly. "That young man is fine all through. He wishes to save his brother the sorrow of fighting on the Sabbath, and he is right; it is the right and manly feeling and does him credit. We will make all possible haste."

Wilson said:

"There is also another reason—a consideration, in fact, which deeply concerns Count Luigi himself. These twins have command of their mutual legs turn about. Count Luigi is in command now; but at midnight, possession will pass to my principal, Count Angelo, and—well, you can foresee what will happen. He will march straight off the field, and carry Luigi with him."

"Why! sure enough!" cried the judge, "we have heard something about that extraordinary law of their being, already—nothing very definite, it is true, as regards dates and durations of power, but I see it is definite enough as regards to-night. Of course we must give Luigi every chance. Omit all the ceremonial possible, gentlemen, and place us in position."

The seconds at once tossed up a coin; Howard won the choice. He placed the judge sixty feet from the haunted house and facing it; Wilson placed the twins within fifteen feet of the house and facing the judge—necessarily. The pistol-case was opened and the long slim tubes taken out; when the moonlight glinted from them a shiver went through Angelo. The doctor was a fool, but a thoroughly well-meaning one, with a kind heart and a sincere disposition to oblige, but along with it an absence of tact which often hurt its effectiveness. He brought his box of lint and bandages, and asked Angelo to feel and see how soft and comfortable they were. Angelo's head fell over against Luigi's in a faint, and precious time was lost in bringing him to; which provoked Luigi into expressing his mind to the doctor with a good deal of vigor and frankness. After Angelo came to he was still so weak that Luigi was obliged to drink a stiff horn of brandy to brace him up.

The seconds now stepped at once to their posts, half way between the combatants, one of them on each side of the line of fire. Wilson was to count, very deliberately, "One—two—three—fire!—stop!" and the duelists could bang away at any time they chose during that recitation, but not after the last word. Angelo grew very nervous when he saw Wilson's hand rising slowly into the air as a sign to make ready, and he leaned his head against Luigi's and said:

"Oh, please take me away from here, I can't stay, I know I can't!"

"What in the world are you doing? Straighten up! What's the matter with you?—*you're* in no danger—nobody's going to shoot at you. Straighten up, I tell you!"

Angelo obeyed, just in time to hear:

"One—!"

"Bang!" Just one report, and a little tuft of white hair floated slowly to the judge's feet in the moonlight. The judge did not swerve; he still stood, erect and motionless, like a statue, with his pistol-arm hanging straight down at his side. He was reserving his fire.

"Two—!"

"Three—"!

"Fire—!"

Up came the pistol-arm instantly—Angelo dodged with the report. He said "Ouch!" and fainted again.

The doctor examined and bandaged the wound. It was of no consequence, he said—bullet through fleshy part of arm—no bones broken—the gentleman was still able to fight—let the duel proceed.

Next time, Angelo jumped just as Luigi fired, which disordered his aim and caused him to cut a chip off of Howard's ear. The judge took his time again, and when he fired Angelo jumped and got a knuckle skinned. The doctor inspected and dressed the wounds. Angelo now spoke out and said he was content with the satisfaction he had got, and if the judge—but Luigi shut him roughly up, and asked him not to make an ass of himself; adding:

"And I want you to stop dodging. You take a great deal too prominent a part in this thing for a person who has got nothing to do with it. You should remember that you are here only by courtesy, and are without official recognition; officially you are not here at all; officially you do not even exist. To all intents and purposes you are absent from this place, and you ought for your own modesty's sake to reflect that it cannot become a person who is not present here to be taking this sort of public and indecent prominence in a matter in which he is not in the slightest degree concerned. Now, don't dodge again; the bullets are not for you, they are for me; if I want them dodged I will attend to it myself. I never saw a person act so."

Angelo saw the reasonableness of what his brother had said, and he did try to reform, but it was of no use; both pistols went off at the same instant, and he jumped once more; he got a sharp scrape along his cheek from the judge's bullet, and so deflected Luigi's aim that his ball went wide and chipped flake of skin from Pudd'nhead Wilson's chin. The doctor attended to the wounded.

By the terms, the duel was over. But Luigi was entirely out of patience, and begged for one exchange of shots, insisting that he had had no fair chance, on account of his brother's indelicate behavior. Howard was opposed to granting so unusual a privilege, but the judge took Luigi's part, and added that indeed he himself might fairly be considered entitled to another trial, because although the proxy on the other side was in no way to blame for his (the judge's) humiliatingly resultless work, the gentleman with whom he was fighting this duel was to blame for it, since if he had played no advantages and had held his head still, his proxy would have been disposed of early. He added:

"Count Luigi's request for another exchange is another proof that he is a brave and chivalrous gentleman, and I beg that the courtesy he asks may be accorded him."

"I thank you most sincerely for this generosity, Judge Driscoll," said Luigi, with a polite bow, and moving to his place. Then he added—to Angelo, "Now hold your grip, hold your *grip*, I tell you, and I'll land him, sure!"

The men stood erect, their pistol-arms at their sides, the two seconds stood at their official posts, the doctor stood five paces in Wilson's rear with his instruments and bandages in his hands. The deep stillness, the peaceful moonlight, the motionless figures, made an impressive picture and the impending fatal possibilities augmented this impressiveness to solemnity. Wilson's hand began to rise—slowly—still higher—still higher—in another moment—

"*Boom*!" the first stroke of midnight swung up out of the distance; Angelo was off like a deer!

"Oh, you unspeakable traitor!" wailed his brother, as they went soaring over the fence.

The others stood astonished and gazing; and so stood, watching that strange spectacle until distance dissolved it and swept it from their view. Then they rubbed their eyes like people waking out of a dream,

"Well, I've never seen anything like that before!" said the judge. "Wilson, I am going to confess now, that I wasn't quite able to believe in that leg-business, and had a suspicion that it was a put-up convenience between those twins; and when Count Angelo fainted I thought I saw the whole scheme—thought it was pretext No. 1, and would be followed by others till twelve o'clock should arrive, and Luigi would get off with all the credit of seeming to want to fight and yet not have to fight, after all. But I was mistaken. His pluck proved it. He's a brave fellow and did want to fight."

"There isn't any doubt about that," said Howard, and added, in a grieved tone, "but what an unworthy sort of Christian that Angelo is—I hope and believe there are not many like him. It is not right to engage in a duel on the Sabbath—I could not approve of that myself; but to finish one that has been begun—that is a duty, let the day be what it may."

They strolled along, still wondering, still talking.

"It is a curious circumstance," remarked the surgeon, halting Wilson a moment to paste so more court plaister on his chin, which had gone

to leaking blood, again, "that in this duel neither of the parties who handled the pistols lost blood while nearly all the persons present in the mere capacity of guests got hit. I have not heard of such a thing before. Don't you think it unusual?"

"Yes," said the judge, "it has struck me as peculiar. Peculiar and unfortunate. I was annoyed at it, all the time. In the case of Angelo it made no great difference, because he was in a measure concerned, though not officially; but it troubled me to see the seconds compromised, and yet I knew no way to mend the matter."

"There was no way to mend it," said Howard, whose ear was being readjusted now by the doctor; "the code fixes our place, and it would not have been lawful to change it. If we could have stood at your side, or behind you, or in front of you, it—but it would not have been legitimate and the other parties would have had a just right to complain of our trying to protect ourselves from danger; infractions of the code are certainly not permissible in any case whatever."

Wilson offered no remarks. It seemed to him that there was very little place here for so much solemnity, but he judged that if a duel where nobody was in danger or got crippled but the seconds and the outsiders had nothing ridiculous about it for these gentlemen, his pointing out that feature would probably not help them to see it.

He invited them in to take a nightcap, and Howard and the judge accepted, but the doctor said he would have to go and see how Angelo's principal wound was getting on.

[It was now Sunday, and in the afternoon Angelo was to be received into the Baptist communion by immersion—a doubtful prospect, the doctor feared.]

CHAPTER 7

When the doctor arrived at Aunt Patsy Cooper's house, he found the lights going and everybody up and dressed and in a great state of solicitude and excitement. The twins were stretched on a sofa in the sitting-room, Aunt Patsy was fussing at Angelo's arm, Nancy was flying around under her commands, the two young boys were trying to keep out of the way and always getting in it, in order to see and wonder, Rowena stood apart, helpless with apprehension and emotion, and Luigi was growling in unappeasable fury over Angelo's shameful flight.

As has been reported before, the doctor was a fool—a kind-hearted and well-meaning one, but with no tact; and as he was by long odds the most learned physician in the town, and was quite well aware of it, and could talk his learning with ease and precision, and liked to show off when he had an audience, he was sometimes tempted into revealing more of a case than was good for the patient.

He examined Angelo's wound, and was really minded to say nothing for once; but Aunt Patsy was so anxious and so pressing that he allowed his caution to be overcome, and proceeded to empty himself as follows, with scientific relish:

"Without going too much into detail, madam—for you would probably not understand it, anyway—I concede that great care is going to be necessary here; otherwise exudation of the aesophagus is nearly sure to ensue, and this will be followed by ossification and extradition of the maxillaris superioris, which must decompose the granular surfaces of the great infusorial ganglionic system, thus obstructing the action of the posterior varioloid arteries, and precipitating compound strangulated sorosis of the valvular tissues, and ending unavoidably in the dispersion and combustion of the marsupial fluxes and the consequent embrocation of the bi-cuspid populo redax referendum rotulorum."

A miserable silence followed. Aunt Patsy's heart sank, the pallor of despair invaded her face, she was not able to speak; poor Rowena wrung her hands in privacy and silence, and said to herself in the bitterness of her young grief, "There is no hope—it is plain there is no hope;" the good-hearted negro wench, Nancy, paled to chocolate, then to orange, then to amber, and thought to herself with yearning sympathy and sorrow, "Po' thing, he ain' gwyne to las' throo de half o' dat;" small Henry choked up, and turned his head away to hide his rising tears, and his brother Joe said to himself, with a sense of loss, "The baptizing's busted, that's sure." Luigi was the only person who had any heart to speak. He said, a little bit sharply, to the doctor:

"Well, well, there's nothing to be gained by wasting precious time; give him a barrel of pills—I'll take them for him."

"You?" asked the doctor.

"Yes. Did you suppose he was going to take them himself?"

"Why, of course."

"Well, it's a mistake. He never took a dose of medicine in his life. He can't."

"Well, upon my word, it's the most extraordinary thing I ever heard of!"

"Oh," said Aunt Patsy, as pleased as a mother whose child is being admired and wondered at; "you'll find that there's more about them that's wonderful than their just being made in the image of God like the rest of His creatures, now you can depend on that, *I* tell you," and she wagged her complacent head like one who could reveal marvelous things if she chose.

The boy Joe began:

"Why, ma, they ain't made in the im—"

"You shut up, and wait till you're asked, Joe. I'll let you know when I want help. Are you looking for something, doctor?"

The doctor asked for a few sheets of paper and a pen, and said he would write a prescription—which he did. It was one of Galen's; in fact, it was Galen's favorite, and had been slaying people for sixteen thousand years. Galen used it for everything, applied it to everything, said it would remove everything, from warts all the way through to lungs—and it generally did. Galen was still the only medical authority recognized in Missouri; his practice was the only practice known to the Missouri doctors, and his prescriptions were the only ammunition they carried when they went out for game.

By and by Dr. Claypool laid down his pen and read the result of his labors aloud, carefully and deliberately, for this battery must be constructed on the premises by the family, and mistakes could occur; for he wrote a doctor's hand—the hand which from the beginning of time has been so disastrous to the apothecary and so profitable to the undertaker:

Take of afarabocca, henbane, corpobalsamum, each two drams and a half; of cloves, opium, myrrh, cyperus, each two drams; of opobalsamum, Indian leaf, cinnamon, zedoary, ginger, coftus, coral, cassia, euphorbium, gum tragacanth, frankincense, styrax calamita, celtic, nard, spignel, hartwort, mustard, saxifrage, dill, anise, each one dram; of xylaloes, rheum ponticum, alipta, moschata, castor, spikenard, galangals, opoponax, anacardium, mastich, brimstone, peony, eringo, pulp of dates, red and white hermodactyls, roses, thyme, acorns, pennyroyal, gentian, the bark of the root of mandrake, germander, valerian, bishops weed, bay-berries, long and white pepper, xylobalsamum, carnabadium, macedonian, parsley seeds, lovage, the seeds of rue, and sinon, of each a dram and a half; of pure gold, pure silver, pearls not perforated, the blatta byzantina, the bone of the stag's heart, of each the quantity of fourteen grains of wheat; of sapphire, emerald and jasper stones, each one dram; of hasle-nuts, two drams; of pellitory of Spain, shavings of ivory, calamus odoratus, each the quantity of twenty-nine grains of wheat; of honey or sugar a sufficient quantity. Boil down and skim off.

"There," he said, "that will fix the patient; give his brother a dipperful every three-quarters of an hour—"

"—while he survives," muttered Luigi—

"—and see that the room is kept wholesomely hot, and the doors and windows closed tight. Keep Count Angelo nicely covered up with six or seven blankets, and when he is thirsty—which will be frequently—moisten a rag in the vapor of the tea kettle and let his brother suck it. When he is hungry—which will also be frequently—he must not be humored oftener than every seven or eight hours; then toast part of a cracker until it begins to brown, and give it to his brother."

"That is all very well, as far as Angelo is concerned," said Luigi, "but what am I to eat?"

"I do not see that there is anything the matter with you," the doctor answered, "you may, of course, eat what you please."

"And also drink what I please, I suppose?"

"Oh, certainly—at present. When the violent and continuous perspiring has reduced your strength, I shall have to reduce your diet, of course, and also bleed you, but there is no occasion for that yet awhile." He turned to Aunt Patsy and said: "He must be put to bed, and sat up with, and tended with the greatest care, and not allowed to stir for several days and nights."

"For one, I'm sacredly thankful for that," said Luigi, "it postpones the funeral—I'm not to be drowned to-day, anyhow."

Angelo said quietly to the doctor:

"I will cheerfully submit to all your requirements, sir, up to two o'clock this afternoon, and will resume them after three, but cannot be confined to the house during that intermediate hour."

"Why, may I ask?"

"Because I have entered the Baptist communion, and by appointment am to be baptised in the river at that hour."

"Oh, insanity!—it cannot be allowed!"

Angelo answered with placid firmness:

"Nothing shall prevent it, if I am alive."

"Why, consider, my dear sir, in your condition it might prove fatal."

A tender and ecstatic smile beamed from Angelo's eyes, and he broke forth in a tone of joyous fervency:

"Ah, how blessed it would be to die for such a cause—it would be martyrdom!"

"But your brother—consider your brother; you would be risking his life, too."

"He risked mine an hour ago," responded Angelo, gloomily; "did he consider me?" A thought swept through his mind that made him shudder. "If I had not run, I might have been killed in a duel on the Sabbath day, and my soul would have been lost—lost."

"Oh, don't fret, it wasn't in any danger," said Luigi, irritably; "they wouldn't waste it for a little thing like that; there's a glass case all ready for it in the heavenly museum, and a pin to stick it up with."

Aunt Patsy was shocked, and said:

"Looy, Looy!—don't talk so, dear!"

Rowena's soft heart was pierced by Luigi's unfeeling words, and she murmured to herself, "Oh, if I but had the dear privilege of protecting and defending him with my weak voice! —but alas! this sweet boon is denied me by the cruel conventions of social intercourse."

"Get their bed ready," said Aunt Patsy to Nancy, "and shut up the windows and doors, and light their candles, and see that you drive all the mosquitoes out of their bar, and make up a good fire in their stove, and carry up some bags of hot ashes to lay to his feet—"

—"and a shovel of fire for his head, and a mustard plaster for his neck, and some gum shoes for his ears," Luigi interrupted, with temper; and added, to himself, "Damnation, I'm going to be roasted alive, I just know it!"

"Why, Looy! Do be quiet; I never saw such a fractious thing. A body would think you didn't care for your brother."

"I don't—to *that* extent, Aunt Patsy. I was glad the drowning was postponed a minute ago, but I'm not now. No, that is all gone by; I want to be drowned."

"You'll bring a judgment on yourself just as sure as you live, if you go on like that. Why, I never heard the beat of it. Now, there—there! you've said enough. Not another word out of you—I won't have it!"

"But, Aunt Patsy—"

"Luigi! Didn't you hear what I told you?"

"But, Aunt Patsy, I—why, I'm not going to set my heart and lungs afloat in that pail of sewage which this criminal here has been prescri—"

"Yes, you are, too. You are going to be good, and do everything I tell you, like a dear," and she tapped his cheek affectionately with her finger. "Rowena, take the prescription and go in the kitchen and hunt up the things and lay them out for me. I'll sit up with my patient the rest of the night, doctor; I can't trust Nancy, she couldn't make Luigi take the medicine. Of course, you'll drop in again during the day. Have you got any more directions?"

"No, I believe not, Aunt Patsy. If I don't get in earlier, I'll be along by early candle-light, anyway. Meantime, don't allow him to get out of his bed."

Angelo said, with calm determination:

"I shall be baptized at two o'clock. Nothing but death shall prevent me."

The doctor said nothing aloud, but to himself he said, "Why, this chap's got a manly side, after all! Physically he's a coward, but morally he's a lion. I'll go and tell the others about this; it will raise him a good deal in their estimation—and the public will follow their lead, of course."

Privately, Aunt Patsy applauded too, and was proud of Angelo's courage in the moral field as she was of Luigi's in the field of honor.

The boy Henry was troubled, but the boy Joe said, inaudibly, and gratefully, "We're all hunky, after all; and no postponement on account of the weather."

CHAPTER 8

By nine o'clock the town was humming with the news of the midnight duel, and there were but two opinions about it: one, that Luigi's pluck in the field was most praiseworthy and Angela's flight most scandalous; the other, that Angelo's courage in flying the field for conscience sake was as fine and creditable as was Luigi's in holding the field in the face of the bullets. The one opinion was held by half of the town, the other one was maintained by the other half. The division was clean and exact, and it made two parties, an Angela party and a Luigi party. The twins had suddenly become popular idols along with Pudd'nhead Wilson, and haloed with a glory as intense as his. The children talked the duel all the way to Sunday school, their elders talked it all the way to church, the choir discussed it behind their red curtain, it usurped the place of pious thought in the "nigger gallery."

By noon the doctor had added the news, and spread it, that Count Angelo, in spite of his wound and all warnings and supplications, was resolute in his determination to be baptized at the hour appointed. This swept the town like wildfire, and mightily reinforced the enthusiasm of the Angelo faction, who said, "If any doubted that it was moral courage that took him from the field, what have they to say now!"

Still the excitement grew. All the morning it was traveling countryward, toward all points of the compass; so, whereas before only the farmers and their wives were intending to come and witness the remarkable baptism, a general holiday was now proclaimed and the children and negroes admitted to the privileges of the occasion. All the farms for ten miles around were vacated, all the converging roads emptied long processions of wagons, horses, and yeomanry into the town. The pack and cram of people vastly exceeded any that had ever been seen in that sleepy region before. The only thing that had ever even approached it was the time long gone by, but never forgotten, nor even referred to without wonder and pride, when two circuses and a Fourth of July fell together. But the glory of that occasion was extinguished now for good. It was but a freshet to this deluge.

The great invasion massed itself on the river bank and waited hungrily for the immense event. Waited, and wondered if it would really happen, or if the twin who was not a "professor" would stand out and prevent it.

But they were not to be disappointed. Angelo was as good as his word. He came attended by an escort of honor composed of several hundred of the best citizens, all of the Angelo party; and when the immersion was finished they escorted him back home and would even have carried him on their shoulders, but that people might think they were carrying Luigi.

Far into the night the citizens continued to discuss and wonder over the strangely mated pair of incidents that had distinguished and exalted the past twenty-four hours above any other twenty-four in the history of their town for picturesqueness and splendid interest; and long before the lights were out and burghers asleep it had been decided on all hands that in capturing these twins Dawson's Landing had drawn a prize in the great lottery of municipal fortune.

At midnight Angelo was sleeping peacefully. His immersion had not harmed him, it had merely made him wholesomely drowsy, and he had been dead asleep many hours now. It had made Luigi drowsy, too, but he had got only brief naps, on account of his having to take the medicine every three-quarters of an hour—and Aunt Betsy Hale was there to see that he did it. When he complained and resisted, she was quietly firm with him, and said in a low voice:

"No-no, that won't do; you mustn't talk, and you mustn't retch and gag that way, either—you'll wake up your poor brother."

"Well, what of it, Aunt Betsy, he—"

"'Sh-h! Don't make a noise, dear. You mustn't forget that your poor brother is sick and—"

"Sick, is he? Well, I wish I—"

"'Sh-h-h! Will you be quiet, Luigi! Here, now, take the rest of it—don't keep me holding the dipper all night. I declare if you haven't left a good fourth of it in the bottom! Come—that's a good boy."

"Aunt Betsy, don't make me! I feel like I've swallowed a cemetery; I do, indeed. Do let me rest a little—just a little; I can't take any more of the devilish stuff now."

"Luigi! Using such language here, and him just baptized! Do you want the roof to fall on you?"

"I wish to goodness it would!"

"Why, you dreadful thing! I've a good notion to—let that blanket alone; do you want your brother to catch his death?"

"Aunt Betsy, I've *got* to have it off, I'm being roasted alive; nobody could stand it—you couldn't yourself."

"Now, then, you're sneezing again—I just expected it."

"Because I've caught a cold in my head. I always do, when I go in the water with my clothes on. And it takes me weeks to get over it, too. I think it was a shame to serve me so."

"Luigi, you are unreasonable; you know very well they couldn't baptize him dry. I should think you would be willing to undergo a little inconvenience for your brother's sake."

"Inconvenience! Now how you talk, Aunt Betsy. I came as near as anything to getting drowned—you saw that, yourself; and do you call this inconvenience?—the room shut up as tight as a drum, and so hot the mosquitoes are trying to get out; and a cold in the head, and dying for sleep and no chance to get any—on account of this infamous medicine that that assassin prescri—"

"There, you're sneezing again. I'm going down and mix some more of this truck for you, dear."

CHAPTER 9

During Monday, Tuesday, and Wednesday the twins grew steadily worse; but then the doctor was summoned South to attend his mother's funeral, and they got well in forty-eight hours. They appeared on the street on Friday, and were welcomed with enthusiasm by the new-born parties, the Luigi and Angelo factions. The Luigi faction carried its strength into the Democratic party, the Angelo faction entered into a combination with the Whigs. The Democrats nominated Luigi for alderman under the new city government, and the Whigs put up Angelo against him. The Democrats nominated Pudd'nhead Wilson for mayor, and he was left alone in this glory, for the Whigs had no man who was willing to enter the lists against such a formidable opponent. No politician had scored such a compliment as this before in the history of the Mississippi Valley.

The political campaign in Dawson's Landing opened in a pretty warm fashion, and waxed hotter and hotter every week. Luigi's whole heart was in it, and even Angelo developed a surprising amount of interest in it—which was natural, because he was not merely representing Whigism, a matter of no consequence to him; but he was representing something immensely finer and greater—to wit, Reform. In him was centered the hopes of the whole reform element of the town; he was the chosen and admired champion of every clique that had a pet reform of any sort or kind at heart. He was president of the great Teetotalers' Union and its chiefest prophet and mouthpiece.

But as the canvass went on, troubles began to spring up all around—troubles for the twins, and through them for all the parties and segments and factions of parties. Whenever Luigi had possession of the legs, he carried Angelo to balls, rum shops, Sons of Liberty parades, horse-races, campaign riots, and everywhere else that could damage him with his party and the church; and when it was Angelo's week he carried Luigi diligently to all manner of moral and religious gatherings, doing his best to regain the ground he had lost before. As a result of these double performances, there was a storm blowing all the time, an ever-rising storm, too—a storm of frantic criticism of the twins, and rage over their extravagant, incomprehensible conduct.

Luigi had the final chance. The legs were his for the closing week of the canvass. He led his brother a fearful dance.

But he saved his best card for the very eve of the election. There was to be a grand turn-out of the Teetotalers' Union that day, and Angelo was to march at the head of the procession and deliver a great oration afterward. Luigi drank a couple of glasses of whisky—which steadied his nerves and clarified his mind, but made Angelo drunk. Everybody who saw the march, saw that the Champion of the Teetotalers was half seas over, and noted also that his brother, who made no hypocritical pretensions to extra-temperance virtues, was dignified and sober. This eloquent fact could not be unfruitful at the end of a hot political canvass. At the mass meeting Angelo tried to make his great temperance oration, but was so discommoded by hiccups and thickness of tongue that he had to give it up; then drowsiness overtook him and his head drooped against Luigi's and he went to sleep. Luigi apologized for him, and was going on to improve his opportunity with a ringing appeal for a moderation of what he called "the prevailing teetotal madness," but persons in the audience began to howl and throw things at him, and then the meeting rose in wrath and chased him home.

This episode was a crusher for Angelo in another way. It destroyed his chances with Rowena. Those chances had been growing, right along, for two months. Rowena had even partly confessed that she loved him, but had begged for time to consider. But now the tender dream was ended, and she frankly told him so, the moment he was sober enough to understand. She said she would never marry a man who drank.

"But I don't drink," he pleaded.

"That is nothing to the point," she said, coldly, "you get drunk, and that is worse."

[There was a long and sufficiently idiotic discussion here, which ended as reported in a previous note.]

CHAPTER 10

Dawson's Landing had a week of repose, after the election, and it needed it, for the frantic and variegated nightmare which had tormented it all through the preceding week had left it limp, haggard, and exhausted at the end. It got the week of repose because Angelo had the legs, and was in too subdued a condition to want to go out and mingle with an irritated community that had come to disgust and detest him because there was such a lack of harmony between his morals, which were confessedly excellent, and his methods of illustrating them, which were distinctly damnable. The new city officers were sworn in on the following Monday—at least all but Luigi. There was a complication in his case. His election was conceded, but he could not sit in the board of aldermen without his brother, and his brother could not sit there because he was not a member. There seemed to be no way out of the difficulty but to carry the matter into the courts, so this was resolved upon.

The case was set for the Monday fortnight. In due course the time arrived. In the meantime the city government had been at a standstill, because without Luigi there was a tie in the board of aldermen, whereas with him the liquor interest—the richest in the political field—would have one majority. But the court decided that Angelo could not sit in the board with him, either in public or executive sessions, and at the same time forbade the board to deny admission to Luigi, a fairly and legally chosen alderman. The case was carried up and up from court to court, yet still the same old original decision was confirmed every time. As a result, the city government not only stood still, with its hands tied, but everything it was created to protect and care for went a steady gait toward rack and ruin. There was no way to levy a tax, so the minor officials had to resign or starve; therefore they resigned. There being no city money, the enormous legal expenses on both sides had to be defrayed by private subscription. But at last the people came to their senses, and said:

"Pudd'nhead was right at the start—we ought to have hired the official half of that human phillipene to resign; but it's too late now; some of us haven't got anything left to hire him with."

"Yes, we have," said another citizen, "we've got this"—and he produced a halter.

Many shouted:

"That's the ticket."

But others said:

"No—Count Angelo is innocent; we mustn't hang him."

"Who said anything about hanging him? We are only going to hang the other one."

"Then that is all right—there is no objection to that."

So they hanged Luigi. And so ends the history of "Those Extraordinary Twins."

FINAL REMARKS

As you see, it was an extravagant sort of a tale, and had no purpose but to exhibit that monstrous "freak" in all sorts of grotesque lights. But when Roxy wandered into the tale she had to be furnished with something to do; so she changed the children in the cradle; this necessitated the invention of a reason for it; this, in turn, resulted in making the children prominent personages—nothing could prevent it, of course. Their career began to take a tragic aspect, and some one had to be brought in to help work the machinery; so Pudd'nhead Wilson was introduced and taken on trial. By this time the whole show was being run by the new people and in their interest, and the original show was become side-tracked and forgotten; the twin-monster, and the heroine, and the lads, and the old ladies had dwindled to inconsequentialities and were merely in the way. Their story was one story, the new people's story was another story, and there was no connection between them, no interdependence, no kinship. It is not practicable or rational to try to tell two stories at the same time; so I dug out the farce and left the tragedy.

The reader already knew how the expert works; he knows now how the other kind do it.

MARK TWAIN

Essays in Criticism

Contemporary Reviews

From *The Athenaeum* (Jan 19, 1895)

The best thing in *Pudd'nhead Wilson*, by Mark Twain (Chatto & Windus), is the picture of the negro slave Roxana, the cause of all the trouble which gives scope to Mr. Wilson's ingenious discovery about finger-marks. Her gusts of passion or of despair, her vanity, her motherly love, and the glimpses of nobler feelings that are occasionally seen in her elementary code of morals, make her very human, and create a sympathy for her in spite of her unscrupulous actions. But hers is the only character that is really striking. Her son is a poor creature, as he is meant to be, but he does not arrest the reader with the same unmistakable reality: his actions are what might be expected, but his conversations, especially with Wilson and the Twins, seem artificial and forced. Wilson, the nominal hero, appears to most advantage in the extracts from his calendar which head the chapters, but as a personage he is rather too shadowy for a hero. And what has to be said about the book must be chiefly about the individuals in it, for the story in itself is not much credit to Mark Twain's skill as a novelist. The idea of the change of babies is happy, and the final trial scene is a good piece of effect; but the story at times rambles on in an almost incomprehensible way. Why drag in, for example, all the business about the election, which is quite irrelevant? and the Twins altogether seem to have very little *raison d'être* in the book. Of course there are some funny things in the story, it would not be by Mark Twain if there were not, but the humour of the preface might very well be spared; it is in bad taste. Still, if the preface be skipped the book well repays reading just for the really excellent picture of Roxana.

From *The Critic* (May 11, 1895)

Pudd'nhead Wilson is no exception to the rule. It is a Missouri tale of changelings "befo' the wah," admirable in atmosphere, local color and dialect, a drama in its way, full of powerful situations, thrilling even; but it cannot be called in any sense *literature*. In it Mark Twain's brightness and grotesqueness and funniness revel and sparkle, and in the absurd extravaganza,

"Those Extraordinary Twins," all these comicalities reach the buffoon point; one is amused and laughs unrestrainedly but then the irksome question comes up: What *is* this? is it literature? is Mr. Clemens a "writer" at all? must he not after all be described as an admirable after-dinner storyteller—humorous, imaginative, dramatic, like Dickens—who in an evil moment, urged by admiring friends, has put pen to paper and written down his stories? Adapted to the stage and played by Frank Mayo, the thing has met with immediate success.

From *Hartford Times* (Feb 18, 1895)

Mark Twain's serial magazine story of Missouri life in a river town, in slavery days "befo'de wah," is now issued in handsome book form by the American Publishing Company of this city, who have once more the right to bring out Mr. Clemens's works. Reading any story in serial form, in a monthly magazine, is a very unsatisfactory way of getting hold of it; and this appearance of Mr. Clemens's latest work in a new volume ought to secure it for many new readers. The marginal vignette pictures, on every page, add nothing to the value or interest of the book, and might as well have been omitted; but the story itself is one of the queerest. One can well believe the author's statement, in *Those Extraordinary Twins*, the roaring comedy which follows what he considers the tragedy of the longer story, that he lost control, both of the characters and the "plot," in *Pudd'nhead Wilson*, and made of it a mixed mess very different from his intention at the start. It would be "easy work" to criticise some of the features of the main story, but who ever feels like criticising Mark Twain?

Pudd'nhead Wilson is not the most prominent character in the book; that place is usurped by the worthless Tom Driscoll, whose one-thirty-second part of "nigger" blood proves, in spite of his octoroon mother's strong character, his bane and his downfall. The practice of Pudd'nhead, in getting everybody, from babies to old people, to imprint the story told in an impression made by the differing lines produced by the ball of the finger on slightly greased glass, and religiously saving every strip of glass thus marked, proves to be the key to the turning point of the story; but it is an improbable practice, for anybody. However, one can't criticise "Mark"--and moreover his own experience of the possibilities of palmistry lends a peculiar interest to this peculiar application of the alleged principle to the purposes of this queer story. As to Angelo and Luigi, the Italian twins and noblemen—well, their appearance as twins of the Siamese sort, in the comedy, is quite as inherently probable as it is in the other way as such a place as Dawson's Landing. But probability, inherent or extraneous, is as soon to be looked in Mark Twain's stories as in the *Arabian Nights*. . . .

HENRY NASH SMITH

[Pudd' nhead Wilson as Criticism of the Dominant Culture]*

* * * The central theme of Pudd'nhead Wilson is still the the corrupt state of the official culture of Dawson's Landing—that is, Hanibal—and the plot of the novel is focused around two acts which, in quite different ways, call attention to evils beneath the apparently placid surface of it. The first act, the slave Roxana's desperate effort to free her son by exchanging him with her master's son in the cradle, is frustrated by the second, which consists in Wilson's detection of Roxy's stratagem more than twenty years later.

* * * Even in this farce [Those Extraordinary Twins], Mark Twain is dramatizing the conflict between propriety and nonconformity that had served him so often before as comic material. The playful fantasy, however, touched off deeper responses—hence the appearance of the three characters who figure in *Pudd'nhead Wilson*. Roxy's son, known as Tom Driscoll during most of the story, is the psychological equivalent of the twins. He is two persons in one: a Negro (according to the definition operative in Dawson's Landing—he "has one thirty-second Negro blood") who appears "white" and is reared as the adopted son of the great man of the town. He is by law a slave but apparently free. The duality of white and Negro introduces the theme of false appearance and hidden reality, which is repeated in Tom's

* *Mark Twain: The Development of a Writer* (Cambridge; The Belknap Press of Harvard University Press, 1962).

activities as a burglar in the disguise of a woman while he is ostensibly leading the life of the idle young heir to the town's largest fortune.

The material drawn up thus into consciousness is not comic, but intensely serious. When Mark Twain has conceived of Tom Driscoll he is launched upon a fable involving the tragic theme of slavery, with all it implies of hereditary but constantly renewed guilt and of perverted social conventions distorting human fact. For what but a morass of arbitrary assumptions makes Tom originally "black" and enslaved, later "white" and free, then converts him back into a Negro and a slave when the "truth" is revealed? The society of Dawson's Landing imposes upon slaves and masters alike the fictions which sustain the institution of slavery. The training corrupts both: the slave by destroying his human dignity, by educating him to consider himself inferior, by building up in him a ferocious hatred of himself as well as of his rulers; the master by encouraging cruelty toward the human beings he is taught to regard as animals, and thus by blunting his sensibilities and fostering an unwarranted pride of place.

Tom's mixed biological heritage points to the further fact that slavery debases sexual relations. To be sure, Mark Twain handles this topic with marked reticence. From the standpoint of imaginative coherence Judge York Leicester Driscoll is the father of Tom just as clearly as Roxy is his mother. But Mark Twain places the unmentionable fact of sexual intercourse between master and slave at two removes from the actual story—first by making Roxy, Tom's mother, the slave of a shadowy brother of Judge Driscoll at the time of Tom's birth; and then by the further precaution of creating an even more shadowy figure, Colonel Cecil Burleigh Essex, to be his biological father.

***

The problem of tone is often difficult in Pudd'nhead Wilson, but

Mark Twain's earlier ridicule of Southern aristocratic pretensions in *Life on the Mississippi* and elsewhere strengthens one's suspicion that he intends to caricature Judge Driscoll's pride of ancestry and his equation of honor with readiness to send or accept a challenge. The Judge is unmistakably an object of satire in Chapter 7, when he shows the newly arrived Italian counts the sights of the town—including the slaughter house and the volunteer fire company—and naïvely tells them "all about his several dignities, and how he had held and that and the other place of honor or profit, and had once been to the legislature." There is some ambiguity in the treatment of the Judge's duel with Luigi; Mark Twain admired physica1 courage, and the reader is expected to feel contempt for Tom because he is too cowardly to challenge the Count. Yet the duel in *Pudd'nhead Wilson* replaces a farcical encounter in "Those Extraordinary Twins" in which Angelo, physically joined to Luigi and therefore exposed to the Judge's fire against his will, dodges about so violently that he frustrates the efforts of both combatants, and finally assumes control of the twins' common pair of legs to run away. And the bit of slapstick that gives rise to the duel in "Those Extraordinary Twins" is retained in the novel. When Tom directs a sneering jest at Luigi from the platform of an anti-prohibition meeting, Luigi "took a couple of strides and halted behind the unsuspecting joker. Then he drew back and delivered a kick of such titanic vigor that it lifted Tom clear over the footlights. and landed him on the heads of the front row of the Sons of Liberty."

Mark Twain's ironic attitude toward the Judge's sense of honor is also indicated by the sequel to the duel. Tom rationalize his refusal to fight Luigi by declaring that the Count is an assassin. Without asking for particulars, the Judge instantly accepts the explanation, and declares: "That this assassin should have put the affront upon me of letting me meet him on the field of honor as if he were a gentleman is a matter which I will presently settle—but not now. I will not shoot him until after the election. I see a way to ruin them both before; I will attend to that first". The Judge waits until the eve of the election and then, still without any effort to verify Tom's slander, repeats it in a campaign speech. The coup bring about Luigi's defeat.

This incident would be more significant than it is if Judge Driscoll were a fully rounded character. But he is not. Mark Twain is not really interested in him as a person; he merely represents the aristocratic part of Tom Driscoll's heritage, which the writer means to satirize in the composite figure of the four descendant of the First Families of Virginia. Yet there is one odd obscurity of outline in the portrait. Pembroke Howard, the Judge's closest friend, is "a devoted Presbyterian" whereas the Judge is a freethinker. The theological difference is of no consequence in the plot. The Judge's unorthodoxy, like his pride in his Virginian ancestry, seems to be a reminiscence of Samuel Clemens' father, John Marshall Clemens. The parallel is a fleeting reminder that as the story of Pudd'nheadd Wilson emerged from the farce about the Italian twins it drew into itself buried memories of Mark Twain's childhood—not always the advantage of the novel.

* * *

The other half of Tom's heritage is that of his mother, Roxy the slave. The two parts of it are at war with each other. When Tom is but an infant Percy Northumberland Driscoll, Roxy's master, threatens to sell some of his slaves down the river. Although he relents and sells them in the town, Roxy suddenly realizes he has the power to carry out his threat: "Her child could grow up and be sold down the river! The thought crazed her with horror." She says to the sleeping infant: "I hates yo' pappy; he hain't got no heart—for niggers he hain't, anyways. I hates him, en I could kill him!" She is the only articulate enemy of the aristocracy of Dawson's Landing. Just as in some not negligible sense Judge Driscoll takes over the function of the Arthurian aristocracy in representing the values of a society stained by tyranny and cruelty, Roxy takes over Hank Morgan's role as adversary of the dominant class. In doing so, she becomes a successor to the vernacular protagonists of earlier stories.

Of course, there are important differences. Because she is a Negro (however "white'" in appearance) and a woman, Mark Twain cannot identify himself with her as he identifies himself with Hank Morgan. And her aggression against the established order is not motivated by a program of reform. Mark Twain has accepted demonstration in A *Connecticut Yankee* that society cannot redeemed. Yet in *Pudd'nhead Wilson* he continues his preoccupation with the question of values, stripping down the fictive world of the Matter of Hannibal to the only vestige of affirmation he can find in it: the warmth, the passion of love and of hate, the sheer personal force in this representative of the submerged slave caste.

Roxy thus represents the last trace of unhandseled nature that has survived the perverted training of society in Dawson's Landing. But with a beautiful irony Mark Twain shows that she has adopted many of the values of the white aristocrats: their pride of ancestry, their code of honor, even their contempt for Negroes. Her denunciation of Tom, setting forth Judge Driscoll's sentiments in her heavy dialect, is one of the great passages in this uneven but often powerful book:

> "En you refuse' to fight a man dat kicked you, 'stid o' jumpin' at de chance! En you ain't got no mo' feelin' den to come en tell me, dat fetched sich a po' low-down ornery rabbit into de worl' Pah! it makes me sick! It's de nigger in you, dat's what it is. Thirty-one parts o' you is white, en on'y one part nigger, en dat po' little one part is yo' soul. 'Tain't wuth savin'; 'tain't wuth totin' out on a shovel en throwin' in de gutter. You

> has disgraced yo' birth. What would yo' pa think o' you? It's enough to make him turn in his grave,"

Roxy herself has stood in range of bullets from the duel in order to watch it, and a ricochet shot has tipped her nose. When Tom asks her, "Weren't you afraid?" she invokes in unconscious parody of Judge Driscoll the absurd pedigree she has invented for herself. She believes that "My great-great-great-gran'father en yo' great-great-great-great-gran'father was Ole Cap'n John Smith, de highest blood dat Ole Virginny ever turned out, en his great-great-gran'mother or somers along back dah, was Pocahontas de Injun queen, en her husbun' was a nigger king outen Africa." It is a sufficient explanation of her behavior that "De Smith-Pocabontases ain't 'fraid o' nothin', let alone bullets."

Except when she is momentarily under the influence of her "strong and sincere" piety, Roxy is indifferent toward property rights; she offers as a matter of course to help Tom in his burglaries when he needs money to pay his gambling debts. But on the crucial occasion of the theft of money that led her master to sell the guilty slaves, she had overcome temptation herself because she had "got religion" a fortnight before at a revival. Mark Twain is at his comic-ironic best in this scene, culminating in Roxy's exclamation, "Dad' blame dat revival, I wisht it had 'a' be'n put off till tomorrow!" Roxy is nevertheless free of the heaviest burden that slavery has imposed on the whites: the sense of guilt. She is not torn by inner conflict, and she conveys the suggestion of subliminal energy, of darkness and mystery, that is attached to women and Negroes in American culture. The aggressiveness of the Judge is controlled by traditional forms, and even on the dueling ground he merely wounds his adversary. But when Roxy, without reference to code or etiquette, conceives the idea of killing her master, or herself and her child, the reader is convinced she is capable of these actions.

There is a haughty grandeur in her character that shines through the degraded speech and manners of a slave, and confers on her an intimation of tragic dignity: "She was of majestic form and stature her attitudes were imposing and statuesque, and her gestures and movements distinguished by a noble and stately grace." We have seen with what assurance she has imagined an Indian queen and an African king among her ancestors. Mark Twain never conceived a more effective passage than the scene, at once tragic and comic, in which she determines to exchange her son with the Driscoll heir, and justifies the action to herself by a process of reasoning both humble (for she takes for granted the inferiority of the Negro—"Tain't no sin—*white* folks has done it!") and arrogant, because she compares herse1f with royalty and even usurps the divine prerogative of arbitrarily conferring free grace on her child:

> "Now I's got it; now I 'member. It was dat old nigger preacher dat tole it, de time he come over here fum Illinois en preached in de nigger church. He said dey ain't nobody kin save his own self—can't do it by faith, can't do it by works, can't do it no way at all. Free grace is de on'y way, en dat don't come fum nobody but jis' de Lord; en he kin give it to anybody he please, saint or sinner—he don't kyer. He do jis' as he's a mineter. He s'lect out anybody dat suit him, en put another one in his place, en make de fust one happy forever en leave t'other one to burn wid Satan. De preacher said it was jist like dey done in Englan' one time, long time ago. De queen she lef' her baby layin' aroun' one day, en went out callin'; en one o' de niggers roun' 'bout de place dat was 'mos' white, she come in en see de chile layin' aroun', en tuck en put her own chile's clo'es on de queen's chile, en put de queen's chile's clo'es on her own chile, en den lef' her own chile layin' aroun' en tuck en toted de queen's chile home to de nigger-quarter, en nobody ever foun' it out, en her chile

> was de king bimeby, en sole de queen's chile down de river one time when dey had to settle, up de estate."

Roxy's subversive threat to the dominant culture is that the only aspect of the material of Pudd'nhead Wilson that stirs Mark Twain's imagination. As a result, she is the only fully developed character, in the novelistic sense, in the book. She has a different order of fictional reality from the figures of fable with which she is surrounded. She resembles a portrait in full color set in a black-and-white background.

Marvin Fisher and Michael Elliott

[Half a Dong Is Worse Than None]*

* * *

Critics who view Wilson as the hero of the story tend to ignore two important factors: first, the inconsistency between the fictional character of Pudd'nhead Wilson in the story and the hazy, transcendent persona responsible for the "Calendar," and second, Twain's own description of what he intended Wilson to be. It would be too much to insist that the bifurcated character of Pudd'nhead Wilson is thematically appropriate to the novel, but it is even less justifiable to view Wilson as a largely sympathetic character reflecting the author's own opinions. Henry Nash Smith has cited Twain's estimate of Wilson as he expressed it in a letter to Livy in 1894: "I have never thought of Pudd'nhead as a *character,* but only as a piece of machinery—a button or a crank or a lever with a useful function to perform in a machine, but with no dignity above that."1 Wilson may be somewhat sympathetic because of his years of neglect but he is essentially unfeeling and only superficially perceptive. In fact, the Wilson who participates in the action of the story does not seem perceptive enough to have uttered the original remark about killing his half of the dog or to understand the moral consequence of such symbolically charged fractional division.

The maxims of the Calendar reflect an aspect of Wilson we hardly see in the events of the novel. It is scarcely possible to imagine that the

---

* The Suthern Review 8(Summer 1972)

1 *Mark Twain: The Development of a Write* (Cambridge, 1962), p.181

Wilson who ostensibly accepts the F.F.V. code and reprimands Tom for not confronting Luigi in a duel could have produced the penetrating combination of disillusioned wit, cynicism, and iconoclasm in the Calendar. And it is scarcely possible to imagine that the Mark Twain who scorned chivalry and dueling in *Life on the Mississippi*, *Huckleberry Finn*, and *A Connecticut Yankee* could admire the spurious nobility of these pretentiously named leading citizens. (In fact such names as Judge York Leicester Driscoll, Percy Northumberland Driscoll, and Col. Cecil Burleigh Essex recall some of the cast in Mark Twain's pseudo-Elizabethan farce *1601* or his burlesques of Shakespeare.) Wilson wants to be recognized and accepted as part of this village elite, he is "deeply gratified" by the invitation to run for mayor of Dawson's Landing, and he considers this political opportunity "a step upward." In the final courtroom scene he serves as protector and supporter of the town's most cherished values and institutions—including the system of slavery. For such a man to commemorate Columbus Day by writing "It was wonderful to find America, but it would have been more wonderful to miss it" is inconceivable. Even the one remark about a dog in the Calendar is out of keeping with the meanings attached to "dog" by Wilson or other members of the community, for the Calendar maxim slyly praises virtuous caninity at the expense of brutish humanity: "If you pick up a starving dog and make him prosperous, he will not bite you. This is the principal difference between a dog and a man." Mark Twain has apparently presented us with two rather separate characters in his portrayal of Pudd'nhead Wilson.

As a consequence of this cleavage, he felt the need to supply some exposition to help the reader join the disparate parts of Wilson's character:

> For some years Wilson had been privately at work on a whimsical almanac, for his amusement—a calendar with a little dab of ostensible

> philosophy, usually in ironical form, appended to each date, and the judge. . . read them to some of the chief citizens. But irony was not for those people; their mental vision was not focused for it. They read those playful trifles in the solidest earnest, and decided without. . . doubt that Dave Wilson was a pudd'nhead.

. .

Quite clearly, this passage, the most extensive of the "unifying" passages, describes the more satanic author of the Calendar, not his notably less visionary counterpart who ultimately thrives so comfortably within the ethos of Dawson's Landing.

And it is in the context of the Calendar that Wilson's original "fatal remark" must be interpreted. We can then treat it as an example of far-reaching, bitterly ironic wisdom—an exposure of what seems at best human folly and at worst the ineradicable evil in man's nature. Like the entries in the Calendar, it is an indictment justified not by any plausible or realistic relationship to the events of the novel, but rather by its moral perception of what makes mankind tick in this Middle-American community and of where the greatest danger to the community lies. When Wilson utters these first significant words, he appears disengaged, not focused on what concerns the citizens he has just met; he speaks "much as one who is thinking aloud." His remark seems to proceed more from the trancelike realm of prophecy than from observation of an immediate situation, as evidenced by its effect on his audience:

> The group searched his face with curiosity, with anxiety even, but found no light there, no expression they could read. They fell away from him as from something uncanny, and went into privacy to discuss him.

As we know, they wholly misconstrue his meaning. For one thing, they miss his irony and ignore his implication; he knows that to kill one half of the dog is to kill the other half too. And as the author of the Calendar he also knows that the citizens are incapable of grasping the moral truth inherent in this graphic image of vivisection—simply that it applies to all aspects of human life, whether physiological, psychological, or social.

The Wilson of the Calendar who can make this point is much closer to Mark Twain than is the unsuccessful lawyer and ardent hobbyist, and only the Calendar character can conceive such a complex analogy wherein for man or for society the whole organism is the fundamental unit of being, and any arbitrary division or artificial quantification for purposes of convenience, profit, or punishment can only mean death. It is doubly ironic that one of the witnesses to Wilson's remark expresses this basic principle when trying to determine Wilson's hypothetical responsibility as a property owner (of his half of the dog): "if he killed his half and the other half died, he would be responsible for that half just the same as if he had killed that half instead of his own." What this man fails to realize is that this idea lies at the heart of Wilson's lesson in fractions. And the society of Dawson's Landing fails to realize that there is little or no moral distinction between the overt violence that can result in physical death and the covert violence that can result in psychic death.

Wilson's "joke," then, describes the essentially destructive effect of division and disunity on certain key, natural relationships symbolically represented in the ideal of the living organism; and the idea behind the joke is closely tied to the twin motif in *Pudd'nhead Wilson.* Even *Those Extraordinary Twins,* the rudimentary farce from which *Pudd'nhead* was extracted, reinforces this suggestion.

* * *

The novel suggests further that arbitrary division is by its very nature a form of betrayal which destroys certain fundamental relations based on family, community, and a larger sense of humanity. The society, irrationally and arbitrarily (as it turns out), makes damaging distinctions in regard to race:

> To all intents and purposes Roxy was as white as anybody, but the one sixteenth of her which was black outvoted the other fifteen parts and made her a Negro. She was a slave and salable as such. Her child was thirty-one parts white, and he, too, was a slave, and by a fiction of law and custom a Negro.

The social effect of these distinctions is to cultivate disunity by elevating to quasi-sacred status this communal code, this elaborate fiction of human fractions. By law and custom the identity of an individual could be quantified by fractional division of blood into categories of white and black. In the scheme of Mark Twain's novel, this sort of behavior is a submerged, slow, unconscious moral masochism—a deep prolonged, unhearing social fracture. The town punishes itself by not only maintaining the false and unnatural distinctions of the slave market, but also by its patently foolish reverence for the F. F. V. pretensions, and their genteel justification of violence. The false Tom, as Henry Nash Smith points out, is really the end-product of Dawson's Landing and, by extension, of the entire region:

> Although Tom Driscoll is evidently the key figure in the imaginative logic of Pudd'nhead Wilson, he is . . . not so much a character as a complex of themes. He incarnates both the tortured paradox of uncertain identity and the perversions resulting from generations of the bad training imposed by slavery.

The most evident source of Tom's duality, according to Smith, is in his "divided" background, one half of which is strictly F. F. V. aristocratic—i.e., the part supplied by his father—while the "other half of Tom's heritage is that of Roxy, the slave. The two parts of it are at war with each other."[2]

The politics of the town sustains the image of an organism in internal war with itself, the traditional "diseased body politic" familiar from Shakespeare. The good fellowship of the Sons of Liberty is shown to be only illusory; the members fight over trifles before their meeting is over, and apparently are not averse to the kind of slanderous, brutal campaigning that the Judge sanctions in order to get Wilson elected mayor. The farcical image of the "antirummies" in the guise of volunteer firemen, joyfully turning their hoses on their political opponents graphically illustrates the notion of the village as an unbalanced social organism working against its own good health and fated to fall victim to its own internal antagonisms. We should not be amused by the bitter truth that "citizens of that village. . . of a thoughtful and judicious temperament did not insure against fire; they insured against the fire company."

There can be no doubt that Pudd'nhead Wilson is a pessimistic book. It moves relentlessly to show that none in "the land of the free" is truly free and the few who are "brave" measure their courage by an inhumane standard. No one is without taint, not the purest descendant of the F. F. V., not the ambitious intellectual, and certainly not the black in bondage. For a variety of reasons and in different ways, the book proves that "the skin of every human being contains a slave." Tom has opportunities along the way to recognize firsthand the essential brutality and inhumanity of accepting and living in accordance with arbitrary labels and divisions. But neither reform nor escape is part of his nature; both have been driven out

---

[2] *Mark Twain.* pp. 176-79

of him by a devastating combination of corrupt training and his own innate, unyielding temperament. Roxy, who alone attempts to stand against circumstance and the continuing heinousness of white domination over her, accepts virtually all of the values and institutions cherished by the slave society in which she finds herself. In the end she fails miserably on all counts, and the novel literally offers no way out, not for the falseTom who gets treated as he was so ready to treat others, nor for the true heir who, despite the fact that he "found himself rich and free" was doubtless doomed to lead a dog's life, for he "could not endure the terrors of the white man's parlor, and felt at home and at peace nowhere but in the kitchen." Mark Twain chooses not to tell this further story, but it is quite clear that if he had, it would be the continuing story of a house divided against itself, some of its inhabitants at home in the parlor, others knowing their place in the kitchen.

That F. R. Leavis should have found *Pudd'nhead Wilson* "a profound study" of an admirable civilization paying homage to art, recognizing excellence in its cultural elite, and exhibiting "the outward signs of an inward grace, " is quite incredible.[3] We cannot help feeling some note of condescension here—toward America, toward American literature, and toward Mark Twain as an indigenously American writer. Rather than deny the frequently satirical and occasionally subversive tone of *Pudd'nhead Wilson*, it might be more accurate to view it as a bitter burlesque of what America was supposed to be and a painful depiction of what it had come to be—one nation, under God, infinitely divisible, with a mockery of justice for all.

---

[3] Introduction to *Pudd'nhead Wilson* (New York: Grove Press, 1955), pp. 13-19

Arthur G, Pettit

[The Black and White Curse][*]

Roxana is more than a bewildering mixture of black and white, however. She is also the most poignant example in Mark Twain's writing of his conviction that the greater crime of the South was not miscegenation but the white Southerners' unwillingness to admit that mulattoes were, after all, the products of their own lust.[1] Since mulattoes offered visible evidence of a covert bond between the races, that bond had to be overtly denied at all costs. The price of such deceit was bound to be paid by Southerners of every hue: all-white aristocrats like Chambers, mistaken for black; supposedly all-white Southerners who must worry whether the stigmata might not turn out to be theirs also; mulattoes like Roxana who are recognized as contaminated; mulattoes like Tom Driscoll who pass the color line only to be brought back across into slavery and blackness. No amount of deceit or dissimulation can guarantee permanent protection from discovery. After twenty-three years of indoctrination into white manners, speech, and decorum, the fair-skinned Tom Driscoll can still be declared tainted. And, conversely, after twenty-three years of indoctrination into black

---

[*] *Mark Twain and the South* (Lexington, Kentucky; The University Press of Kentucky, 1974)

1. In 1906, in response to William Lecky's remarks in his history of *European Morals, from Augustus to Charlemagne*, 2 vols. (New York, 1903; Clemens's copy in MTP), that "the chastity of female slaves was sedulously guarded by the Church," Clemens scrawled in the margin: "This is better the Southern Protestant Church of America ever did, *nicht wahr?*"

manners, speech, and decorum, the fair-skinned Chambers is beyond redemption. Neither environment nor heredity can match Southern prejudice.[2]

In its exposure of the Southern racial trauma, *Pudd'nhead Wilson* anticipates one of the obsessive themes of Southern writing in the twentieth century. The legacy of slavery and concubinage is one of fear, suspicion, false accusation, hypocritical exoneration, and guilt—a legacy that can be wiped out only by putting an end not to miscegenation but to discrimination. In a society of mixed blood in which the central preoccupation is with purity of blood, denial of the dignity and worth of blacks and mulattoes becomes, inevitably, a denial of the self. If some blacks are partly white, then some whites must be partly black. If some whites are slaves, then some blacks must be free. Who are they? And how many? And how long is this self-defeating denial going to go on? The fear and the hypocrisy seem endless: by rejecting blackness by day and embracing it by night, white Southerners have planted a lie in the soul of their progeny, cut themselves off from a vital part of their past, and locked themselves into a dilemma which will last as long as the blood curse itself.

For Mark Twain this was the central tragedy of the Southern experience—the curse of blood. The problem was not one of racial mixture, but the destructive emphasis on purity of blood of any sort. Injustice toward blacks springs from intraracial as well as interracial discrimination. The whole business of "born a gentleman, always a

---

[2] Robert Wiggins, in *Mark Twain: Jackleg Novelist* (Seattle, 1964), p. 107, points out that Mark Twain is inconsistent when he argues that environment (what he called training) determines human behavior exclusively. With Chambers, Mark Train's deterministic theory is convincing; slavery ruins him. But Tom Driscoll is carefully shown to be wicked before his white training has the opportunity either to uplift or to damage him. With Chambers, environment is the determining factor; with Driscoll, both environment and heredity (including six generations of white blood) could be said to determine his behavior.

gentleman," or Marshall Clemens's efforts to compensate for poverty by assuring his family they were "blood-pure," or the blood feud of the Grangerfords, or Pap Finn's hatred of black skin when his own was "a white to make a body's flesh crawl," or Roxana bragging to her mulatto son about his FFV blood—all this adds up to an intolerable burden imposed by white on black, white on white, and black on black. Tainted blood goes far beyond color; indeed it may have nothing whatever to do with race. But from blood consciousness springs the stultifying pride of those who believe they are pure and the paralyzing fear of those who believe they are not. Southern pride in blood and Southern fear of miscegenation are two sides of the same sword and the sword cuts black and white alike. More than any nineteenth-century novel except Gable's *The Grandissimes, The Tragedy of Pudd'nhead Wilson* implies that the greater tragedy of the South is not miscegenation but the curse that white Southerners have placed upon it; and, therefore, upon themselves.

편저자 : 유 영 종
Saint Louis University (학사)
Saint Louis University (석사)
Purdue University (박사)
인하대학교 문과대학 영어영문과 교수

논 문 : 젊은사탄으로부터 No. 44까지: 마크 트웨인의 카니발적 웃음
연구동향: 미국문학의 로맨스 소설 이론
마크 트웨인의 남부유산: 남서부유머와 *아더왕궁전의 코넷티컷 양키*
헬렌이전의 헬레나: H.D.의 "이집트의 헬렌"

저 서 : *서양문화와 예술*, 공저. 인하대학교출판부, 2005.
19세기 미국소설 강의, 공저, 신아사, 2003.

Mark Twain
Pudd'nhead Wilson
푸든헤드 윌슨

1판 1쇄 찍음 · 2007년 8월 25일
1판 1쇄 펴냄 · 2007년 8월 25일

편저자 · 유 영 종
발행인 · 정 현 걸
발 행 · 신 아 사
인 쇄 · 예지인쇄

출판등록 · 1956년 1월 5일 (제9-52호)
서울특별시 은평구 녹번동 28-36번지 2F
전화 (02)382-6411 · 팩스 (02)382-6401
홈페이지 · www.shinasa.co.kr
E-mail · shinasa@chol.com

ISBN: 89-8396-070-2

정가 12,000원